Passage to Intimacy

Lori H. Gordon, Ph.D.
with Jon Frandsen

A FIRESIDE BOOK
Published by Simon &Schuster
New York London Toronto Sydney Tokyo Singapore

FIRESIDE
Simon & Schuster Building
Rockefeller Center
1230 Avenue of the Americas
New York, New York 10020

FIRESIDE and colophon are registered trademarks
of Simon & Schuster Inc.

Designed by Marysarah Quinn.
Cartoon illustrations on pages
73 and 74 created by Sally Pierone.
Manufactured in the United States of America

1   3   5   7   9   10   8   6   4   2

Library of Congress Cataloging-in-Publication Data
Gordon, Lori Heyman.
Passage to intimacy / Lori H. Gordon with Jon Frandsen.
p.   cm.
Includes bibliographical references and index.
1. Marriage—Problems, exercises, etc.   2. Communication in marriage—Problems,
exercises, etc.   3. Intimacy (Psychology)—Problems, exercises, etc.   I. Frandsen,
Jon.   II. Title.
HQ734.G64   1993   92-33219
646.7'8—dc20   CIP

ISBN: 0-671-79596-1

This book is dedicated to

My teachers and mentors

Virginia Satir
Daniel Casriel
George Bach

whose indelible footprints pointed the way to a true
I-Thou dialogue between intimates

and to

Morris Gordon

my husband and dearest friend

ACKNOWLEDGMENTS

For much of my life, I have been deeply curious about what makes relationships work and what causes them to fail. I have searched for understanding. I have sought to use my understanding to help others prevent breakdown in important relationships. I hope that through this book some of the heartache, the waste, the tragedy of unnecessary loss will be prevented.

I wish to express my appreciation to all those who so openly shared their stories with me. The richness of their lives, their struggles, their joys, their often painful discoveries in transformation, represent the accumulated wisdom of this book. To the Monday Night Group, to the NIP participants, to the PAIRS participants, to all of my clients, colleagues and friends of the Family Relations Institute, I think of you with deep warmth and appreciation.

I wish to pay tribute to those who most influenced my professional learning and growth: I thank particularly Virginia Satir, who generously shared her wide-ranging knowledge, practical wisdom and remarkable inventiveness in developing experiences to deepen perceptions and who chaired the PAIRS Advisory Board; George Bach, for his important work on the love/hate paradox and his rituals and exercises for managing conflict nondestructively; Daniel Casriel, for his essential focus on Bonding, the honest expression of intense emotions and levels of emotional maturity; Paul MacLean, for his unique understanding of the Triune Brain; Murray Bowen, for his concepts of individuation, differentiation and the use of the genogram in family systems; James Framo, for his integration of psychodynamic object relations theory with family of origin exploration; John Bradshaw, for so clearly defining the issues for adult children and pointing out the need for new learning and skills; Ivan Boszormenyi-Nagy and Geraldine Sparks, for illuminating the concepts of Invisible Loyalties and the Revolving Ledger through the generations; Hugh Missildine for his early work on the "Inner Child"; Roger Gould; for his insights into adult stages of growth and change; Bernard Guerney, for his sensitive work on expressive and listening modes; Jean Houston, for her original work on imagery, human potential and empowerment; Norman and Betty Byfield Paul, for their focus on the impact of past loss and grief on present relationships; Bernie

Siegel, for his emphasis on love as healing; Lonnie Barbach and Bernie Zilbergeld, for their warmly human approaches to sexuality and pleasuring; John Gray, for his focus on letting go of grudges through the "Love Letter"; Nathaniel Branden, for demonstrating the power of sentence completion exercises for surfacing hidden thoughts and feelings; Ira Progoff, for his focus on Journaling and the Time/Life Dimension; Clifford Sager, for his clear work on couple contracting; and Richard Stuart, for his work on helping couples change with important focus on caring behaviors. I thank each of them for their contributions to decoding the puzzle of intimate relationships and charting new and more fulfilling paths.

I wish to express my thanks to Cornell University, Department of Child Development and Family Relationships, for nurturing my early interest in intimate relationships, and the Graduate School of Social Work at Catholic University for honoring my eagerness to learn by awarding me the National Public Health Stipend.

I wish to thank my colleagues: Gerard V. D'Amore, whose lucidity, writing skills and support were invaluable in the inception and development of the PAIRS materials (Jerry invented the PAIRS acronym, for Practical Application of Intimate Relationship Skills); John D. Robinson, who first invited me to develop the prototype of this course for the Graduate School of Counseling Education at American University; Israel Charny, who invited early presentation of my work at an International Family Therapy Conference in Jerusalem and also at Tel Aviv University; Diane Sollée, who strongly encouraged public and professional presentations to the American Association for Marriage and Family Therapy.

I offer my deepest thanks and appreciation to Carl Nissen, Ann Ladd, Frank Roberts and Richard Robertson, who were the first to take PAIRS out into the world. And to each and every one of the Leaders who have taken the PAIRS Professional Training since, and whose experiences and enthusiasm for this program convinced me that PAIRS fills a universal longing—I thank you. I am especially grateful to each of you who are teaching the PAIRS program around the world:

Pete Adams and Dee Jones (*Baton Rouge, LA*)
Teresa and Jesse Adams (*New Orleans, LA*)

Paul Allsop (*London, England*)
Zev Appel (*Natanya, Israel*)
Yardena Arnon (*Givataim, Israel*)

Bud and Michele Baldwin (Chicago, IL)
Shanti Bannwart (Santa Fe, NM)
Judy Beebe and Norm Kummerlen (Lorain, OH)
Allison Bell-Schrag (Mt. Kisco, NY)
Philip Belzunce (Rocky River, OH)
Judy Berg (Highland Park, IL)
Frances Bernfeld (Tucson, AZ)
Rachel Bolless (Yavheh, Israel)
Jill Bourdais (Paris, France)
Naughné Boyd (Richland, WA)
Holly Brown (New York, NY)
Cheryl Castille (DeRidder, LA)
Naomi Cohn (Milwaukee, WI)
Judith Collignon (Paris, France)
Joseph Costanzo (Hampden, MA)
Joan Marie Cook (Waxahachie, TX)
Terry Cooper (London, England)
Rita DeMaria (Philadelphia, PA)
Richard Dicker (San Diego, CA)
Bunny Duhl (Boston, MA)
Fred Duhl and Verne Cooper-Duhl (Newton, MA)
Carlos Durana (Falls Church, VA)
Eric Ehrke (Milwaukee, WI)
Bonnie Eisenberg and Frank Doyle (Bethesda, MD)
Joyce Elijah (Federal Way, WA)
Peggy Errington and Joe Sanders (Alexandria, VA)
Pam Evans (DeRidder, LA)
Ines Fahrner (Germany)
Lane Franz (Falls Church, VA)
Ben Fuchs (Forres, Scotland)
Ruth Gilat (Tel Aviv, Israel)
Julia Gippenreiter (Moscow, Russia)
Lalei Guitierrez (Rocky River, OH)
Greg and Ellen Haag (Ft. Lauderdale, FL)
Meg Haycraft (St. Louis, MO)
Gary and Deanie Hurst (Fairfax, VA)

Jan Wendy Itzkowitz (Highland Park, IL)
Linda Kibrick and Bill Rhoads (East Windsor, NJ)
Sheldon Kramer (San Diego, CA)
Ann Ladd (Falls Church, VA)
Noreen LeGare (Tallahassee, FL)
Marvin Leiner (New York, NY)
Mary Madland (Wenatchee, WA)
Gloria Mahdesian (Encino, CA)
Derk and Cindy Manley (Austin, TX)
Ernest and Lalla Mellor (Memphis, TN)
Oriel Methuen (London, England)
Alexey Morozov (Moscow, Russia)
Carl Nissen (Falls Church, VA)
Richard Passoth (Denver, CO)
Carolyn Perla (New York, NY)
Claude Phipps (Santa Fe, NM)
Claire and Yossi Rabin (Tel Aviv, Israel)
Marc and Bonnie Rabinowitz (Norfolk, VA)
Lynda Rees (Toronto, Canada)
Mariene Rees-Newton (Toronto, Canada)
Frank Roberts (Falls Church, VA)
Pat Rubinstein (Encino, CA)
Ruth Russell-Stern (Cary, NC)
Clifford Sager (New York, NY)
Lorraine Sando (Federal Way, WA)
Jonah Schrag (Mt. Kisco, NY)
Suzanne Scurlock-Durana (Falls Church, VA)
Audra Seagle (Roanoke, VA)
Barbara and Fred Seldin (South Bend, IN)
Joanne Sorenson (Littleton, CO)
Onnolee Stevens (Milwaukee, WI)
Lynn Turner-Bielenberg (Falls Church, VA)
John and Natalie Tyler (Maui, HI)

Patricia Walochik *(Vienna, VA)* Cynthia Williams *(Ft. Worth, TX)*
Suzanne Walsh *(Towson, MD)* Haya Yaniv *(Ayalon, Israel)*
Beverly Weaver *(Boston, MA)* Tom and Jane Smith Young
Nancy White *(Houston, TX)* *(Boise, ID)*

My thanks and love to my four children, Beth, Jonathan, David and Seth, who patiently accepted my long absences and my search for answers, and to their beautiful loved ones, Daniel, Ron, Rob, Lisa, Fran and Peggy. And to my grandchildren: Jessica, Lauren, Evan, Adam, Benjamin, Sara, Alex, Michael, Ronnie, Donna, and Guy; to my parents, Bertha Hahn Heyman and Dr. Julius Heyman, whose loving encouragement, despite their early loss, gave me a lasting foundation of self-worth; and to my sister, Selma, who taught me of sibling rivalry and loving friendship. My deepest thanks to Maybelle Charley, who lovingly cared for my children, which enabled me to pursue my studies and career. And to my friends through the years in the Satir AVANTA and IHLRN groups—thank you for your support.

Words cannot express my appreciation to Pat Swift for her dedication and hours beyond the norm in transforming these often illegible pages into a beautifully presented manuscript and to Kumi Herat and Cris Cassidy as well. The graphics and imaginative ideas of Bevi Chagnon, Sally Pierone and Christy Piper beautifully illustrate the PAIRS concepts. I thank Toni Sciarra and Barbara Gess for their clear, lucid editing. I thank agents John Brockman and Katinka Matson who diligently searched me out to elicit this manuscript.

Special thanks to collaborator Jon Frandsen for his deep personal concern, thoughtful writing and eloquent metaphors, which clearly enhance this manuscript.

Most of all, I thank my husband, Morris, whose deep belief in the power of love and personal search for those understandings that sustain love supported the development of PAIRS from a small private gathering in a corner of the Family Relations Institute into a publicly funded, psychoeducational foundation whose work is available to all. His unswerving love, devotion, and support of me and my work illustrate the truth of these pages.

For all those whose relationships begin in hope—and must be sustained by understanding—and to their children, I dedicate this book.

—*Lori Heyman Gordon*

TABLE OF CONTENTS

PREFACE

As we moved into the twentieth century, there was a very clearly prescribed way in which men and women were to behave with one another in marriage. The man was the undisputed head of and authority in the family. In addition, he was to provide for and protect his wife and children.

The woman's role was to obey her husband, to take care of him, to take charge of the house, to bear and care for the children and to be responsible for setting the emotional tone in the family. She was also responsible for the sexual fidelity of the home. In the marriage vows of that time, the woman pledged to love, honor and obey her husband. He had only to love and cherish her.

Since women were not expected to be educated, and divorces were possible only on the grounds of adultery, insanity and desertion, the wife was completely dependent on her husband. She had no other means of support nor a right to manage her affairs. If the marriage became difficult, she felt obliged to stay. Once married, she had to endure her lot. A further deterrent was that divorced women were ostracized and often looked upon as sexually loose.

The society of that day only gave recognition and status to those who married. The others who did not marry, especially women, were considered misfits and were objects of pity and sometimes scorn. As a result, women scrambled to get married. To be respectable, a woman had to have a Mrs. in her name.

A new era has dawned since then. This began when women got the vote in 1920. That gave them control over their lives. Slowly, states began to liberalize divorce laws as well. Always permitting divorce under the grounds of adultery, insanity and desertion, these laws were being extended to neglect and abuse.

In World War II much of the work formerly done by men was being successfully done by women. This gave women a new sense of confidence. They learned they could be successful heads of families themselves. When the men returned from war, the climate of relationships had changed and women were no longer willing to be submissive.

The women's rights movement emerged soon thereafter. The end of the dominant-submissive model in relationships was certainly in sight. However, there was very little that had developed to replace the old pattern. For the last thirty years, couples have been floundering. New forms for the new values have not yet emerged, and the old ones are no longer acceptable.

The aim was to develop a new kind of equality, based on equal value of each person. The old role definitions were no longer appropriate and chaos set in. Retrospectively, one could have expected that there would be a lot of chaos and a lot of fallout; the change from the dominant/submissive model to one of equality of value is a *monumental shift. We are in the beginning of learning how a relationship based on genuine feelings of equality can operate practically.*

PAIRS is a splendid preparation toward enabling couples to develop new satisfying patterns of relationship based on high self-worth for each one. The program of PAIRS touches all the significant variables in the marital relationship. This program came from a gifted therapist /educator, Lori Heyman Gordon, who conducted several hundred seminars with ordinary couples who wanted to reshape their patterns of relationship. PAIRS is the outcome of the experiences of those couples.

In a world where equality between human beings is generally not practiced and maybe not known, the material contained in PAIRS is a truly significant, pioneering effort.

—*Virginia Satir*
Palo Alto, California

(This book was in process when Virginia Satir died. This is the preface she wrote for it. PAIRS is a legacy to her work.—**Lori Gordon**)

BEFORE YOU BEGIN THIS BOOK

This book is about avoiding quicksand, as well as other dangers that cannot be seen. It is about providing the tools to find and protect those rare joyful things, the unicorns of our souls, that can come from the union of two people. It is about making love last.

—Jon Frandsen

For a long time, I had a vision of a perfect spot on which to stand. It was in a heavily wooded area in the rear of my house, looking out onto a lake. From there I would be able to view rustic steps carved into a rocky hillside that led to a clearing from which one could see a natural island that was a wild bird's paradise. It was beautiful, restoring. That was where I wanted to stand. *The problem was that there was nothing to stand upon.* It was simply space in the air. Nonetheless, I could see the spot from the window of my house. I could visualize the beauty of that place. I did that often.

Eventually, after thought, planning, searching, and imagining the design countless times and ways, I found a carpenter who shared my vision and who built my dream structure: a cedar deck that extended far into the trees. It first had to be designed and sketched. There had to be a plan. We had to negotiate the terms. The foundation had to be poured, the supports set, the planks installed. But it was worth it. It was truly beautiful. And I not only could stand there, I could return there again and again. It is a place of renewal.

I see PAIRS this way. PAIRS is an acronym for Practical Application of Intimate Relationship Skills. It offers a beautiful new view of what is possible in relationships. But you need to take specific steps to get there. PAIRS provides tools, concepts and the experiential learning to enable you to build a solid foundation. It offers a framework for learning the language of the heart. It offers the skills needed to sustain pleasure in intimate relationships.

I learned early about both love and loss. My parents died while I was in my teens. My father died suddenly of a coronary when I was fifteen. He was a silent, but affectionate, father. He taught me to play chess on his knee when I was six. He validated my intelligence.

My mother died at home a year-and-a-half later of cancer, after a long and painful illness. I had been very close to her. At the end, it was a relief that she was no longer suffering. I learned early about the unpredictability of life and to wonder what life was about and why.

I became a doer of puzzles—intrigued with putting together picture puzzles. Eventually, the puzzles became so large and complex, with so many obscure pieces to locate, that I spent sleepless nights obsessed with finding each missing piece. Finally, I gave up picture puzzles. Intimate relationships became my next puzzle.

At the end of my sophomore year of college, I met and married a young law student I'd known for less than three months. That marriage lasted seventeen years. It was not a source of pleasure. I knew nothing about how to handle differences, how to argue, how to speak in my own behalf to a distant, angry, unloving partner. It wasn't what I had seen in my parents' affectionate marriage. And I had no one to turn to for help.

While raising four children, I entered graduate school hoping to find answers. I didn't, and, finally, I gave up on my marriage. It was too unrewarding, too lacking in the intimacy I deeply yearned for and in the affection I had known as a youngster and had seen in my parents' marriage. I simply didn't know how to make it happen. I was lonely with him, lonelier than I had ever been without him.

I set out on a search for answers. I met with couples and families, singly and in groups. I searched out innovative teachers, everyone I could find who had useful insights about people, relationships, marriages and families. I searched and I questioned.

What do men and women seek in relationships with each other? What sustains pleasure? What does it take to *sustain* love—not just fall in love? What are the fears that paralyze or sabotage?

I didn't know when I began my search how complicated these issues were. I didn't know that we need to know not only about love and affection and sensuality and sex and passion, but also about how to deal with the entire range of emotions—anger and pain and resentment and disappointment and worry and fear and excitement and joy. How to deal with differences in ways that build rather than destroy. How to confide in each other and how to *listen* to each other. How to recognize that our *style* of communication is often more of a problem than *what* we are trying to communicate.

We don't know how many hidden expectations we have about each other until we are suddenly upset and realize that what we expect is not what our partner expects or may be capable of. We don't understand our history, our conditioning, our past hurts, the scars we bear, the grudges we hold, our "dark side" or that of our partner. We don't understand the decisions we reached early in life that secretly govern our rules for living.

How do we learn? That's what I set out to discover.

Along the way I became a skilled marital and family therapist. I founded the Family Relations Institute in Falls Church, Virginia (now the PAIRS Institute). I sponsored and studied with those who were pioneers in the field: Virginia Satir, George Bach, Daniel Casriel, Ira Progoff, Jean Houston and many others. And I integrated what I learned into my personal life and work.

I became an insightful and effective presenter of this material. In 1975, I was invited to become adjunct professor at American University for their new graduate program on marriage and family, to develop their first course. I decided to build into the course everything I had learned that was effective in helping couples move to a better place in their relationship. I wanted it to be practical, clear and experiential; to offer new perceptions and effective skills for creating new, more positive, more pleasurable attitudes and behavior in intimacy. I wanted it to be a preventive maintenance course, one that could help partners to avoid the pitfalls of relationships before it was too late.

Shortly after I began teaching this course, the graduate students began telling me how enormously useful it was in their personal relationships with their mates, parents, children, lovers, friends. I made the critical decision to adapt it and teach it at the institute to those couples (and later, by demand, to singles as well) who came for help, often with the belief that it was too late to save their relationship. Too much had gone wrong, too much water was under the bridge. It became a crash course in intimate relationship skills for those who most needed them.

The course began very quietly with six couples. I had the supportive help of Jerry D'Amore, who collaborated with me in preparing early written materials. He invented the PAIRS acronym. The course quickly grew in popularity. It spread by word of mouth. It was unique in its range and depth. It wove together the best from the educational, therapeutic and human potential fields, integrating them into an experiential whole. My puzzle-doing perfectionism had served me well.

Shortly, I was teaching PAIRS twice a year. Each class was four months long—one evening per week and one weekend per month. Those who came ranged from those early in marriage to those married over forty years; from those hoping to save a deteriorating relationship to those who wished to enrich an ungratifying relationship; from those who had been divorced and wanted to be sure that the same things didn't go wrong again to those who had never been married and wanted the knowledge to prevent problems.

In 1984, we established PAIRS as a separate educational foundation. In 1986, we began training therapists to teach it all over the world. It was a stunning experience for me. I never dreamed when I developed the course that the insights and experiences that had changed my own life would have such significance to so many others. The following statement was written at the end of the course by an attorney, married nine years and father of two children. It represents many that I receive:

> PAIRS was the most useful educational, practical and relevant experience I've had—far and away more significant to me than my college, law school and professional experiences. In fact, PAIRS helped undo what I "learned" about people, the world and myself as a person in the world, through the dehumanizing experience of law school. Without PAIRS, we would never have gotten closer, as I believe we have; we would never have become intimate, as I believe we are becoming; I would never have felt a sense of loss when she is away from me as I do now.

My second marriage, in 1982 to Morris Gordon, has been a source of incredible joy and companionship. The skills and understandings in PAIRS are second nature to us—as they have become to many others. And, finally, the demand to know what is in the course has become so great that I have joined with Jon Frandsen to offer you in book form the best, most useful parts of PAIRS.

HOW TO USE THIS BOOK

PAIRS is a language and a tool kit. PAIRS speaks the *language of the heart* as well as of the mind. I have included carefully sequenced, step-by-step experiential exercises that we have found most helpful in offering you new understandings about yourself and others. They are designed to provide experiences between partners and explorations within yourself that can lead to excitement, discovery, pleasure and love. We have included stories, descriptions and instructions to help the material come alive for you. (The stories are composites. The names and many of the circumstances have been changed in the interest of confidentiality.)

The riddle of relationships is that the self and the self in a relationship are in a series of interlocking spheres—each one a world in itself with its own rules, customs and unique history. Some of the spheres are easily visible, some can become visible if we know how and where to look for them. All are always present in some fashion. A disturbance in any one of them can cause a spiraling downward in all of them. The spiraling downward can be triggered by anything that diminishes self-esteem or by any circumstances that affect the self or the relationship.

Just as a relationship can spiral steeply downward, it can also spiral upward—particularly when given knowledge, skill, goodwill—and a willing partner. That is what PAIRS is about.

This book attempts to offer the PAIRS concepts in linear fashion. The book is designed to be interactive and interdimensional. It is between you and yourself, you and a partner, you and this book as your own personal journey of discovery. It is designed to be reflected on in times to come—when old ways of thinking and behaving threaten to overpower new decisions.

None of the exercises or descriptions in the book are terribly complicated. Some of them may even seem obvious. *Implementing them in your life is the challenge and the reward.*

The book is organized to flow in a structured sequence. You are welcome to read sections out of sequence if there are some parts that particularly interest you, but the book is designed to weave everything together into an integrated, meaningful whole, so I encourage you to read it all.

To use this book most effectively, a journal will help you. Go out and buy a notebook. Any notebook will do, so long as it is one in which you can keep private notes and responses. You may choose to share it with someone else, but you don't have to unless you so wish. Each chapter concludes with a suggestion that you record your understandings in your notebook.

Each section has its own exercises, skills and understandings. Do the exercises. They offer you a very personal set of discoveries. If used, they can transform your relationship and your life.

Section I explains the emotional aspects of intimate relationships and offers a Relationship Road Map as the conceptual guide for PAIRS.

Section II focuses on communication: the art of talking, the art of listening, mind reading, fair fighting and other skills needed to avoid misunderstandings and to resolve conflict nondestructively.

Section III offers a guide to understanding ourselves and our partner through exploring our conditioning, our beliefs, our invisible ledgers, our hidden expectations, the rules we learned that may limit us today and the interaction of our unique personalities.

Section IV invites pleasuring through bonding, sensuality and sexuality.

Section V offers easy access to PAIRS concepts through the PAIRS Tool Kit.

Among other things, the PAIRS exercises are designed to help you:

- Satisfy your biological need for that combination of physical closeness and emotional openness which is called "bonding"
- Recognize when your communication style is more of a problem than the actual problem about which you are communicating
- Develop the ability to feel genuine empathy for your partner, instead of secret resentment

- Express your feelings so that they can be recognized without causing your partner to feel resentful, overwhelmed, manipulated or inadequate
- Avoid the mind reading that so often leads to misunderstanding between couples, learn to avoid assumptions and not to expect that "if you loved me, you would know"
- Express and accept anger without destroying love
- Fight in such a way that you actually resolve the issues at hand
- Acknowledge and enjoy the differences between you and your partner, rather than see them as threats
- Trace your family's emotional history so that you can uncover the hidden expectations that may be influencing your relationship
- Recover past decisions that may be sabotaging your relationships today
- Recognize the different roles you and your partner play, and how they work or don't work together
- Learn the difference between affection, comfort, tenderness, bonding, sensuality, and sexuality so that sex is not your only avenue to closeness
- Negotiate a relationship you can both live with joyfully

Sprinkled throughout the book are questions, set apart in boxes, designed to help you apply the material to your own experience. Some you will be able to answer easily; some will require reflection. This offers another opportunity to use your journal.

Except when asked not to, read through each chapter once before doing the exercises. Then allow yourself a lot of time to do and reflect on the exercises. You're worth it. Your life is worth it.

As human beings, we are all miracles, capable of remarkable learning, growth and change. You *can* understand what went wrong in previous relationships or what is going wrong now. You *can* make changes *if* you choose to learn how to use what you've learned.

Although a book cannot take the place of a group experience in a professionally guided course, it can move you far along the path. In reading this book, you may wish to take the PAIRS course, which is being taught in many places.

We are all pathfinders today, working our way through uncharted territory as we seek to build *coequal relationships* for the first time in human history. As many explorers and ships went down in the Atlantic during the search for new worlds, many relationships fail today because we have no current, reliable maps. Many of us have wandered into unknown jungles and got caught in quicksand. Some come back with new delights, rare jewels.

This book is for all whose relationships begin in hope and must be sustained by knowledge, skill and goodwill.

The Relationship Road Map

■　　　■　　　■

I have sought love, first, because it brings ecstasy—ecstasy so great that I would often have sacrificed all the rest of life for a few hours of this joy. I have sought it, next, because it relieves loneliness—that terrible loneliness in which one shivering consciousness looks over the rim of the world into the cold unfathomable lifeless abyss. I have sought it, finally, because in the union of love I have seen, in a mystic miniature, the prefiguring vision of the heaven that saints and poets have imagined.

—*Bertrand Russell*

The Logic of Love
and Other Emotions

■   ■   ■

*M*any of our deepest and most intangible desires, many of them not even fully formed thoughts, are wrapped up in our dream of an ideal relationship. We count on feeling safe and content. We expect passion and excitement. We hope for an end to loneliness. We fantasize about having all of our sexual needs fully met, on demand. We seek an end to acrimony and discord. We envision lives without masks, being seen and appreciated for simply being what we are. We dream of feeling whole.

But we aren't always ready for the dreams we have.

That's because right behind our most profound and cherished dreams, locked to us like shadows, are our deepest fears.

Each of us tends to hope for three things in a love relationship:

That all the good things I have had in my life, such as freedom, autonomy and the power to make my own decisions, I will continue to have

That everything I ever wanted but didn't have, I will find with you—whether it is affection, sex, friendship, loyalty, devotion, trust, a playmate

That everything bad or upsetting that ever happened to me before will not happen with you, such as disappointment, betrayal, fear, misunderstandings, arguments, violence or abandonment

And right behind these hopes lurk their opposite—the fears:

That I am liable to lose all the good things I had before—my freedom, my other relationships, my power to decide
That I will not find with you the things that I have wanted
That everything bad that ever happened to me is about to happen again with you

Seeing the connection between our feelings of love and fear—our dreams and nightmares—and understanding how we respond unconsciously to that connection invites us to reconsider the way we understand emotions. That is the first step toward keeping our dreams and hopes alive.

That understanding requires a fresh look at the way our brains work—the relationship between our conscious, our subconscious and our emotions. One of the most eloquent theories about the way we think was developed by Dr. Paul MacLean, formerly chief of the Laboratory of Brain Evolution and Behavior at the National Institutes of Mental Health, who developed the concept of the triune brain.

MacLean sees the brain as being composed of three primary parts, superimposed on each other, that developed at different times in evolution. The earliest, the one that we inherit from the reptiles, is the reptilian or old brain, and it is the most primitive part of our response system. It coordinates our automatic movements and reflex actions and is concerned with instinct, territory and repetition, lacking the ability to learn to cope with new situations. It asks only about self-preservation: Is it safe? Will I survive? It orders human response based on the answers it gets. The second part of the brain, which we inherit from the warm-blooded creatures, is the early mammalian brain, which surrounds the old brain. It also can be called the emotional or "creature" part of the brain because it is believed to be where our capacity to love and hate, be sad and be exhilarated, to feel grief and joy lies.

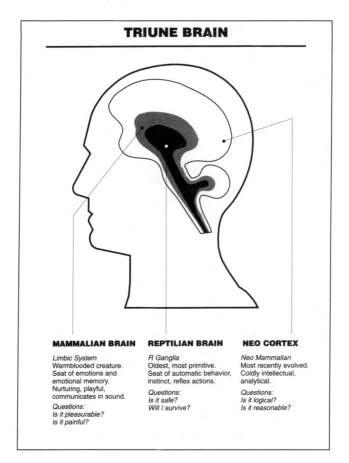

TRIUNE BRAIN

MAMMALIAN BRAIN	REPTILIAN BRAIN	NEO CORTEX
Limbic System Warmblooded creature. Seat of emotions and emotional memory. Nurturing, playful, communicates in sound. *Questions:* Is it pleasurable? Is it painful?	*R Ganglia* Oldest, most primitive. Seat of automatic behavior, instinct, reflex actions. *Questions:* Is it safe? Will I survive?	*Neo Mammalian* Most recently evolved. Coldly intellectual, analytical. *Questions:* Is it logical? Is it reasonable?

In this part we can experience humor and playfulness, communicate in sound, bond with and nurture our young. Emotions reside in this part, including emotional memory. This part is generally concerned with the basic questions: Is it pleasurable? Is it painful? It is concerned with self-survival and species survival, and it remembers anything that was ever painful to us in order to protect us.

The third and most recently evolved part of the brain is the one with which we are most familiar, the neocortex or intellectual part. It is the part that has the ability not only to ask innumerable questions, but to gather the resources to answer many of them. It asks: Is it reasonable? Is it logical? It is the part of you that is reading this book.

Seeing our brain as having what amounts to three separate control centers with three separate need systems helps explain why we sometimes do things that are contradictory or don't seem logical, like getting angry over something our intellect is saying is minor or wolfing down a piece of cheesecake when we are dieting. Our behavior, at that time, is being controlled by our old or creature brain, not our intellect. The difficulty of having three centers to our behavior and thinking is compounded when we recognize that the more severe a given situation is, the more stress we are under, the more our old or emotional brains get into the act. When our lives are in danger, our old brain virtually takes over. This is the state people are in when they describe going on "automatic pilot" or reflexively taking actions (like turning a steering wheel sharply) that our intellect has not had time to think up and demand. When we are under emotional forms of stress (like sadness, disappointment or fear), our "creature" part might take charge.

If you accept MacLean's theory, as many psychologists now do, it becomes obvious that the key to changing behavior is accessing and understanding the oldest parts of our brain, as well as the newest.

The part of the brain that causes us the most havoc in relationships is the part that deals with emotions. In part, that's because of our lack of control over our emotions. When an emotion arises that we are uncomfortable with or that feels inappropriate, we feel out of control. In a society that tends to value reason over emotion, our need to somehow control these uncontrollable feelings is even more pronounced—and we feel even more frustrated, uncomfortable and out of control.

We are unable to exercise such control over emotions because they have their own logic, quite distinct from the logic our intellect uses to puzzle our way through day-to-day life. This is something few of us were ever taught. Almost all of our training, from learning how to use a toilet and tie our shoelaces, to balancing budgets and managing an office staff, was aimed at our intellect. But many of the skills we develop for the office or for dealing with people out in the world are the opposite of the skills we need to sustain our intimate relationships.

When I make this point in PAIRS, I ask the class to give me examples of skills and characteristics that serve well in the workaday world. The answers I get include:

Competitiveness
Ambition
Discretion in what you say
Emotional guardedness
Being hard working
Being serious
Knowing how to manipulate, manage and control others
Taking and giving orders in a hierarchy

When I ask for skills and characteristics that are important in sustaining love relationships, the answers include:

Cooperation
Confiding
Emotional openness
Spending time together
Fun and playfulness
A relationship between equals
Affection, tenderness and sex
Trust
Mutual respect

Whenever our hopes start to dissolve into our fears, our emotional brain kicks in and instinctively deploys the skills we know best, which are often our highly developed work skills. These are generally our most highly developed and familiar skills, abilities that we use naturally and with ease. For instance, if we think our partners are angry or unhappy with us, or perhaps losing their feelings of love for us, we might do everything we can to *control* and *manage* their feelings. If our own feelings start to wane, we may become secretive, closed and stoic—businesslike—and keep our fingers crossed and hope that things will right themselves. If we are jealous of our partners, we might become competitive to catch up to them, or be sarcastic and belittle them. If they aren't doing what we think needs to be done, we might become bossy and aggressive.

Generally, we discover that these qualities don't bring us happiness as a couple.

We become disappointed, despondent or unfulfilled. We grow apart. This is often when people turn to me or to my colleagues in the counseling field.

My office is near Washington, D.C., which is a pressure-cooker of a professional town where the work skills I described are honed to a fine edge.

Many of my clients are powerful and talented men and women who have risen to the top echelon of government, the military, the legal profession or the media. They are often shell-shocked when they come to see me because they cannot understand why, with all their proven and prized abilities, they could not save their marriages, their families and their dreams.

THE LOGIC OF EMOTION

One way to understand love is to understand what it is not. Love is not a commitment. Love is not a relationship. Love is not a responsibility. You may choose to make a commitment based on feelings of love, but you cannot commit yourself to feel love for another person. *Love is a feeling.* All feelings, including love, wax and wane. The only promise that we can make and keep is to create an atmosphere between us that allows for feelings of love to continue to flow between us.

Since love is just one of a wide range of emotions, we need to understand how emotions work—what they tell us, how they influence our behavior, how they can and cannot be controlled—before we can learn about sustaining love in long-term relationships.

We can understand the logic of love if we understand the logic of emotion. The logic of emotion is actually very simple: It is the logic of pleasure and pain. We are drawn to what gives us pleasure and tend to avoid what gives us pain. What gives us pleasure at the simplest level is to have our needs met. Unfulfilled needs give us pain.

Beyond our most rudimentary survival needs, such as food, water and shelter (the needs the reptilian brain looks out for), there exists another level of "creature needs"—the more subtle but no less demanding needs for closeness, communication, nurturing, safety and emotional warmth that are required by the emotional or creature part of the brain. Experts are just coming to recognize that among the most powerful of these creature needs is the *need for bonding*—a combination of physical closeness and emotional openness. While it has long been known that consistent bonding is necessary for infants and children to thrive, it is only recently that we have started to understand that the need for bonding extends throughout our lifetime.

There is growing evidence that bonding is built into the human species as a biologically based need. And as with other biological needs, the inability to fulfill this need easily and comfortably often gives rise to symptoms. Instead of feeling hunger pangs or thirst, we feel unsettled, anxious or even depressed.

As children, we depend upon other people to fulfill many of our needs. A child needs to be cared for, protected, nurtured, guided. While growing up, we developed a series of attitudes and beliefs about people that were shaped by whether and how those needs were met and whether they were met at a cost. If you were raised in an unstable family, you might have difficulty trusting anyone to provide for your needs. You may have learned that the surest way *not* to get your needs met was to ask. Or you might believe that you have to be perfect to have your needs met. Or you might think that needing another person for anything is dangerous or wrong or weak. Now that you are an adult, however, you can fulfill all of your needs yourself—except the need for bonding. You have the ability to earn a living, keep a roof over your head, keep your body fit, feed yourself, dress yourself. You can learn what you choose. You can even have sex by yourself. *But you can't bond with yourself.* So all of the feelings, attitudes and beliefs about how your needs were responded to by other people become attached to the one need that you still have of others, that of bonding.

THE NATURE OF BONDING

The fulfillment of bonding has two basic elements: physical closeness and emotional openness. One without the other is not enough. If you are emotionally close to someone and confide in that person, that's friendship. While important to all of us, friendship only partially fills the need for bonding. If you are physically close to somebody who is emotionally distant or closed, it's like hugging a tree or a stone. It takes the two together—emotional openness that elicits mutual confiding, combined with physical closeness—to fill the creature need for bonding.

Bonding is the heart of intimacy. More encompassing and enduring than passion or lust (though at times it may include them), bonding is a source of total body pleasure that remains, even when sexual capacity is diminished because of illness or age. It's a closeness that fills both skin hunger and the need to feel safe in the world, to feel that you can trust another person with your whole being, your laughter, your tears, your rage, your joy. It's the deep satisfaction of all three parts of your brain. At its most heightened level, it's as close as most of us get to the exquisite experience, however temporary, of fusion with another being.

Many of us are so busy that we don't take the time for this kind of mutual nurturing. Some of us don't even know it exists. It is a powerful buffer against the stresses of daily life—and nature's best remedy for depression. The inability to meet our need for bonding is often at the heart of depression, yet people who are depressed rarely know it.

While bonding may be shown by such simple gestures of warmth and affection as hugs and kisses, true bonding is much more than that. Its essence lies in total certainty that your partner is emotionally fully there with you and for you—open to you in body, heart and mind—and knowing that you can offer the same to your partner. It's the ability to lower your defenses and share yourself fully with another human being, knowing that you are accepted and loved for what you really are, and knowing that you don't have to pretend.

It's when you combine confiding with physical closeness that you get the intimacy that lies at the heart of bonded love. It's when people lose this unique combination that they begin to say, "There's something missing. I'm not happy."

If in your early life it wasn't safe to confide in another person, or if you felt humiliated or rejected or betrayed, you can feel emotional pain or the anticipation of pain when you consider trusting, when you have the opportunity to be close or even when you anticipate being close. When we feel we are in danger, nature predisposes us to react in one of three ways: we run, we fight or we freeze. And this is the way we may treat our intimates.

If, on the other hand, you grew up in a safe and warm environment where trust and closeness were a pleasure, then being close in the present can give rise to feelings of pleasure. The anticipation of being close is felt as desire. That desire, that anticipation of pleasure, gives rise to feelings of love.

In a relationship, we need to explore what gives us a sense that we can love and trust the other person and what makes us suspicious or resentful, causing us to lash out (fight), turn our attention elsewhere (run), or withdraw (freeze). To do this, we need to take a careful look at our personal history—from our earliest memories to the present—because we tend to treat the person who is with us now on the basis of our experiences in the past.

THE RELATIONSHIP ROAD MAP

The Relationship Road Map, which I will refer to and build on throughout this book, is the foundation for the intimacy lessons we learn in PAIRS. It illustrates those behaviors and attitudes that prevent us from experiencing pleasure in intimate relationships and offers new attitudes and behaviors needed to sustain loving relationships. At the very center of the map is bonding. We find ourselves on the pain side or the pleasure side of the map depending on how we deal with our need for closeness or love. If both people in a relationship can confide, can be expressive and open to each other with their bodies, hearts and minds, they will generally experience and display "symptoms" of happiness and fulfillment: health and energy, flexibility, creativity, responsibility for self and a capacity for intimacy. If the relationship is marked by caution, anger and mistrust it will grow more and more difficult to experience pleasurable bonding. The symptoms we develop in a relationship where we are unable to fulfill our needs for love and bonding tend to be fatigue, depression, rigidity, addictions (to drugs, alcohol, food or work) or isolation.

The emotions and symptoms we experience can indicate to us where we are on the Relationship Road Map now. Our emotional past—our personal history—is what led us to one side of the map or another. The resulting attitudes and behaviors we rely on now are what keep us there. If you are unhappy in a relationship, you can choose to learn new ways of thinking, feeling and behaving that will allow you to establish more pleasurable, loving bonds.

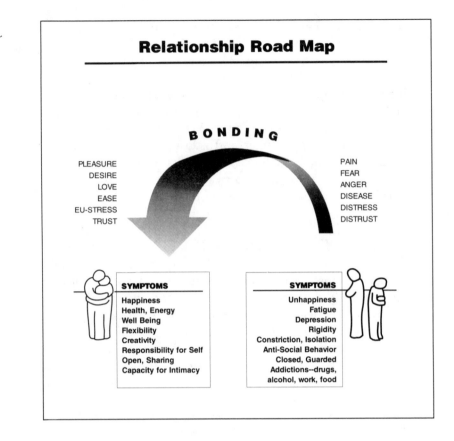

Relationship Road Map

B O N D I N G

PLEASURE
DESIRE
LOVE
EASE
EU-STRESS
TRUST

PAIN
FEAR
ANGER
DISEASE
DISTRESS
DISTRUST

SYMPTOMS

Happiness
Health, Energy
Well Being
Flexibility
Creativity
Responsibility for Self
Open, Sharing
Capacity for Intimacy

SYMPTOMS

Unhappiness
Fatigue
Depression
Rigidity
Constriction, Isolation
Anti-Social Behavior
Closed, Guarded
Addictions--drugs,
alcohol, work, food

Look at the Relationship Road Map.
- On which side would you place yourself?
- What emotions tend to prevail in your relationship?
- What "symptoms" do you show?
- What symptoms would you prefer to have and what emotions do you wish would predominate in your relationship?

Take a moment to write a few sentences in your notebook about your response thus far. You might start out by writing, "I am beginning to realize . . ."

2

The Mechanics of Emotion: Emotional Allergy and Intimacy

■   ■   ■

*T*he human nervous system has not changed much over thousands of years, although it developed at a time when the human condition and human needs were drastically different. The pleasure part of the system probably evolved to meet the species' need for survival and procreation. Pleasure—a wide array of feelings ranging from excitement, passion, euphoria and wonder to comfort and safety—is an emotional way to tell our creature brain that we can or should keep doing whatever it is we are doing. Through those feelings, our body ensures that it mates, gets fed, is safe from harm, has companionship and, in general, has its needs met. Because they provide the fuel that drives us, feelings have enormous energy. Our defense-related emotions—fear (for detecting danger), pain (for knowing we are in the midst of danger) and anger (for responding to danger)—are the body's way of advising our brain how to respond to things that could cause injuries. When we feel threatened, the brain unleashes powerful hormones into our bloodstream. Our heart beats more quickly, our blood pressure rises, and blood flows to where it is needed the most (away from the skin and the stomach to the muscles). We sweat and our feet turn cold, our eyes dilate to better see what threatens us, our skin turns pale, we get that "sinking feeling" of a knot or butterflies in our stomach, and our mind races as our body mobilizes for the coming "flight or fight" responses needed to cope with danger.

The problem is that the body and its emotional responses were designed for more primitive conditions than those in which we live. We're not out hunting or avoiding bears or tigers anymore and we rarely have to physically fight one another. But evolution has yet to catch up with the times, so that our hormonal bodies behave much as they did when we lived in the wild.

That leaves us with instincts that are often inappropriate at best and dangerous at worst. When we are passed up for a well-deserved promotion, our gut reaction might be to take a poke at our boss. But such a response is likely to lead to the loss of our livelihood and perhaps our freedom if we end up in jail.

How do we handle the dangers of the gorillas in the boardroom and the ghosts in the bedroom? How do we handle our fears and the pain of betrayal or loneliness or disappointment? The statistics on divorce, drug and alcohol addiction and overall mental health indicate that we don't handle them well.

Our difficulty in handling emotions isn't caused by weakness or character flaws. It exists because emotions work in a subtle but powerful way that most of us are never taught to understand. It's almost as if we think of our feelings as something that happen to us, like being stuck in a rainstorm or being tripped in a grocery aisle. But emotions are signals that demand expression and attention. If they are neglected, they keep returning, or they find ways to leak out, with even more force, nit-picking, criticism, withdrawing, displacing, withholding, footdragging or even rage or violence.

EMOTIONAL ALLERGIES

What happens with difficult emotions is similar to what happens during an allergic reaction. You can be exposed to something like ragweed for years without a hint of a problem. Then one day, you've had too much of it, your system can't tolerate it anymore, and suddenly, you are made miserable by sneezing, headaches and congestion. From then on, exposure to even a tiny amount of ragweed can touch off a full-blown allergic reaction.

Emotions work the same way. Anything in our lives that has hurt us, caused us pain or disappointment or distrust can develop into an "emotional allergy." Our emotions do not care whether we are conscious of the source of that past pain or it is buried deep in our unconscious, whether it is from a recent event or from the distant past. Later on, one hint of a similar thing happening—even if it's nowhere near the same—will catapult us into anticipating the same kind of pain or fear and can launch us into a full-blown anxiety attack.

Think about what you have wanted most from a relationship.
- To be special to someone?
- To be cherished?
- To be trusted or to be able to trust?
- To have a playmate or friend?
- To have a sexual partner?

Think about what scares you the most about being close to someone.
- How can that person hurt you the most?
- How do you respond when you suspect you're going to be hurt?

When our partner does something that sets off an invisible warning (ignores us when we need attention, speaks sharply or dismisses us when busy), we very often find ourselves reacting as if our partner were the enemy. And we don't treat enemies like friends or lovers. We hide, demand, capitulate, blame, avoid, ignore, distrust, threaten, attack, destroy, keep secrets, nitpick, criticize, interrogate, label and call them names. We distance and withhold, often saying things like:

I don't love you anymore.
Don't bother me.
You've changed.
Not tonight. I don't feel like it.

You don't understand me.
Who would want to be with you?

We may even develop a Revolving Ledger and displace the blame for past hurts onto our present partner, which we discuss in more detail in Chapter 12.

Our partner is likely to respond to what we say or do by getting angry in turn or withdrawing as well. And neither of us understands the true spark of the conflict. We are hurt and baffled.

Anne Marie was raised by a responsible and hardworking mother. Her father was an alcoholic who offered little help around the house and who eventually left her mother for another woman. Anne Marie grew up and married Pete, who was a loving and attentive husband. Whenever Pete happened to forget a household chore like taking out the garbage or picking up the dry cleaning, Anne Marie would fly into a rage. Inevitably they would end up in an hours-long argument. While on the surface she was furious, beneath she was panicked. On an unconscious level, she was panicked that his forgetfulness was simply the first sign that he was the same kind of selfish, unthinking man her father was and eventually he would abandon her just as her father had abandoned his family. It took some detective work for her to pinpoint her emotional allergy.

Terri and Charles, beginning their second marriage, provide an even more dramatic example of the damage that can be caused by an emotional allergy. They came to my office not long after Charles had written her a note saying that he was leaving. Terri was in shock. She had believed that they had a good marriage. She loved Charles and believed he loved her. When urged to present his complaints so that at the very least she would know what had gone wrong, his first and strongest resentment centered on an event Terri did not even remember. Charles had called her at work one day to touch base, to feel a sense of connection between them. Rushed that day, she had responded in a businesslike manner. What Charles essentially heard was, "Why are you bothering me? What do you want now?" As he tearfully related that incident, Charles revealed that his mother had left home when he was three and he had been raised in a series of foster homes because his father could not keep him. Even when his father remarried and might have brought him home, he didn't. Charles's picture of himself as unwanted and abandoned was triggered by Terri's cool response to his phone calls. Terri had thought nothing of her response on the phone, having no way of knowing the importance Charles placed on such ordinary contact. When she realized how painful it was for Charles to even discuss his childhood, she could see the link between her responses and his easily triggered sense of abandonment.

Armed with that knowledge, it was easy for her to decide to be more receptive and affectionate to Charles on the phone. Opening himself to his past and sharing it with Terri allowed Charles to see how he was responding to his historical emotional allergies. His ability to share this self-awareness with Terri gave them crucial information that breathed new possibilities into their relationship. The emotional allergy to abandonment, his reaction to it and his initial inability to confide in Terri about it were what kept Charles on the pain side of the Relationship Road Map. He was able to begin moving to the side of pleasure only when he could take the risk of confiding and asking for the reassurance he needed.

Intense emotional responses require careful examination because they can lead us to knowledge about ourselves and ourselves in the world. Such knowledge empowers us and gives us the opportunity to choose. When we react blindly to such emotions, we allow circumstances to make choices for us.

Imagine that you're camping deep in the woods. The fire has gone out and you're just drifting off to sleep. Suddenly there is a loud howl and it doesn't sound very far away. The hackles go up on your neck and you bolt upright in your tent. Your emotional response is telling your body to do something, to protect yourself. If you are with an experienced camper, he or she will give you information and advice you need to make a decision. "Don't worry, it's just a coyote. They never attack people." With that knowledge, you can now make a choice. Do you trust that person's knowledge? If the answer is yes, you can decide that there is little to fear. Your heart stops racing, your breath evens out, you feel calmer. If you hear the howl again, it doesn't startle you in the same way. You may even be able to enjoy listening to it for its strangeness and beauty. If you were alone and ignorant of the ways of the forest, however, and could not tell what the noise was, you would have difficulty being calm. If the howl came again, but closer this time, you would probably grow more frightened. Sleep would be out of the question; you might, like Charles, just pack up and leave. If you never gained knowledge about what that noise was and whether it was a threat, you might never go camping again.

Understanding what touches off our emotional allergies is the only way to decide whether the haunting sound you hear is a harmless coyote or a man-eating wolf. In a relationship, that determination can be made only through honest self-exploration, openness, trust and honesty.

Think about a recent argument you had with your partner or someone else you are close to.
  • Do you know what that fight was really about?
As you replay the fight in your mind, don't think in terms of who started it or whose fault it was. Think about how you felt before it started.
  • Were you hurt by something? Scared? Angry?
Think about other times in your life that felt the same way.
  • Who else did you have similar fights with or whom did you observe having similar fights?
  • Is there a relationship between these episodes?

EMOTIONAL BLOCKS

We tend to fall into one of two patterns—and sometimes both—when we lose touch with our feelings (which most of us do at some time in our lives).

First, we may bottle them up so tightly that we stop feeling altogether. In effect, we deep-freeze our feelings. The ability to go numb can be a valuable mechanism for those times when we are overwhelmed by tragedy. It allows us to survive, but it is not a way to thrive. When we are numb, we block not just fear, anger and pain, but also all feelings of pleasure and love. If this pattern is not changed, many of us eventually move from being numb to being depressed—an overwhelming but vague feeling of despair for which we can find no single explanation or cause.

Second, our feelings of pain and anger can leak out, often in destructive ways. This is especially common for those of us who try to "protect" our partners from problems, such as mounting bills or conflict at work. We return home after a particularly rough day and pretend that everything is okay. But if we go into the bathroom and find the sink filled with pantyhose or the garbage overflowing in the kitchen or a TV dinner, we may turn suddenly bitter or sarcastic. We may nitpick, harangue, pick fights.

Pain leaks out as well. Many of us find that almost any sad movie or song can invite tears. Unacknowledged fear can make us chronically anxious, listless or tentative, unable to rise to challenges.

Jesse went through both phases. Jesse had a difficult time expressing any of his emotions to Carol, especially his fears. When his company was failing, he grew panicked about their future. Wanting to protect her from those fears, however, he never mentioned them. Jesse later acknowledged that he resented that she could be so calm. He resented that she seemed oblivious to his problems— even though he hadn't mentioned them or his concerns. He began to attack and criticize Carol for the slightest mistake. He provoked bitter fights when she lost her car keys. Once, Carol asked why he got so upset by something so minor and his response was: "Because I'm so tired of you being so stupid."

Jesse realized that his marriage was collapsing and he blamed himself. He decided that his seemingly uncontrollable anger was the biggest obstacle and vowed to not get angry with Carol anymore. He stopped being sharp and sarcastic. Eventually, he stopped talking to Carol almost entirely. He lost all desire for sex. Jesse grew distraught and, convinced that there must be more to life than the thin, closed-off existence he was leading, left the marriage. The feelings of numbness were so strong that it took years, and dozens of therapy sessions, for him to begin experiencing remorse and loss over the dissolution of his marriage.

THE EMOTIONAL JUG

If you were to pour your emotions into an Emotional Jug, they would look multilayered. The cork at the top of the jug would be indifference or ambivalence; these feelings essentially are decisions to cover up and control our upsetting feelings. If you "pop your cork" or "blow your lid," right beneath it often lies a layer of anger. When we first begin exploring our emotions, anger is often at the top, the first to reveal itself. When Charles first started to list his complaints about Terri, for example, he talked angrily about how cold and unfeeling she was. It was only after he expressed his anger about that that he was able to get to the next level—fear and pain. Those feelings lie beneath anger, near the middle of the jug, sometimes far out of our reach.

EMOTIONAL JUG

Lid of Indifference

Blowing your top
Popping your cork

Stiff Upper Lip

ANGER

FEAR Pain

Pleasure

Tenderness

Love

Once anger, fear and pain are released, there is room to feel love.

For some, especially those who were taught that anger was a dangerous, forbidden feeling, it is much easier to feel and express pain than it is to get angry. For them, the top layer of the jug might be pain and fear, with anger buried underneath. The difficult task they face is learning that it is okay—even necessary—to get angry, even to the point of being furious, if that's what's there.

Beneath these feelings, buried deeply, are our feelings of tenderness, desire, pleasure and love. The only way to find out if they're there is to uncork the lid of indifference and release the difficult feelings of anger, pain and fear. To look at Charles one last time, it was only after he worked his way through indifference (it doesn't matter anymore; I'll just leave), anger (you're thoughtless and cold), pain (nobody cares; I'll be alone) and fear (you'll leave me just like everybody else did) that he was able to rediscover and reclaim feelings of love for Terri.

The peculiar logic of emotion is sometimes at odds with the logic of our thinking brain. Our logical thinking brain tells us that pain should be avoided, dispensed with, ignored and buried as quickly as possible. Unfortunately, avoiding pain simply tends to prolong its effects and can mean depriving yourself of pleasure and love as well. For when you are filled with pain, fear and anger, there is no room to feel love. The way to move from the pain side of the Relationship Road Map toward pleasure is to allow ourselves to experience the pain and its companion emotions of fear and anger instead of suppressing them. The corrosive nature of these feelings can be checked once they are brought out into the open, accepted, understood and confided in an interested, empathic partner. That is what the two PAIRS Museum Tour exercises are designed to help you do.

PAIRS Exercise: A Museum Tour of Past Hurts

This exercise, one of several I use in PAIRS that are based on the pioneering work of George Bach, gives us an opportunity to bring to the surface and reflect on sources of pain and disappointment in our lives. It requires two steps and some time in which to be reflective.

STEP ONE:

In your journal, write a list of "pictures" in your Personal Museum of Memories of things that happened in your life that were hurtful, dangerous or scary. Think of each event as a painting that hangs on a wall of your museum. These can be single events, such as being sick and alone in a hospital, an accident, an abortion, a divorce, being forced to move away from close friends; a series of related or repeated events (incest, alcoholism, staying up nights and listening to violent arguments between parents, endless nights of being left home alone); slights ("I'll never forget how you refused to postpone a business trip to attend my graduation"); times of loss or rejection (death of a family member or friend, a broken relationship); or acts of betrayal (an affair by a spouse; abandonment by a parent, partner or friend; the refusal of one parent to protect you from the abuse of another; slander by a friend).

Think about events that occurred in connection with parents, siblings, friendships, work, school and childhood. Pay special attention to current and past important relationships. Don't dismiss anything because it seems "silly" (like being disappointed that you didn't get a particular birthday present as a child or feeling sad at being left home alone sick while your partner plays tennis) or seems as if you are being unfair ("I know she was gone during our anniversary, but that was a very important business trip for her"). Things that may seem trivial can still feel devastating emotionally. You will have an opportunity later to examine the reasons why you may have felt a particular way. Write as little or as much as it takes to have a good sense of what each "painting" looks and feels like.

Here are some sample entries:

> Having my wife harangue me and scream at me on our honeymoon because of the awful way my uncle behaved when he got drunk at our wedding. It was like she had turned into some kind of monster I could never have made up, even in my nightmares.
>
> Having a dog follow me home when I was nine. I wanted to keep it but Dad took it to the pound because it was too much trouble. I'll never forget the look of betrayal on that creature's face when he was thrown into the back of the station wagon and I didn't go with him.

Watching my mother get suddenly ill and being sent to camp because I would "wear her out." I remember her asleep in bed looking fragile and thinking that I could make her feel better if they would just let me.

STEP TWO:
This step involves more searching. Look at each incident and ask yourself these questions about it. Write down your answers in your journal.

What was I upset and angered by?
What was I hurt by?
What was I scared, anxious, frightened about?
What did I want or need?
What do I realize?

Using the "painting" of the troubled honeymoon as an example, we find answers that might look like this:

I was angry that she blamed me for something I had no control over, my drunken uncle.
I was hurt that she would not stop talking about it and that she could not overlook such an incident on such a special occasion.
I was scared by how volatile she seemed. I was scared that our life together might always be like this.
I needed her understanding. My uncle is an alcoholic but I love him despite his problem. I need to trust that she will not take every mishap that happens to us out on me. I need sympathy sometimes instead of blame.
I realize that she was angry because she had worried about his behavior before we invited him. I know she has an allergy to that kind of behavior because her father was an alcoholic.

How did it feel to think about past painful episodes? Were there connections between incidents in your childhood and your more recent past? Do you still hold grudges against some of the people you wrote about? Are there any attitudes you have now about trust or confiding or about the opposite sex that are linked to these incidents and might be sabotaging pleasure and trust in your relationship today?

We examine painful periods in our lives to help us determine which events may still be causing us pain now and which might be the basis for an emotional allergy. But moving to the pleasure side of the Relationship Road Map also means learning about the things that bring us joy. If we take note of the things that add pleasure to our lives, we can make more good things happen instead of waiting for luck or fortune. We do this by not just looking at the things that have us stuck on the pain side of the Relationship Map, but by actively moving toward the side of pleasure.

PAIRS Exercise: A Museum Tour of Past Joys

STEP ONE:
Turn to a new page in your journal. List the various incidents and people that have been sources of joy for you. Think of each as a painting or portrait and write enough to conjure up a complete picture. These can be childhood memories, romantic encounters, gestures by a partner when you felt hurt or scared, accomplishments and pastimes, trips, discoveries, things grandiose and things simple. While you review your life, pay special attention to your current relationship or past important relationships. Let yourself experience again the things that make you happy with another person.

Cheryl wrote:

> I remember how it started to rain while we were camping. You said you were going to take me to dinner at some cheap diner so we could get warm and instead you had made reservations at a nice hotel for the night. It even had a private whirlpool and you bought soap bubbles.
> I remember how, even though he didn't like the idea, Dad convinced Mom that it should be my decision to go to music school part-time and pursue my career in the band instead of going away to college.
> I still love to look at the cabinet that I spent almost a whole year making and refinishing.

STEP TWO:
Now, ask yourself these questions about each incident:

How did I feel (valued, respected, satisfied, special, and so forth)?

What did I appreciate (that you went out of your way, that you considered my feelings, your thoughtfulness)?

What do I realize (you were busy; you disagreed with me; it was just as much fun for you)?

Using the example of the aborted camping trip, we might find answers like this:

I felt that you turned a major disaster into a wonderful experience. It made me feel special and loved.

I appreciated your spontaneity and inventiveness.

I realize that it was a difficult decision for you to pay for that room. We were broke and you brown-bagged to work for two weeks afterward. How sick you must have gotten of bologna and peanut butter.

- How did it feel to bring up pleasurable memories?
- Did it help to ease the uncomfortable emotions brought out by the previous exercise?
- Did it help restore good feelings about people at whom you were angry or who hurt you?
- Did you find yourself wondering why you haven't done some fun or pleasurable things recently?
- Do you recall more easily the small things that brought you a great deal of happiness?

The memories in our Museum of Past Hurts are of experiences that we hope to prevent from happening again. These memories and the intense emotions they arouse can be triggered by an incident in the present to which we react with an emotional allergy—often without our making the connection between the current event and our past. Sometimes we are drawn to recreate the circumstances of those incidents with the hope that this time they will have a better ending. The Museum Tour of Past Joys not only helps us pay attention to and search out the things that bring us pleasure, but also can help us to discover a different kind of emotional allergy as well. If we had good things happen to us in our lives, we want them to keep happening. We experience disappointment if they do not— often without understanding the source of our feelings. For instance, if Jim saw how happy it made his father when the family was waiting for him when he came home from work, Jim might feel hurt and annoyed if his wife and children are busy elsewhere when he comes home. He might be irritable and cranky when the family finally does get together, without clearly knowing why.

- Can you see which events of pain and pleasure from your past may be influencing your feelings now?
- How do they affect what you are drawn to and what you are turned off by?

The good and bad things that happened to us as we grew up also deeply affect the way we look at ourselves now. We will look at the effect our view of ourselves has on us in the next chapter.

Take a moment to write in your journal notebook about what you are beginning to realize.

3

Self-Esteem:
The Indispensable Foundation

■   ■   ■

*N*othing is more important to intimacy than your sense of self-worth. How you feel about yourself in relation to other people is a major factor in the quality of your intimate relationships. And trouble in a relationship almost always involves a problem with self-esteem.

To have a sense of self-worth, you need to believe that you are both good enough and lovable. While growing up, you need to develop confidence about your competence and mastery of the world—your ability to do well in school or in athletics, to cook or ride a bike or fix an engine or use other skills. The attention and approval you received as a child from your parents and other adults helps you develop confidence in your ability to cope with the world.

You also need to feel that you are lovable whether you are competent or not. When your lovability is validated, you grow up feeling confident about yourself as a man or woman, as a sexual being and as a friend—as someone worth spending time with and confiding in.

What often happens is that we are validated in one area and not the other. We may be praised for our good grades in school, for example, but not for being pretty or handsome, or because someone would want to be with us or spend time with us. Men in particular often tell me, "I don't have any doubts about myself. I'm doing very well. I have a good job, I'm in a good position, I make enough money—so *I* don't have any problems," when in fact, they often have not been validated as a sexual, lovable person: someone with whom you would want to be close; someone whom you would treasure and enjoy, not for their achievements, but simply because they exist. Unconditional love is something we need as adults, but we need it especially when we are small. If we don't develop the sense that we are lovable creatures when we are children, the question of our lovability becomes crucial in our future interactions with people.

In her book *New Peoplemaking*, Virginia Satir tells a story about a huge three-legged caldron that sat on the porch of the farm where she grew up. At different times of the year there were different things in the pot. In the summer, her mother used it to make soup for the farm workers who did the threshing. In the winter, she used it to make soap. And in the fall, her father used it to store manure for her mother's plants. (It came to be known as the three-S pot: soup, soap and shit.) So the question around their house tended to be "What's in the pot and how full is it?" Obviously, when it was full of soap or fertilizer, it wasn't going to hold soup. Each of these things had a value of its own, but when the pot was full of one thing, there was no room for anything else. Virginia adapted the pot image to the measure of self-worth, for which the appropriate question became, "What's in your pot and how full is it?" Within yourself you might have soup, which is very nourishing, or soap, which is neutral, or shit—and if someone gets near you, that's what's going to come out. Virginia Satir talks about not only what's in your pot, but also whether you are "high pot" or "low pot": If you are low pot, you don't really feel good that day, and if you are high pot, you feel great. That pot on Virginia's farm was never empty— it always had something in it. And your metaphorical pot is the same; within the self, there is always something going on.

When you are "low pot" (when you don't have a lot of self-confidence), you tend to be so preoccupied with questions of self-worth that, when you interact with someone else, especially some-one who is important to you, you may not perceive what is going

on very accurately. Your mind will be filled with questions about
your sense of worth and lovability:

Am I good enough?
Will he like me?
Will she want me?
Do my feelings matter?
Am I safe?
Will I be hurt?
Will I be laughed at or humiliated?
Is it safe to ask for things?
Can I trust you?
Will you leave me?

When we are nagged by such doubt-inspiring questions, we
likely view reality differently: a smile that seems comforting to you
may seem condescending to me; a criticism that I construe as being
informative may knock the wind out of your sails. This is one way
that simple day-to-day events can seemingly erupt from nowhere
into devastating arguments.

Household chores, one of the mundane things that often becomes a marital battleground, are a good example.

For years, it may have been common for you to ask me to take
out the trash. But if your self-esteem is at a low ebb and you feel
that I have been taking advantage of you by leaving it to you to
remind me every few days that the trash needs to be taken out, you
might attack me the minute I get in the door, saying things like:
"You never help around here" or "You can't even handle a little chore
like getting rid of the trash." It is likely such a statement will trigger
my "flight or fight" response and I will either say something sharp
in return or shut down emotionally and withdraw.

It may be that my own self-esteem is low so that when you ask
me to take out the trash, instead of hearing a simple request, I feel
as if you are bossing me around or doubting my ability to remember
simple tasks. Since I believe that I am a mature, reasonable person,
however, I decide that I won't snap at you. Instead, after dinner, I

bring up the fact that you are always overspending and have no sense when it comes to money.

In these examples, several things have happened:

People with low self-esteem were *unaware* of the real cause of their discomfort.

They *assumed* that their partner was to blame for the bad feelings they were experiencing.

They *acted* on those feelings and took their partner to task for them.

Rather than directly address the way they felt, they *created an issue* in which they felt they had the upper hand, regardless of whether the issue was the genuine source of concern or irritation (the trash).

You can see how rapidly a chain of negative events can be set into motion by one small comment. Part of the work of a relationship is to learn how to short-circuit these chain reactions. By "short-circuit" I do not mean trying to set aside or stuff down the feelings that you have, trying to pretend they did not occur. I mean using those feelings to detect the source of the problem so that you can deal with it directly.

There are three things you can begin doing right away to prevent the havoc that comes from mindlessly acting on the emotions you experience and to begin moving away from the pain side of the Relationship Road Map.

First, recognize your emotions as a signal that something is wrong. Ask yourself *why* you think you are so upset or angry: Be a detective in your own behalf. Do you feel threatened? Diminished? Controlled? Uncared for? Ashamed? Guilty? Incompetent? Unloved?

Second, keeping in mind whatever answers you come up with, ask yourself if what happened or what was said was the sole source of your feelings, or if other things that occurred recently were a factor. Had an emotional allergy been triggered? Remember that the conclusions you reach are nowhere near as important as the process of learning to stop the automatic reaction and think things through. You may discover that you have legitimate reason to be upset. That's fine; you now have the information you need to tackle that problem directly and clearly.

Third, talk to your partner regularly, daily, about how you feel, particularly about yourself. Your partner needs to know whether your "pot" is high or low. This gives him or her clues about your behavior. As you make discoveries about the things that affect your self-esteem, such as doubts, let your partner know what you have learned. Such confiding provides your partner with invaluable information about what is going on inside the person he or she loves.

As you begin practicing these techniques and the others to follow, remember that you are combating decades of habit and conditioning and cannot expect that they will change overnight. Habits, even negative ones, feel natural to us even when we can see clearly how they interfere with our lives. Be patient with yourself and your partner. Give each other a break if you find yourselves falling back into old patterns. Under stress, we regress. You will know that you have changed the old patterns when you can sustain the new way under stress!

Can you think of a recent fight you had with your partner that had more to do with your self-esteem than with the issue you were arguing about?
  • Would you handle it any differently now?
  • Is it difficult to tell your partner when you feel taken for
    granted or mistreated? If so, why?

SELF-ESTEEM PATTERNS AND CONTROL

Persistent low self-esteem causes problems that can go far beyond misunderstandings and temporary flare-ups. When your self-esteem is solid, you are likely to choose a partner because he or she has qualities that bring you pleasure. You have a clear sense of your own power—you neither cede power to nor seek control over your partner.

If your sense of self-worth is low, however, you may become involved with someone for the wrong reasons. You may marry someone who bolsters your ego with constant admiration, devotion and flattery. But if your partner's love or admiration appears to waver (if she flirts at a party or he has lunch with his pretty new officemate), you may be tormented by jealousy and suspicion or even panic or depression. On the other hand, you may look to marry someone who makes you look good because of his or her good looks or status or achievements. It then becomes very important that he or she continue to make you look good. It can even become important for your children or your friends to make you look good. You may see them as extensions of yourself and become very controlling, rigid or manipulative.

The confusion that stems from such blurred distinctions can be enormous and displays itself in many ways.

If you learned while growing up that your worth was tied to your productiveness ("idle hands are the devil's workshop"), you may find yourself feeling bad when your partner seems "lazy" and will forever be searching out things for him or her to do. If you believe that "clothes make the man" or that women should always dress attractively and neatly, you might constantly monitor your spouse's and children's appearance and feel that it reflects badly on you if they appear slovenly. If you feel unsure of yourself, others' opinions and thoughts about everything from politics to theater feel like a challenge to your own, not just a matter of differing tastes. It becomes very important that those close to you present themselves to the world in the way you want them to. *People with low self-esteem can be very controlling.*

Oddly enough, low self-esteem also can lead to seemingly opposite behavior. Some allow themselves to be easily controlled and pliable, or as one friend says, "Please feel free to walk all over me with cleats on." If people treat you badly, you don't speak up or object because you don't really believe you are entitled to be treated any differently. You may go out of your way to please and comfort others without seeking the same for yourself. Feeling needed is the way that many people bolster their self-esteem. Sometimes they seek to make the other person feel "indebted" to them. Unfortunately, such a constant preoccupation with others will probably prevent you from experiencing the joys of being cared about. If you are a "caretaker" type and someone should express an interest in your needs, you may become suspicious ("What do you really want?" or

"When will you stop caring?"), never believing that you are worthy of someone's attention and love for your own sake. You constantly question the offer of love, which can finally discourage the lover. Being cared for may make you feel uncomfortable and vulnerable, because when someone else is tending to your needs, you no longer feel in *control*.

Both cases are really different sides of the same coin. Each type, feeling a lack of control and mastery over his or her own life, seeks control over those closest to him or her—either actively (by being demanding and bossy) or passively (by caretaking).

We tend to mix and match these traits. Many people in PAIRS have reported being mostly one way in one relationship and mostly the other way with a different partner. People with low self-esteem often find one another and compensate for their traits—one playing the role of the dependent, needy person while the other plays the caretaker.

- Is it important to you to always have things your way?
- Does the threat of losing an argument or not having things done the way you always do them make you feel as if you are losing control or are diminished?
- Does a compromise feel like a retreat instead of an agreement that helps keep the relationship in balance?
- Are you a caretaker? Do you always put someone else's needs before your own?
- Do you spend more time trying to "fix" other people than you do yourself?
- Do you find it difficult to tell people when you feel hurt or angry?

MAKING RULES ABOUT EMOTIONS

One of the most troublesome symptoms of low self-esteem is having rules against certain feelings. You may feel somehow defective or ashamed or bad because you're feeling the "wrong" thing.

This is especially true of anger, pain and fear, but also can be true of any emotion. Even love can be an upsetting feeling if you anticipate rejection or if it is for the "wrong" person. In essence, you end up doubting your own perceptions. When you feel angry about something, you might chastise yourself: "That's ridiculous, this is nothing to be angry about." The truth is, the only way you can determine the validity of a feeling is to experience it and then try to discover the validity of its source. There is nothing wrong with feelings themselves; the question is how do you express them?

Low self-esteem can exhibit itself in any or all of the ways described in this chapter. If you mix two people with low esteem into one relationship, the room for confusion becomes an entire mansion.

Lucille is a beautiful woman who never felt confident about her own worth. As a child she had learning disabilities and could never read or spell well, which made her feel defective and unlovable. She came to see me when her current relationship had collapsed, having already gone through two failed marriages. Her boyfriend had been abandoned by his parents as a child and needed enormous amounts of reassurance that he was wanted and loved. Lucille, believing that her opinions and emotions never counted for anything, didn't know to offer that reassurance. He left.

This is why confiding is so essential to the well-being of an intimate relationship. No matter how silly or vulnerable you may feel at the time, confiding not only provides your partner with valuable information, but also teaches you how to accept the full range of your own emotions.

IMPROVING SELF-ESTEEM AND BECOMING NONDEFENSIVE

There is no easy trick or exercise that will raise your self-esteem. Taking *risks*—doing something that feels unnatural or uncomfortable at first and allowing yourself to *be imperfect* and learn—is the path toward changing the way you feel about yourself. Many of us are anxious about trying something—be it skiing, playing the piano or even having sex—because we are afraid we won't do it "right." All beginnings are clumsy, even for adults. Through risk taking, we challenge and change disabling attitudes that prevent us from having pleasure. What often prevents us from taking risks are internal messages—negative attitudes—that tell us there is no point in taking risks: We will fail, we will be hurt, we don't deserve the experience. Developing and practicing positive attitudes to replace those messages helps us to do things that feel risky.

The chief negative attitudes that accompany low self-esteem are *"I'm not good enough," "I'm not lovable,"* and *"I'm not entitled to be happy."* We can deliberately practice changing these attitudes and replacing them with more positive ones:

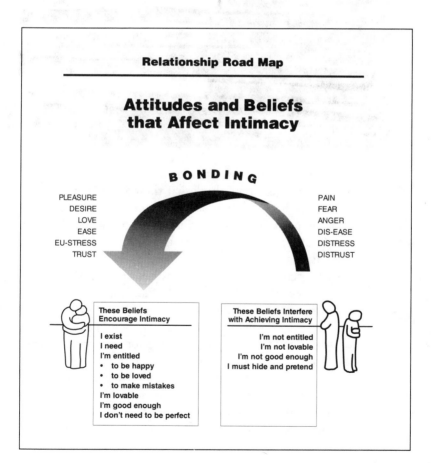

Relationship Road Map

Attitudes and Beliefs that Affect Intimacy

B O N D I N G

PLEASURE	PAIN
DESIRE	FEAR
LOVE	ANGER
EASE	DIS-EASE
EU-STRESS	DISTRESS
TRUST	DISTRUST

These Beliefs Encourage Intimacy

I exist
I need
I'm entitled
• to be happy
• to be loved
• to make mistakes
I'm lovable
I'm good enough
I don't need to be perfect

These Beliefs Interfere with Achieving Intimacy

I'm not entitled
I'm not lovable
I'm not good enough
I must hide and pretend

"I exist." By virtue of being born, I exist. I am a separate person. I have my own uniqueness. I have a right to exist. I can make my own judgments, choices and decisions.

"I need." By virtue of existence, I have needs. In addition to needing shelter and food, I have emotional needs for closeness and intimacy. I am entitled to have them and to try to get them met. I can help other people, but I will not wrap my identity up only in meeting other people's needs. I will not wait for someone else to come along and take care of me. I am in charge of myself.

"I am entitled." I am entitled to pursue getting my needs met, to be happy, to be imperfect.

"I am lovable." You may not love me, but I *am* lovable. I may even have unattractive qualities, but if I can begin to be honest about revealing who I really am and stop presenting my defenses to the world, you will find that I am lovable. First I have to realize it myself.

"I am good enough." I do not have to be perfect, I am certain to make mistakes, I may well need help and I may not be the best at any given thing, but I am good enough.

When we discuss these new attitudes in PAIRS, participants at first seem uncomfortable. Some think that these statements are obvious and almost childish. As we discuss each one in detail, however, almost everybody in the room makes a personal connection with at least one, if not all, of these attitudes. They begin to understand the misapprehensions under which they have been operating.

For those who tend to be docile and unassertive, the assertion "I exist" ("I don't need to apologize for the fact that I am here" is how one person put it) is often the eye-opener. For workaholics and perfectionists, "I am good enough" liberates them and allows them to see that they can do things for fun, not for accomplishment. They can take risks and be open to learning new things even if they are clumsy at first. Caretakers can see that they have as much right to have needs—and to have them met—as anybody else.

In relationships, the biggest risk for those of us with low esteem is confiding our needs, foibles and fears. We are accustomed to always putting our best face on for our partner; we don't like to feel weak or vulnerable. But without taking the risk of revealing ourselves fully, we can never find the intimacy and trust that enrich a relationship and help it keep growing. Such self-revelation can also allow partners to bolster each other during periods of low self-esteem.

Here is how one PAIRS participant, Sara, explained it:

> When I'm in a bad mood or irritable with the kids, Frank will now say, "I'm not going to let you pick a fight. I want to find out why you're so upset." And I really need for him to do that; it's one of the things that I really love about our relationship now—to have someone who knows me so well that he can more often than not put a finger on what's really happening with me. And the reverse is beginning to happen, too. When he's in a bad mood, I am more inclined to become curious or sympathetic than to get defensive. That allows him to feel freer and more open, and the tough times pass by more quickly. There is very little tension between us now.

4

Confiding:
The Daily Temperature
Reading

■   ■   ■

*C*onfiding—the ability to reveal yourself fully, honestly and directly to another human being is the lifeblood of intimacy.

It's frightening to be in a close relationship in which silences, hidden agendas, contradictions and inconsistencies are a steady diet. No matter how much in love two people are or how well suited to each other, no relationship can flourish under that kind of strain. Clear, regular communication is needed to live and work together with satisfaction.

In relationships that go well, couples tend to maintain an easy, flowing communication about the big and little things that are going on in their lives. On the basis of this observation, Virginia Satir developed a technique for keeping each other up-to-date, which she called the Daily Temperature Reading. This simple technique has become a major source of relationship pleasure for many couples. It also works well in other settings and in other relationships.

PAIRS Exercise: The Daily Temperature Reading
PAIRS graduates tell me two things about the Daily Temperature Reading: that it is one of the most important techniques they have

for staying close and that all too often, when they get busy, they let it slide.

Don't let it slide!

Take a Temperature Reading on each other once a day. This is an important way to maintain or develop open, flowing communication in your relationship. You will evolve your own style for doing it, but here's the basic format you will want to work from.

STEP ONE:

Appreciation. We need to be told what's good about us, and nobody is better equipped to tell us than the person who is closest to us. We hear much about what's wrong with us, both from the world at large and from ourselves (we're usually own worst critics). When you see something in your partner that you appreciate, express it—

either with words or with a gesture, but express it. Many of us also have to learn to accept our partner's appreciation. Often we have a conditioned response of brushing off compliments ("Oh, this old thing?" or "It was nothing"). We need to accept what they say and to thank them for saying it.

STEP TWO:

New Information. When we fail to provide routine information about what's going on with us, there's too much room left for making assumptions. Intimacy thrives only when partners know what is happening in each other's lives—the trivial as well as the important. It may be related to work ("I finally got that new contract"), family ("Aunt Maude's getting married again"), mutual concerns and interests ("I'm worried about that mole on your neck" or "Here's an article I think you'd enjoy reading") or friends ("I had lunch with . . ."), whatever it takes to keep contact alive and let your partner in on your moods, states, experiences—your life. Many problems and misunderstandings arise because we make *assumptions* about what's going on with our partner, since no one is providing actual information.

STEP THREE:

Puzzles. If there are things you don't understand (why your partner seemed so down last night, the latest news about the office reorganization, why Mary and Pete broke up) and your partner can explain, ask. Don't assume that your partner knows that you are interested. Not asking might well be seen as indifference. Some believe, "If you wanted to know, you would ask me." Others think, "If you wanted me to know, you would tell me." Thus do many puzzles go unresolved and questions unanswered—a ripe situation for assumptions and mind reading to develop. If there are things you don't understand that your partner could help to clarify, ask for clarification.

This is also an opportunity to explore and voice any puzzling questions you may have about yourself. ("I'm really far behind on that project at work and I don't understand why I can't sit down and get it done. I seem to have a real block." "I'm really not sure why I got so angry last night while we were trying to balance the checkbook." "Somebody snapped my head off at work over something minor and it really upset me. I don't know why it bothered me so much, since it was a small thing and something obviously was bothering me.") Bringing up such personal quandaries doesn't mean you will suddenly find answers, but discussing them can give your partner more insight about your conflicts and thoughts. Your partner also might have insights about your thoughts.

STEP FOUR:
Complaints with Requests for Change. These need not be blaming or judgmental. Simply say, "This thing happened that bothered me, and I would feel better if you did this other thing instead." When you state your complaint, *be specific* about the *behavior* that bothers you and state the *behavior* you are asking for instead. All too often, we subject people to long lists of "don't do this" and "don't do that" without ever telling them what we *do* want. Yelling, "Why don't you ever come home on time?" won't get the same response as, "If you're going to be late, please call. That way I can make my own plans and I won't worry about you." If emotional or touchy issues come up that need long discussion, you might want to set aside a more appropriate time to deal with them in depth.

The Daily Temperature Reading is intended to provide information. It is not intended to serve as a serious conflict-resolving tool—its purpose is to help prevent misunderstandings. Later chapters provide a variety of methods to prevent touchy issues from erupting into full-scale battles in which you drag every grudge you've ever had into play.

STEP FIVE:
Wishes, Hopes and Dreams. Our hopes and dreams are integral, vital parts of who and what we are. If we don't share them with our partner, we are depriving him or her of an important part of ourselves. In a world where much of our time is spent reacting to various immediate pressures, we rarely have time to think beyond the moment. This part of the Daily Temperature Reading gives us a chance to reflect on what *we* want—from ourselves, from our partners and from life. The more we can bring our expectations and hopes into our own and our partner's awareness, the more likely it is that we will find a way to realize them. They can extend from the mundane to the grandiose: "I hope you can get this weekend shift off so we

can spend more time together." "I hope we can have a baby." "I wish that someday we could have a house in the country." "I dream of having the time to leave for a month and go hiking in Alaska." "I wish I had time to concentrate on my painting."

It may seem awkward and artificial to do the Daily Temperature Reading at first. Don't let that prevent you from using it. As you become accustomed to it, you will find yourself touching on most areas automatically. You won't always have something to say in all five categories each day, but I encourage you to set aside a brief period of time every day to give yourself the opportunity to think about each area. Appreciations nurture the relationship, New Information, Puzzles and Complaints prevent misunderstandings and solve problems, and Wishes, Hopes and Dreams offer a future to look forward to.

Some people who take the PAIRS course initially resist this idea because it seems to run counter to the spontaneity they want in their relationship. But they have found that if they stick with it, the structure gives way to real sharing and allows just the spark of spontaneity they are seeking. Many people are surprised to discover that when they think about it, their day at work wasn't as boring as they believed, or that it is easier than they ever thought to be both direct and kind when they tell somebody they love that they are doing something annoying or irritating—and they get results. If you did not give yourself time to be fanciful and to share fantasies with your partner, you may never have discovered that you both dreamed about opening a bed and breakfast and that maybe you will be able to pull together the resources to give it a shot.

In his book *I and Thou*, noted philosopher Martin Buber said that when two people can be together without any masks, without any pretense, it is one of the most vitalizing experiences in life. Treating the other as someone from whom you don't have to hide your true self increases your flow of energy and your pleasure in all of life.

- Are there specific steps in the Daily Temperature Reading that made you uncomfortable or that you would prefer to avoid?
- Do you find it hard to find things that you appreciate in your partner or to voice complaints?
- Do you worry that you will feel silly or stupid or weak because of some of the questions you might ask, the dreams you have or the fears you might express?
- Have you explored where those concerns may have come from and shared them with your partner?

Take a moment to write in your journal notebook about what you are beginning to realize.

SECTION II

*I*ntroducing the Arts

■   ■   ■

A good relationship is based on mutual respect and a relatively equal balance of power.
It involves concern for and sensitivity to each
other's feelings and needs, as well as an appreciation of the things that make each partner so special. . . . Within this idea, there is
room for arguments, bad moods, differences
of opinion, even anger. However, loving
partners find effective ways of dealing with
their differences; they do not view each encounter as a battle to be won or lost.

—*Susan Forward*

5

What's Your Stress Style?

■ ■ ■

"*I*s that a new dress? We just agreed to stick to a budget! How could you be so irresponsible as to spend so much money? What's the matter with you?"

"Please don't get upset. If you don't like it, I'll take it back. I'm sorry."

"Everybody knows that unless you stick to a budget, your entire financial picture goes down the drain."

"Let's get Chinese food tonight. How do fried dumplings and won ton soup sound to you?"

We act out this kind of only slightly exaggerated dialogue in PAIRS, as you will later on in this chapter, to demonstrate the various stress styles that people use to communicate when they are upset or feel defensive. Two things are readily apparent: First, it would be rare for any of us not to be able to identify with some element of the above exchange and, second, the styles do little to enhance communication, provide information or solve problems.

Virginia Satir observed that people tend to react to stress and threats to their self-esteem with one of four different defensive communication styles: Placating, Blaming, Computing (also known as being Super-Reasonable), and Distracting (also known as Irrel-

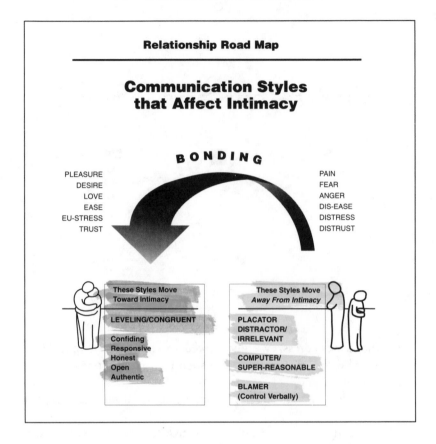

Relationship Road Map

Communication Styles that Affect Intimacy

B O N D I N G

PLEASURE	PAIN
DESIRE	FEAR
LOVE	ANGER
EASE	DIS-EASE
EU-STRESS	DISTRESS
TRUST	DISTRUST

These Styles Move Toward Intimacy

LEVELING/CONGRUENT

Confiding
Responsive
Honest
Open
Authentic

These Styles Move Away From Intimacy

PLACATOR DISTRACTOR/ IRRELEVANT

COMPUTER/ SUPER-REASONABLE

BLAMER (Control Verbally)

evant). They become so accustomed to using these communication styles during periods of tension and to protect themselves that they don't even realize they are alienating their partner. Eventually, they use the style so automatically that *the style itself becomes the core problem.*

All four stress styles mask insecurities that keep us from understanding each other and hold us on the pain side of the Relationship Road Map.

As you read the following descriptions of the four defensive styles, label the style used in the dialogue at the beginning of the chapter. All four are represented. Then pick out the ones that you tend to use. Think of specific incidents in which you used that particular style and try to recall the way you felt at the time. What were the circumstances that led up to that incident?

THE FOUR STRESS STYLES

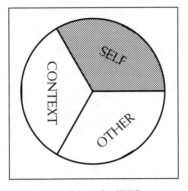

The PLACATER
cancels out SELF.

The *Placater:* Ingratiating, eager to please, apologetic, a "yes" man or woman, the Placater tends to be, at extremes, a bootlicker and a martyr. You'll often hear Placaters saying things like: "Whatever you want." "Without you, I'm nothing." "Don't make waves. Don't rock the boat." "Never mind about me. It's okay."

Inside, the Placater is feeling "I am nothing. Without him [her], I am helpless, worthless. Peace at any price." The Placater derives a sense of value only from the love and approval of others. Because the Placater has difficulty expressing anger and holds so many feelings inside, he or she tends toward depression and is prone to illness.

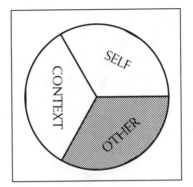

The BLAMER
cancels out OTHER.

The *Blamer*: a fault-finder who can be a dictator, the blamer controls, nitpicks, criticizes relentlessly, and speaks in generalizations: "You never do anything right." "If it weren't for you . . . [everything would be all right]." "You're so stupid" (sick, bad, crazy, sinful and so forth). "You're just like your mother" (or father or whoever).

Inside, the Blamer is feeling "I am lonely and probably unlovable." The Blamer is angry because he or she anticipates not getting what he or she wants or needs, and he assumes that, given a problem or a threatening situation, the best defense is a good offense.

Often described as controlling, disagreeable, hostile, tyrannical, nagging, nitpicking, fault-finding, and at extremes, paranoid or violent, the Blamer goes on the attack and resorts to anger. The Blamer is unable to deal with or express pain or fear.

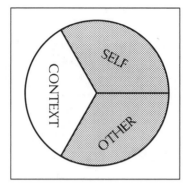

The COMPUTER
cancels out
SELF and OTHER
(all emotion).

The *Computer* (the Super-Reasonable style): Calm, cool, collected and super-reasonable, the "Computer" carefully chooses the right word, expects people to perform and to conform, avoids admitting mistakes, denies feelings, tends to cite facts, statistics, authorities and tradition. You'll often hear the Super-Reasonable Computer saying things like: "Upset? I'm not upset? Why do you say I'm upset?" "Everybody knows . . ." "It says in this book . . ." "The right thing to do is . . ."

Afraid of emotion, the Super-Reasonable operates on this principle: Given a problem or any stress, the best thing to do is deal with authority, facts and statistics, never emotions. Emotions are unreliable, unpredictable and dangerous. "I don't reveal my emotions and I'm not interested in anyone else's."

People who adopt this style are often described as legalistic, militaristic, compulsive, dogmatic, obsessive, opinionated, rigid, principled, insensitive, unfeeling, lacking in empathy, sympathy or compassion—at the extreme, a robot.

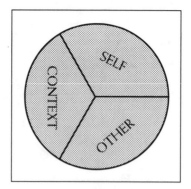

The DISTRACTOR
cancels out
EVERYTHING
(all three).

The *Distractor* (the Irrelevant style): Talkative, unfocused, often frantically active, the Distractor avoids direct eye contact and direct answers, and is quick to change the subject or ignore the point being discussed, as if to say: "Problem? What problem? Let's go to the movies" (or get drunk, have sex, invite friends over and so forth).

Inside, the Distractor is frightened and distrustful and worried. The underlying principle of this style is: If I ignore the problem, it doesn't exist. Maybe it will go away or take care of itself. Confronting the problem would certainly lead to a fight, which would be dangerous and could end up with me or someone being hated, or even left.

A Distractor often is described as erratic, inappropriate, talkative, frantic, hyperactive, purposeless and sometimes out of touch with reality.

Few of us stick to just one fighting style. These styles can be mixed and matched. There are many combinations and patterns, but some are more common to each sex. Men generally don't acknowledge their pain or fear, and women tend to be afraid of anger. That leads to a tendency in men to be Super-Reasonable Blamers, more in touch with performance and conformity (the tyranny of "shoulds"), because our society rewards men's career effectiveness.

Women tend to be Irrelevant Placaters because they have been afraid to show their power or their anger. Generally, women have been conditioned to believe that their success in life depends on being loved, cared for and approved of by a man.

We're talking about typical patterns here. They certainly don't hold true for everyone, and gender roles are changing so quickly that such distinctions are becoming more blurred every day. (Unfortunately, that often means that instead of producing more people who don't rely on these styles, we now have more women Blamers and male Placaters.)

PAIRS Exercise: It's My Style!

This exercise will appeal to the playful thespian in all of us. Acting out the various styles is much more fun and instructive than experiencing them day to day. Even if you don't closely resemble any of those types, allow yourself to participate in the exercise as vigorously as you can. You may notice one or two that come much more naturally to you than you would think.

Embellish your performance by using the exaggerated body language postures associated with each style:

PLACATER: *Cowering, cringing, on knees, pleading, apologetic.*

BLAMER: *Angrily pointing finger, stern and belligerent expression.*

DISTRACTOR: *Irrelevant, shifting gaze, avoids eye contact, vapid expression, quick and jerky gestures, frantically wandering limbs.*   COMPUTER: *Super-reasonable, stiff, rigid posture, superior and aloof expression.*

Ideally, you should begin this exercise when you have about forty-five minutes available, since, for optimum impact, we suggest that you also read the next chapter and do the next exercise during the same extended session.

With your partner or a friend, make up a scenario that you can see easily leading to an argument (housework, a problem child, planning leisure time, money, visiting in-laws). Don't try to work on a "hot spot" in your relationship during this exercise. Pick something that is not a major issue in your own life. Now, decide, *without saying it out loud,* which style you will begin with. For no more than five minutes you are both to deal with that issue in each of the four styles, switching or matching them in whatever sequence you wish.

You might start as a Blamer, for example, and talk for about thirty seconds; your partner might respond as a Placater. Then you switch to Super-Reasonable, he becomes a Distractor, and so on.

Again, the content of your interaction is not important; spout whatever you wish as long as you dramatically convey the style. Don't forget to adopt the appropriate stances and gestures. Focus on carrying out your own performance with conviction, but also be aware of the impact of your partner's performance on you. Complete the entire sequence (each using all four styles) without any break or out-of-role comments.

You can use the dialogue at the beginning of this chapter as a model. As adults, we rarely allow ourselves to play-act like this. No one's watching, so have fun.

- Did any of the styles promote understanding or help the characters in your skit resolve whatever issue you picked?
- Did the issue seem to take a backseat to whatever you felt?
- Which style or styles felt most natural? Which felt unnatural?
- Which seemed the most natural for your partner?
- As your partner moved from style to style, how did you feel during each one?
- Which styles do you and your partner tend to use together in everyday life?
- Did any of them solve the initial issue?

LEARNING FROM OUR STYLES

When we do this exercise in class, the reactions are almost universal. People report that being a Placater "almost made me physically ill," "felt like I had no personality of my own." Blaming generally feels "powerful," "frightening," "didn't have to worry about anyone else," "free of responsibility." Computers described feeling "robotized," "detached," "safe." Distractors say they "wanted to leave the room," "felt antsy," "only felt comfortable with another Distractor."

All of these comments make it clear that when we use our stress styles, we are not really trying to communicate a *concept*. Instead, we are—in a very distorted and unclear manner—expressing our *emotional state under stress.* We are using an issue to express the way we feel, and *our style becomes the problem.*

Studying these styles can give us important clues about the nature of our own emotions and the behavior that results.

Remember, emotions operate on their own logic: the logic of pleasure and pain. If we are experiencing pain or danger, our "fight-or-flight" response is activated. These styles are all forms of fighting, freezing or fleeing. Each one is a unique response to pain, anger or fear.

The Placater is afraid to show anger and runs like a rabbit.

The Blamer is afraid to show pain or vulnerability and fights like a tiger.

The Computer is afraid that responding to feelings will mean losing control and avoids them, like a robot.

The Distractor is afraid of fear. He sees any sign of difficulty as danger and deals with it by hiding his head in the sand like an ostrich.

I compare the responses to animal behavior not to make fun of these styles, but to point out how natural and instinctual our responses to emotions can be. Animals have no control over their environment and have no choice but to follow their instincts. As humans, however, we have the ability to use our emotions as clues. Once we pinpoint what is causing our particular feeling, we have the power to think about it, to talk about it, to change it, or to decide how best to deal with it.

So if we find ourselves fighting like a tiger, or blaming, we know that there is something painful or scary occurring and can try to figure out what it is. If it is our partners who are blaming, we now can realize that rather than simply attacking us because they are aggressive or mean, they are probably hurting or scared. If we can find a way to make it safe for them to talk about their pain or worry, or simply ask if something is bothering them, they might learn to deal with their underlying feelings more directly. Placaters need to know that it is okay to express anger, that they don't have to run. Blamers need to be able to speak in their own behalf, without blaming. Computers might need someone to ask them how they *feel* about certain things—not what they think—so they don't have to avoid feelings. They may have to learn the difference between a thought and a feeling. Distractors need to know that they are safe, that they are not helpless, that they can think things through, that problems can be solved, and that conflicts can be resolved so they don't have to automatically run and hide and avoid being in touch.

One word of caution: don't take to labeling or dismissing your partner's behavior, as in, "There you go Placating again" or "You're nothing but a bullying Blamer" or "Oh, stop being such a scared rabbit." That's simply a way of assigning blame, not a way to promote understanding.

Learning to identify our stress communication style is not a way to find out what's wrong with us. It's about learning to pinpoint and change the habits that contribute to our unhappiness. The stress styles are just paths on the Relationship Road Map that all of us find ourselves on from time to time. The trick is learning that while these particular paths may feel natural and comfortable, they keep us in distress, pain and difficulty. The only way to leave the pain side of the Relationship Road Map is by following a new road. When it comes to communication, this path requires learning a different stress fighting style—the Leveling or Congruent style—explained in the next chapter.

Take a moment to write in your journal notebook about what you are beginning to realize.

6

The Art of Talking

■   ■   ■

Only one communication style is truly useful in confiding, in solving problems and in conveying information. We call it the Leveling or Congruent style, congruent because what you express in words and behavior fits with what you actually feel inside. Oddly enough, it works because it draws from some of the qualities of the four stress styles covered in Chapter 5. Each of the styles has a positive version. In Leveling, the four styles are humanized, or presented in their positive version.

The Placater in its positive form is our capacity to be sensitive, loving and caring and to have empathy for our partner, to act not out of fear but out of a genuine desire for our partner to be happy.

The humanized Blamer is our ability to speak on *our own behalf*, to say our truth—without blaming. We all need to be able to do this, to speak our own feelings and thoughts. Others are not mind readers. We are not transparent.

The positive version of the Computer (Super-Reasonable) style is our ability to use our intelligence and logic to solve problems as long as our logic includes feelings, ours and our partners.

The Irrelevant style, in its positive form, is our capacity for fun, for play—our ability to balance pleasure and purposefulness; to say,

"I'm not going to deal with that tonight because I want to enjoy myself; I can deal with it tomorrow, and I will."

When you combine these traits, you have a "Leveler" who can say:

"I can be sensitive and caring without placating, I can accept your anger, and my own, as a natural way to express discomfort and need.

"I can say how things are for me, especially when something hurts me or worries me, without blaming.

"My feelings and yours are important information that I can use in increasing understanding in our lives.

"I can choose to be playful, have fun and let things go. I can choose another appropriate time to deal with them and I will. My behavior and responses reveal what I am thinking and feeling; I don't wear a mask or hide behind a smile, a glazed look, a blank or icy stare or impassiveness. I won't tell you I am fine when I am not."

I also refer to this as the Congruent style. When we speak directly and our words match our emotions, we are speaking congruently. We are not masking feelings with a style that expresses another kind of emotion. Neither are we blowing one event out of proportion because we are upset about something else that we would rather not discuss or that we are not fully aware of.

The Leveler's relaxed perspective makes it possible to deal with others, even on stressful topics, without resorting to pretenses, defenses, assaults, evasions or game playing. The constant underlying assumption is: "On balance, I'm okay and therefore what I think or feel must also be reasonably normal and acceptable—and even if it isn't or even if I'm wrong, I have the power to think about it and make changes if what I learn suggests that it is wise." The Leveler's intent is to share real information in order to arrive at workable solutions. Frequently used phrases of a Leveler include:

"I realize you see it differently but what I think is . . ."

"I see—what you're saying is . . ."

"Hey, I think you're right! I never thought of that."

"No, you misheard me or I misspoke. What I meant was . . ."

THE ''I'' POSITION

Almost everybody who takes PAIRS grasps the importance of Leveling right away. But people often come back into class or into private sessions saying things like: "I can't seem to get it right" (Placating); "My partner won't cooperate" (Blaming); "This feels artificial—I keep thinking there must be a more practical way to do this" (Computer); "Communicating isn't our problem. We really need help with our sex life" (Distractor). And they say these things without any idea that they are slipping back into familiar stress styles!

These styles cannot be erased overnight. It takes practice and it takes a substitute technique that can be learned. The key thing to remember is that the ultimate goal of Leveling is to explain yourself—to let your partner know what is going on with you.

Leveling means speaking mainly from the "I" position. "I feel," "It hurts me when," "I am afraid." Messages that start with "you" often involve assumptions or blaming—or both. They also sound as if you are delivering a final, seemingly irrevocable judgment: "You always . . ." "You'll never learn to . . ." When you start with "I" the potency of the message is limited to your own perceptions, which renders it less threatening and more easily considered or discussed.

It's important to remember the spirit behind the "I" technique. If I say to you, "I never want to see your socks on the floor again," I may seem to be talking about my reaction to your socks, but what I'm really talking about is who has the right to tell whom what to do—and there's a pretty good chance my statement is not going to alter your sock-dropping habits. Your partner will be able to hear you better if you can say what you want without blaming and without issuing demands. So you might say, "It bothers me when you leave your dirty socks on the floor." If your partner requires more information, you might add, "I end up feeling like you don't care what our home looks like." Don't say, "It feels terrible for me and it's all your fault," but rather, "It feels terrible for me, and what I'm asking of you is . . ."

Leveling means being able to avoid vague or hurtful statements (like "You bother me," "I can't stand you," "You're impulsive," or "I don't want anything to do with you") and saying instead that this thing that you do bothers me. As during the Daily Temperature Reading, be specific and offer a remedy: "This is what bothers me and what I'm asking of you is . . ." This is the beginning of learning to fight fair, which we'll discuss in more detail in Chapter 10.

Most of us are often good Levelers without even realizing it. In part, this is because most of our messages deal with information, simple observations or everyday feelings ("Barry called" or "I dread going to work"). It's when we try to talk about powerfully emotional issues or our deeply private feelings or thoughts, disclosure of which may make us feel vulnerable to hurt, rejection or ridicule, that we tend to abandon our Leveling skills.

EXPLAIN YOURSELF

Sometimes we have to tell our partners how our early conditioning affects our fight-or-flight reactions now. One PAIRS participant grew up with a father who would issue a decree, "I want to talk to you," in a stern voice, meaning, "You've done something wrong and you're going to get it." So whenever this man's wife said, "We need to talk," it was as if she had made that awful sound chalk can make on a blackboard, and he would go out of his way to avoid her. Once he confided this aspect of his conditioning to his wife, it was an easy matter for her to choose a less charged phrase when she wanted to talk to him. "Can we talk about," for instance, sounded more like an invitation and clued him in on the subject matter. That prevented him from feeling as if the boom were about to be dropped.

People sometimes complain that if you really love each other you should be able to say and do anything and your partner will accept and understand. That's not true. We have to be aware of how our words and behavior are going to be *received*. If you hear "Do you admit" as threatening "courtroom" language, it's not that difficult for me to switch to an alternative phrase that doesn't trigger your emotional allergy, such as "I would like to check out with you if."

For many people, the *quality* of another's voice may carry a much stronger, unintended message. A stern tone might remind someone vividly of scoldings (or abuse from parents or authority figures). If this happens to you, it's important to remind yourself, "He is not my father" or "She is not my mother." It's also important to tell your partner, in a way that makes it clear that you are just sharing an insight, about the effect that a certain tone has on you. You might say, for example, "I need you to understand that when your voice gets shrill, I can't listen to what you are saying. So if you want me to be able to hear you, it will help if you don't scream."

If your partner is unaware of speaking sharply or loudly, the two of you might agree on a way in which you can unobtrusively bring this to your partner's attention, such as by an agreed-upon gesture. Also, now that you know your partner's voice rises when he or she is upset and that your partner is not trying to intimidate you, you might find it easier to just ride things out until it is out of your partner's system. We will learn more about ways to handle such expressions of anger in the following chapters.

LEARNING TO LEVEL:
THE "DIALOGUE GUIDE"

We often have trouble Leveling about certain feelings or issue because we ourselves often cannot put our finger on what is wrong. We may feel overwhelmed by rage, hurt, fear or confusion but find it difficult to explain why. Unable to find the right reasons or words, we tend to lapse into our old defensive patterns and never really make our point.

After outlining a typical conflict-laden scenario, I'd like to share with you the Dialogue Guide, a guide for Leveling that PAIRS graduates have found to be one of the most valuable resources for talking about uncomfortable subjects.

Pretend you're Jim, married to Jane. You've just finished dinner on a rainy Friday evening and are starting to relax in your favorite chair with the newspaper. You're peripherally conscious of the rain beating on the windows. You glance up as Jane enters the den and sits on the sofa. She looks over at you and leans forward in a posture that lets you know that she is about to speak: "Alex [your brother-in-law] called. Robin and he went to see a new comedy playing at the Avalon last night. He says it's hilarious and we ought to see it."

If Alex thought the movie was funny, you think, "it's probably a lot of cheap slapstick"—but you assume Jane wants to go to the movies tonight, although she knows that you'd rather stay home and get to bed early because you've got a lot of work to do around the house tomorrow. You think, "If I say that I don't want to go, either we'll argue or I'll get the deep-freeze treatment, and that'll ruin the weekend. If we do go, it's almost certain that we'll have to stop at Alex and Robin's afterward, and we'll be late getting home, not to mention soaked. But if I put up a fuss now, Jane might not feel like going bowling tomorrow night." You feel annoyed and disappointed (the simple, comfortable evening at home is spoiled either way); impatient (Jane should have known what you preferred to do and should share your feelings); confused (as you are torn between several conflicting impulses); and a little guilty (because she so seldom asks you to do anything special). You want to stay home but not at the cost of an argument, so what you *really* want is for Jane to change her mind without blaming you for it.

You plop the newspaper down on your lap, indicating resignation. You raise your eyebrows, sigh and say, "Welllll, if you *really* want to go, on a night like this . . ."

In situations such as these, you are aware of the half-formed thoughts that flit through your mind. But most of us have not trained ourselves to deliberately bring them to our awareness in a manner that permits us to weigh everything and rationally control the outcome. Your final statement, for example, is not a real solution. By sending contradictory and essentially dishonest messages, you're continuing the game Jane started. (She could have said, "I'd like to see the show at the Avalon tonight, but I have a feeling you'd rather stay home.") The predictable outcome to this kind of scenario is more shadow boxing, with a crescendo of angry exchanges as you each become increasingly frustrated by the incompleteness and dishonesty of the information being given and received.

Jane's response to your "well, if you *really*," for instance, would likely be either a shrug of the shoulders and withdrawal or an angry, blaming response along the lines of: "Fine. I don't care if you never get out of that chair. But I'm going to that movie tomorrow no matter what and the hell with bowling."

Both of you are trying to "win" (that is, trying to make the other person want what you want) without stating what it is you *do* want.

If Jim were a Leveler, he'd probably put the newspaper down without any dramatics, sit back for a moment and look at Jane thoughtfully as he checked out his feelings and weighed the options. He might eventually say, in a calm, direct tone of voice: "I have mixed feelings. I wonder if you remember what Alex's sense of humor is like, although we might agree with him this time. Also, it's so nasty out that I really would prefer to stay home and go to bed early. But I know you really want to go and I don't want to disappoint you. Besides, I'm still hoping you'll come bowling tomorrow. Finally, the one thing I am most afraid of is going to their place and staying up real late. I've got a lot things I need to get done in the morning. How about this? Suppose I call the theater? If this weekend is the last weekend that the show is playing, we'll go, but come straight home; if not, we'll go after the weather clears—and tonight we can watch that movie on Channel Four."

Communicating as a Leveler and learning to think through all the possibilities takes knowledge and practice. That is why I developed the Dialogue Guide.

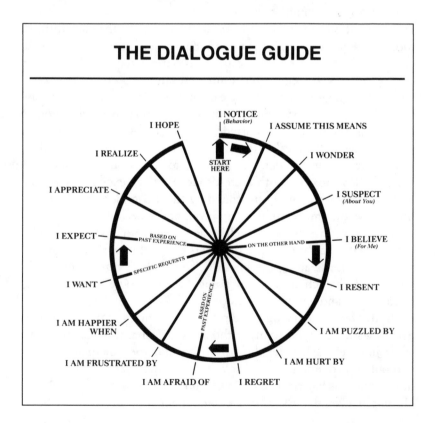

THE DIALOGUE GUIDE

PAIRS Exercise: The Dialogue Guide

The Dialogue Guide will help you to fine-tune your thoughts and feelings about a situation and to present them in a nonthreatening manner.

The guide provides starter sentences, arranged in an order that helps you sort out and describe your perceptions, thoughts, feelings and requests—the elements present in any issue. Because the Dialogue Guide helps you to be very specific about situations that feel vague, it is likely that by using it you will discover nuances in your reaction of which you have been unaware.

When the two of you have something important to discuss, I suggest that you sit facing each other and hold or touch each other's hands while you talk. Why? Because when you maintain physical touch and eye contact, there is much less chance of garbled messages and misunderstanding. For some couples, touching and looking directly at each other is the last thing they want to do when they feel at odds with each another. If you practice staying in touch physically—despite your instinct to withdraw or look away—you eventually will find that it is easier to work through anger and pain and avoid misunderstandings.

It is much harder to misunderstand each other when you make eye contact and hand contact. Many issues that seemed unsolvable have been resolved this way.

Set aside one hour for you and your partner to practice using the Dialogue Guide. Both of you should read through the following directions and examples and have the Dialogue Guide at hand for easy reference.

Select an issue or a behavior of your partner's that at times bothers you or upsets you. This shouldn't be something of cosmic proportions. Start with something relatively trivial, such as "Why don't you take out the trash without being asked?" or "Why don't you ever tell me when you write a check?"

Allow ten minutes for reflection (look at the Dialogue Guide to help you organize your thoughts). With the Guide at your side and sitting comfortably facing and touching each other, one of you begins by voicing your issue: "I notice (behavior)," "I assume (that means)," and so on around the wheel. Your partner's only job is to listen attentively. He or she must not interrupt with any advice, rebuttal, judgment or comment. Your partner may ask you to repeat or rephrase something if you say something that he or she does not understand. Your partner may ask you to pause after two or three items so he or she can remember and accurately repeat all of what he or she heard before you continue.

Remember that what you say should be phrased in a low-key, nonargumentative fashion: Neither of you is trying to win or prove anything. You are simply trying to exchange information.

Now your partner tells you what he or she heard. Fill in whatever your partner left out until you know he or she heard it all, then thank your partner by words or gestures, such as a touch, or an embrace for listening and hearing you accurately. It is a gift to be confided in and it is a gift to be heard accurately. Acknowledge this.

It is now your partner's turn. Your partner may, using the Dialogue Guide, either respond to what you said or select an entirely different subject.

This is how it might go the first time:

"*I notice:* that you constantly give me advice when I drive, telling me to look out for this or that, how fast to go, when to pass a car and when not to."

"*I assume:* this means that you think I need advice about my driving."

"*I wonder:* why you do that. I've been driving for more than twenty years."

"*I suspect:* that you are used to giving directions."

"*I believe:* that I don't need directions when I drive. If I want them, I'll ask for them."

"*I resent:* your giving me directions."

"*I am puzzled:* by your insistence on doing this."

"*I am hurt:* by the implication that you do not trust my ability to drive."

"*I regret:* having to even talk to you about this."

"*I am afraid:* that I will not want to drive with you in the car or that one of these days I will have an accident because I get so rattled when you do this."

"*I am frustrated:* that you do not see how irritating this is for me."

"*I am happier:* when I make the decisions while I drive and you make the decisions while you drive."

"*I want:* you to stop it even if it is difficult for you."

"*I expect:* that you will remember for about a week and then you'll forget."

"*I appreciate:* that you're a very caring and kind person and that you don't intend to insult me or upset me."

"*I realize:* that you are used to giving directions and it will be hard for you to change this."

"*I hope:* that you will change your behavior, because it really matters to me."

When both of you have taken your turns, take five or ten minutes to hold a general critique. You are not to talk about the issues again, but rather discuss the experience—how it felt for each of you to use the guide, the degree to which new information was exchanged or old data was better understood. It would also be useful to share how using the guide actually put you in touch with feelings that perhaps you didn't realize you had. Discuss how well you followed the general principles of communication outlined here. For instance, your partner might say, "I have to admit that it was hard for me to listen because you started out by saying 'you never help out in the kitchen.' It would be easier for me if you tried not to speak in absolutes." Or, you might say to your partner: "I was wondering if you were really listening? At one point it seemed you were going to burst because you wanted to interrupt me. It made me feel like you were just waiting for me to finish so you could start arguing."

The Dialogue Guide may strike you as an artificial structure. If you keep practicing it, however, I would be surprised if you don't discover how it allows you to expand the dimensions of your dialogue. It is amazing how much information it will pull out of you that you didn't even realize was there.

You won't always need to use all of the guide's elements, but try to do so the first few times you use it. You may decide to alter certain parts to make the format better fit the circumstances. For example, you may add, "How does this feel for you?"

Differences in individual desires and needs are common even in the most ideal relationships. No two people can ever be wholly alike. When you sense that you're getting into an "issue" area where there is a real or potential conflict, making the conscious effort to check all of the points on your Dialogue Guide can save both of you time and grief.

- How did it feel to use the Dialogue Guide? Was it comfortable or awkward?
- How did you and your partner sit while you were talking? Were you touching?
- Have you ever had a discussion like this while you were touching and looking at each other?
- Did you find yourself getting angry or upset or nervous?
- Did you tell your partner of your feelings during or after you did the Dialogue Guide?
- Did you feel as if you got your point across? Were the results different than when you raised this or a similar issue in the past? How so?
- Did your partner appear to be listening more carefully?
- Did you thank him or her for listening?

Take a moment to write in your journal notebook about what you are beginning to realize.

7

The Art of Listening

■　　　　■　　　　■

*C*onfiding is much more than being able to reveal yourself to another. It is knowing with absolute certainty that what you think and feel is being *heard and understood* by the person you have chosen to share with. It also means that person can count on us for the same kind of undivided attention. We should be able to both give and expect empathy.

We tend to be passive listeners, picking up only on those things that have some direct bearing on *us* rather than listening for *how things are for our partner.*

- What are your listening habits?
- Do you interrupt often?
- Do you listen for openings or points that you can rebut?
- Are you listening for the meaning things have to your partner, or for the impact their words will have on you?
- Do you listen as much to humor your partner as to learn?

Like Leveling, listening with empathy is a learned skill, not something we develop automatically. The two crucial ingredients are:

Undivided attention: Never *assume* that you know something unless it is clearly stated by your partner. Always ask for clarification if you are not clear on something or if you find yourself filling in blanks for your partner.

Empathy: You need to understand fully what your partner's thoughts and feelings mean to him or her. Resist the instinctive response to search for the effect that your partner's words have on you. Put yourself in your partner's shoes. Notice his or her emotions, facial expression, levels of tension. Feel what your partner feels.

MIXED MESSAGES

Most of us listen by inference. *We add our own agenda to what is said or change its meaning altogether.* We interpret body language and tone. In short, we often don't offer our partners the courtesy of truly listening to what they say. Instead we run it through our brains like an apple through a food processor and end up examining the apple sauce we made instead of the apple they gave us.

Here is an example of how easily things can go awry:

Jane: Mom asked me today whether we were thinking about having a baby. I told her you were ambivalent. (Her intended meaning: He has mixed feelings about it.)

Jim: Thanks a lot! Why the hell did you tell her that! (Jim's interpretation: His wife has just told his mother-in-law that he is opposed to having children.)

Jane: What are you getting so huffy for? She has a right to know.

Jim: Right to know! Sure. Just like she noses into all of our other affairs, like our finances.

Jane: At least she didn't call us on our honeymoon like your mother did.

Jim: What's the point of talking to you? You are always blaming me for things I can't control. *You* can control what you tell your nosy mother.

Neither is aware of the mistaken impression that led to their argument. They slid right past it into a fight neither sought but both are conditioned to expect. All that was needed was that Jim ask what Jane meant by "ambivalent." Perhaps he would have asked had his self-esteem been a notch higher, so he would not assume that he was somehow being attacked or criticized. Or, had her fuse not been so short, she might have asked, "Hey. What did you think I meant by 'ambivalent'?"

It's up to each partner to be aware of possibly misinterpreted thoughts and words and to be vigilant about making sure that things are understood. The challenge, clearly, is learning awareness so that you realize when you are mind reading or making assumptions. Ask questions. Ask questions. Ask questions! About anything and everything. Also begin practicing Empathic Listening.

LISTENING WITH EMPATHY AND SHARED MEANING

Empathic Listening means being willing to listen *solely* to understand what your partner means and feels—not to judge, rebut, advise or contradict. Instead of hearing only part of what is said, guessing at the remainder and immediately beginning to frame your reply, you need to silence your critical voice and focus entirely on what your partner is trying to tell you. For a moment, it's as if you become your partner, achieving in the process a high degree of intimacy.

The greatest impediment to empathic listening is our self-interest and self-protective mechanisms. We listen for what is of interest to us; we listen for things that enhance or affirm our position or qualities, and we listen for openings to jump back into the conversation, to relate our own views or experiences. This is natural enough, but it is a barrier to intimacy. There is no way that your response can be helpful or make sense unless you've first truly understood what your partner actually meant.

The Shared Meaning technique enables you to share the meaning of what you heard and check out if what you heard is what your partner meant. Often it is not. Many of us have seen the poster that says, "I know you think you heard what I said, but I don't think you realize that what I said is not what I meant." The first step to successful listening is to not even bother discussing something that is important until both of you have time and energy to give each other your undivided attention. The chances for misunderstanding grow geometrically when we are listening to one thing while thinking about (or doing) something else. Once you have set aside at least ten or fifteen minutes, the person who asked to be heard explains what is on his or her mind, in very simple and short segments, perhaps using the Dialogue Guide, and the partner repeats what he or she heard without embellishment, comment or advice. As simple as this sounds, couples in PAIRS practice this for half an hour together and, because our old communication habits are so strong, it's usually not until the end of the session that a couple can stick to the rules. By forcing themselves to think only about what is being said, PAIRS participants find themselves hearing things they never allowed themselves to hear before.

PAIRS Exercise: Empathic Shared Meaning

Until this technique (or a modified form of it) becomes second nature, make a conscious decision to use it whenever either of you thinks it is important for your partner to hear what you have to say.

After reading through the following instructions, try the Empathic Shared Meaning exercise with your partner.

STEP ONE:

The First Message. Face and touch each other. The partner who raised the issue begins by stating the message as simply as possible. If it is complicated, it should be expressed in sections, as many as it takes, to ensure that everything you have to say is heard. The listener's job is to do just and only that: listen. The listener will get an opportunity to respond later on.

He: It's very upsetting for me if you bring up a difficult problem late at night, say after ten o'clock, particularly on a weeknight. There's never time to

discuss it thoroughly and it
often keeps me from going to
sleep. (Pause.) There's more.

STEP TWO:
First Empathic Response. Hearing the signal that there is more to come, the listener now repeats the gist of the message and shares the meaning they heard. A mere parroting of the words would display good memory, but not understanding. The listener does not in any way expand or comment upon the message or try to anticipate the rest of it. In word, tone and manner, she simply verifies that the speaker was heard and understood.

> *She:* It bothers you a lot when I start talking about some controversial issue late at night because we can't resolve it and then it keeps you awake.

STEP THREE:
Continuation of the Message. The speaker verifies that he was correctly heard, thanks the listener and continues with the next part of the message. If he is not satisfied that he was wholly heard and understood, the speaker repeats the part omitted until the listener's response is accurate. It may also happen that, upon hearing what he said repeated out loud, he realizes that what he said is not what he really meant. If so, the speaker acknowledges the mistake and restates the message.

He: Yes. Thank you. I realize
that it's tough on you. By the
time I get home and we eat
and clean up it's often already
almost ten and by then I usually have my nose in the paper.
So if something bothersome
happened during the day it
must seem like there's never a
good time to tell me about it.

She: You understand it from my point of view—that quite often it's late by the time we finish the evening routine. So there's never a good time for me to tell you my troubles.

He: No. That is, the first part was right, but then I said it must *seem* to you that there's never a good time to tell me.

She: Sorry. You realize it's difficult for me since it's usually so late by the time we finish up— and you're concerned that I must feel that there's never an appropriate time to talk about problems.

He: Right. Thank you. When I think about it like that, I realize it's unfair. If something goes wrong at the office, I don't hesitate to unload it on you.

She: But I don't mind. I want you—

He: Hold it. Please stick to the rules. (She broke the rules by starting to respond, rather than reflecting his meaning.)

She: Whoops, sorry. When you look at it objectively you feel sort of guilty because you always feel free to tell me about office problems.

He: I didn't actually say "guilty."
But you're right. Thanks. Anyway, I'd like to do something
about the unfairness of it and
am open to suggestions.

She: You'd like to discuss some
ways that we could handle it
more fairly.

He: Hey, right. Thank you.
That's it.

STEP FOUR:
Synthesis. If the message is quite long or complex the speaker should
restate it, reducing it to a brief and comprehensive message. The
listener responds as above.

STEP FIVE:
Reversal. When the speaker's complete message is transmitted and
understood, the process is reversed.

STEP SIX:
If the thought expressed was a problem in the relationship, you are
now free to explore solutions. In the chapters that follow, you will
find a range of strategies for doing this.

How effective was the Empathic Shared Meaning exercise in
helping you and your partner exchange significant information?
  • How did the level of tension, confusion or animosity
    compare to what happens when you usually discuss dif-
    ficult issues?
  • Was it difficult for either of you to stick to the format?
  • Did you argue about the rules?

Like several of the tools used in PAIRS, this one may feel forced at first, appearing to replace spontaneity with rigidity. In fact, however, this structure is intended to help spontaneity enhance rather than disrupt relationships.

Alice's comment typifies the reactions of PAIRS couples after they have practiced this kind of listening. "I used to be marshaling my rebuttal while Bill was talking, but I realized that you can't listen while you do that. So I stopped. Now when Bill has a long face, I ask him what's wrong and he goes through a laundry list [of gripes]. I used to spot items and get defensive about them. Now I don't, and he feels better when he's finished because (a) he can say the whole list and (b) I don't try to correct him."

The remarkable thing about Empathic Shared Meaning is that, often, we discover that all we need to do in order to resolve a problem is to *listen* to our partner. What once felt like an enormous burden or a dangerous issue to raise can diminish once your partner feels that he or she has been heard. This is a two-way street: Just knowing that your partner understands how you feel can ease your pain or anger.

Take a moment to write in your journal notebook about what you are beginning to realize.

8

Relationship Landmines, Assumptions, and the Art of Mind Reading

■　　　■　　　■

*A*ll of us bring certain expectations to our intimate relationships, expectations that we don't have of anyone else. They are specific to those to whom we are closest. Frequent positive expectations are undivided attention, words and gestures of love and caring, loyalty, constancy, sex, companionship, agreement, friendship, fidelity, honesty, trust, respect, acceptance. The negative expectations are their opposites. These expectations are like hidden landmines waiting to go off. They often explode unexpectedly. And the misunderstandings they lead to can cause endless turmoil.

We often don't think about what these expectations are—but when the positive ones aren't fulfilled we quickly feel angry, disappointed, hurt, resentful, bitter, worried. And how we react to our feelings becomes the key to the outcome.

It is important to become aware of exactly what expectations and assumptions we have of our intimates. Often one would have to be a mind-reader to know. Picture the following scenario.

Martin and Pamela, upon moving into a new home together, decided to spend an afternoon rearranging furniture, which until now had been placed with expediency rather than decor in mind. The more they moved things around, the more agitated Martin grew. Pamela tried to calm the brewing storm by throwing herself even more into the task, saying "Let's try this chair over here and that table in this corner," all the while chit-chatting cheerfully to lighten the atmosphere. Suddenly, Martin exploded, angrily announcing that he didn't have any more time to waste fiddling around with furniture. He stormed into his den and started on some paperwork. Pamela, knowing that there must be something else eating him, waited until she felt he had calmed down and asked him why he had gotten so upset. He grew furious again, snapping at her: "Why can't you ever leave me alone? In fact, why can't you ever leave *anything* alone? Why do you always have to change everything?" Shocked that her attempt to reach out had been seen as unwelcome intrusiveness, Pamela left the room. Neither of them spoke of the incident for months.

When we began addressing this material in PAIRS, Pamela told Martin it was very important for her to understand what had happened that day because she had been uncomfortably wary of him ever since. Were there some expectations or unwritten rules that she had not lived up to?

Martin, unaware until that moment that the incident had been major and had eroded her trust in him, reflected.

"This was the third time in less than three years that I moved. I also had just started a new job. The living room was the only room in the house that felt entirely together and was a place where I could relax. As silly as it sounds, I needed the sense of being settled that that room brought me. That's why I got upset. I got even angrier when you pretended to ignore me. I exploded when I felt like you were shoving me around, trying to control me by telling me how to move the furniture."

If we could break all of this down into a series of expectations or attitudes, Martin's hidden expectations would be:

1. Loving me means knowing that I need to feel settled and not taking things away from me that make me feel secure.
2. Loving me means paying attention to me. You should have known I was getting upset and why. Since you ignored me, you obviously didn't care about how I felt.
3. Loving me means not trying to control me. Trying to make

moving the furniture fun when I was angry felt like you were manipulating me, treating me like a child.

"As I look at this list, I'm sorry it took me so long to think about what really bothered me," Martin said. "I guess I expect things of you that are unrealistic."

This is the way they reworked his expectations to help them avoid similar misunderstandings in the future:

1. If I expect you to understand what I need, I have to tell you. That means that *I* have to figure out what I need. If I had thought about it first instead of blaming you, I would have understood why I got angry while we were moving the furniture.
2. I can't expect you to care about how I feel unless I tell you how I feel in the first place.
3. If I had asked you why you were ignoring me and trying to make something that I was not enjoying fun, I would have understood that you were trying to avoid a fight, not trying to manipulate me. I realize I have a choice about what I do for and with you, and that asking me to do something does not mean that you are trying to control me.

This discussion helped Pamela recognize some of her own hidden assumptions. She told Martin that only now did she realize that if she had worried less about avoiding a fight (her thought had been: Anger is dangerous and should be appeased) and more about finding out what was going on, she might have discovered what was bothering him. They agreed that if he had volunteered his anger and discomfort, or if she had asked, they probably would have agreed to try rearranging the furniture some other day.

While we all have our own hidden assumptions and expectations, there are many that we have in common. Here are some examples:

- *Loving me means . . . not interrupting me*—when I'm talking, thinking, working, relating.
- *Loving me means . . . knowing what I want and what I feel.* If you don't know what I want or how I feel, then it is obvious that you don't love me. In that case, there is no reason

for me to care about what you want or feel, even if you tell me, so don't bother telling.

- *Loving me means . . . not trying to control me*—and that is what you are doing when you tell me what you want. When I feel controlled, I feel weak, inadequate or manipulated. If I give you what you want, I feel resentful.
- *Loving me means . . . agreeing.* When we don't agree, then one of us is wrong. Obviously, it can't be me because that would mean that I am stupid or inadequate. That means that it must be you and I will prove it to you in any way that I can.
- *Loving me means . . . needing you.* If I let myself get close to you, I will become dependent upon you, I will not be able to survive if you leave me. I cannot allow myself to be that close to you, or to anyone. I will distance, care less and not let you know how I really feel so that I will not come to depend on you and risk being hurt.

Many "landmines" are set off by the way we deal with our partner when he or she *does* express feelings of anger and pain:

- *When I try to tell you how I feel, you criticize, advise, judge or dismiss my feelings.* I feel frustrated, betrayed, and not listened to. I stop telling you how I feel.
- *When you are in pain, I feel that it is my responsibility to fix it for you, but I don't know how to fix it for you, so I feel inadequate.* When you are in pain, I get angry at you for making me feel inadequate.
- *When you are unhappy, it must be because I am not doing something right.* I feel inadequate when you are unhappy, so I withdraw from you.

Sometimes, our assumptions operate in groups, presenting a set of circumstances that puts our partner in a no-win situation. For example:

- *When I tell you what I want and you do it, it doesn't count, because I had to tell you.* When I don't tell you what I want and

you don't do it, I feel misunderstood and angry. When you do what I want but not the way I want, it still doesn't count.
- *When you tell me how you feel, I get angry because I can't fix it or I feel blamed.* When you don't tell me how you feel, I get angry because I feel left out and mistrusted.
- *When I tell you how angry I am at you, you distance from me.* When I don't tell you how angry I am with you, I distance from you.
- Finally, we often keep people at arm's length because we fear that: *If you knew too much about me, you couldn't really love me.*

(For a more complete list of relationship landmines, see *Love Knots*, by Lori H. Gordon, Dell, 1990.)

We may also find it difficult to love people who love us because we secretly believe that anyone who loves us must have something wrong with *them.* We have to learn to give ourselves a break. We have the same rights to be happy and to make mistakes and to be vulnerable as anyone else. We must learn to risk being rejected when someone gets to know us, because when we are accepted after confiding our weaknesses, we are finally free to fully trust in a relationship.

DIGGING UP THE LANDMINES

Ferreting out these landmines can be difficult because one action can trigger a series of internal reactions such as anger, anxiety, fear or sadness. As the emotion builds, it is easy to release that tension by blaming the other person. We say or think *"You* make me so angry" or *"You* are so frustrating." When we do this, we are handing responsibility for our feelings to our partner. We regain that responsibility by accepting a particular feeling as our own; as something that comes from within us, although triggered from outside.

One way to dredge up our assumptions and expectations is to link an event to our feelings by completing sentences. Here are some possible sentence stems to complete:

WHEN YOU

1. Are late . . .
2. Spend money . . .
3. Discipline the kids without talking to me . . .
4. Refuse sex . . .
5. Cry, yell, are rude . . .
6. Spend time with other people . . .

I FEEL

1. Taken for granted
2. Taken advantage of
3. Powerless
4. Rejected
5. Controlled
6. Jealous

BECAUSE I THINK IT MEANS

1. You don't think that I am valuable or that my time is important.
2. Spending money is more important to you than my feelings.
3. You don't think I know how to deal with the children.
4. You don't want me anymore.
5. I must do something about it.
6. You would rather spend your time with someone other than me.

As scary as it may seem, expressing your feelings about a given situation and asking for your partner's honesty in return is the only way to discover truth in your relationship. But the majority of communication between intimates is nonverbal and leans heavily on mind reading. The only thing you have to go on is internal information that could easily be skewed by any number of factors. This is also why genuine responses are so important. Telling someone what you think he or she wants to hear, instead of what is really going on, complicates and postpones a useful solution to a problem.

It is critical to keep in mind that while some assumptions may be faulty or unrealistic, that does not invalidate the feelings that helped you discover them in the first place. When we experience a rush of emotion over something that we do not understand, we often either suppress it or act on it impetuously. Ignoring or dismissing an emotion because it seems silly, inappropriate or out of proportion to a given situation cheats us of a chance to understand more about ourselves. If Martin continued to ignore the discomfort he felt while moving furniture, he would be setting himself and Pamela up for repeated flare-ups and misunderstandings that would drive a deeper wedge between them. By using the incident to understand his basic need to have a place that felt safe and secure while the rest of his life was in flux, Martin and Pamela were able to take simple steps to fill that need. They created a routine that gave them time together and made a place in their home that was entirely his. These actions gave Martin the sense of security he needed to be more open to change, such as the newly arranged living room. It also prepared him for dealing with much larger later issues, such as having a child.

LANDMINE TRIGGERS

Landmines often appear around several key areas that cause friction or disappointment.

Differences of opinion. A great deal of havoc is caused in relationships because many of us believe that disagreement is a sign of waning love. Many of my clients cite differences (over taste, child-rearing philosophy, politics) as evidence that their partner does not love them. Differences *can* cause problems, and couples have to negotiate solutions to them. But we cannot *expect* differences not to arise. It's been said that "If the good Lord wanted us to be the same, he would have made only one." Moreover, we cannot *assume* that such a difference means lack of love. Sometimes we feel that when a difference arises, it must mean that one of us is wrong. We may yell, act rude and use any means we can think of to prove that it is not we who are wrong. This stalemate can be avoided if we understand that our goal in trying to settle a difference is to *improve the relationship for both*. Finding out who was wrong or right seldom accomplishes this; understanding and empathy do. We will teach negotiating skills for handling differences in Chapter 10.

Power imbalances. Friction often develops when one of us believes the other is trying to control, change or smother the other. For instance, many men tell me that their wives try to smother them. Eventually, they often reveal that they fear being trapped or smothered in any relationship. The only way to change this is by changing their attitude. They need to understand that, as adults, we have our own power and the ability to be independent. No one can take that away. If we avoid being intimate because of this fear, we are depriving ourselves of one of life's most exquisite pleasures. It is often by changing that attitude, more than by a change in the partner's behavior, that people can stop feeling controlled or powerless in relationships.

Emotional issues. "She cries all the time. I just can't make her happy." "He gets so angry. He must hate me." Many of us have a peculiar notion that when someone is upset, we must fix it, or fix ourselves. When we can't fix it, we feel resentful or inadequate. To avoid feeling like that, we decide we don't want to hear about our partner's feelings. This attitude leads to alienation and isolation. We need to be able to listen to and confide in our partners. The listening partner must learn that he or she has no obligation to *do* anything but listen and try to empathize. Later, that partner can see if, in reality, he or she can comfortably *do* something—but listening and empathy are the most important parts.

Self-esteem problems. Many landmines are connected to low self-esteem. Sometimes we expect our partner to succeed in order to make us look good, instead of being satisfied with what we ourselves can accomplish. Sometimes we feel competitive with our partners, believing that they somehow diminish us when they succeed and we don't. Sometimes we believe that our partner would be happy if only we were everything we should be. Sometimes we take criticism as an attack on who we *are*, not as a critique of what we *do*. True success can only be measured by goals we set for ourselves, by seeing where we have been compared to where we are, by how we ourselves are learning and growing—not by looking for someone else to meet our goals and not by comparing ourselves to others.

The best way to avoid relationship landmines is to openly check out your own and your partner's assumptions. Any time that you are confused about something your partner did or said (and sometimes even when you aren't confused), ask what's going on. This is one of the greatest values of the "Puzzles" in the Daily Temperature Reading. Another surprising way that PAIRS participants have learned to enjoy their relationship more and avoid landmines is through the Mind-Reading Exercise I'll be explaining shortly. This exercise is designed to check out whether assumptions we have about what our partner thinks and feels are true. Often our assumptions are not correct, and if we don't check them out, we can't really know or react appropriately. And reactive behavior based on erroneous assumptions leads to enormous misunderstandings and alienation. One typical assumption of intimates is:

Assumption: When you tell me what you think or feel, I believe you *want* my reaction—whether it is agreement, disagreement, advice or judgment.

Typical reaction: Not true. I just want you to *listen*, to want to know and understand. If I want your advice, I'll ask for it!

Another typical assumption is:

Assumption: When you are upset or unhappy, I believe you want me to fix it. And since I can't, don't know how or don't want to fix it—I believe you're disappointed and angry at me.

Typical reaction: Not true. When I'm upset, I just want you to be *interested in what's wrong*, to ask me, perhaps put your arm around me, to offer some sympathy.

Think of assumptions you have. Examples might be:

1. When I make a long-distance call, you hover over me because you resent my spending time and money on the telephone.
2. When I come home late, you think I'm inconsiderate and even lying as to why I'm late.
3. When I take time to be with the children, you feel neglected. You think I care more for them than for you.

Bringing assumptions into your awareness is an essential first step in checking them out. The next step is to ask your partner, to say,

"I'd like your permission to mind-read you," and then state your assumption and find out. George Bach believes that mind reading of your partner without permission and without checking it out is a form of assault. He called it mind-raping. We do this with our intimates all the time. And alienation in marriage is often caused by misunderstandings and mistaken assumptions.

- When you suffer a disappointment in your relationship, do you automatically think that it wouldn't have happened if only your partner (or you) were different?
- What have been the biggest disappointments you have suffered in your relationships?
- What expectations did you have that were not met?
- Were they clearly expressed, either before or after you were disappointed?
- Were they clear to you?
- What do you think your partner's expectations and assumptions about you are?

Here are two examples of the Mind-Reading Exercise:

MIND-READING EXERCISE

SAMPLE DIALOGUE I

Sender: Do I have permission to read your mind?

Receiver: Sure. Go ahead.

Sender: I think that you think that whatever I do is *never good enough.*

Receiver: You think that I think that whatever you do is never good enough.

Sender: Yes. Whatever I do—I hear criticism for what I didn't do or that I didn't do it right!

Receiver: Whatever you do, I criticize you for what you didn't do or didn't do it right.

Sender: Yes. When I get home, I'm told I'm late. When I buy something, it's not exactly what you wanted. When I clean or pick up, you point out what I left out. When I fix food, there's another way you like it. When I relax, you say I should be working.

Receiver: (Repeats, then goes on.) But that's not true. I like a lot of things that you do . . .

Sender: That's not true. You like a lot of things that I do.

Receiver: Yes.

Sender: Then tell me what you like. Tell me what you appreciate. Stop telling me what else I haven't done.

Receiver: Then you want me to tell you what I like. What I appreciate. And stop pointing out what you haven't done or what else I'd like you to do.

Sender: Yes.

Receiver: Okay. I didn't realize I was doing that. (Hugs)

SAMPLE DIALOGUE II

Sender   Do I have permission to read your mind?

Receiver: Okay.

Sender: I think that you think that whenever I tell you what I want or how I feel that I am criticizing you and putting you down.

Receiver: You think that I think that whenever you tell me what you want or how you feel that you are criticizing me and putting me down.

Sender: Right.

Receiver: Well. I do like to please you. I do like you to be happy. And you do complain a lot.

Sender: You like to please me. You want me to be happy. And I do complain a lot.

Receiver: That's right.

Sender: Well . . . I would like to be able to tell you what I want or what upsets me without you hearing it as a criticism.

Receiver: (Repeats.)

Sender: That's right.

Receiver: Well—then—how about saving your complaints or "requests" for when we talk on Sunday and let me know before you say them—what you appreciate about me—then I can listen better.

Sender: (Repeats.)

Receiver: That's right.

Sender: I'll try that. But I want you to know that when I tell you what I want, I am *not* criticizing *you*. I *am* telling you what pleases me or upsets me. *It is not a putdown of you.* I love you. I want us to be happy together.

Receiver: (Repeats.)

Sender: That's right.

Receiver: Well, maybe I need to hear more about what's right. It sounds like I'm always doing something wrong.

Sender: (Repeats.)

Receiver: That's right.

Sender: It's *because* I love you that I tell you my feelings.

Receiver: It's because you love me that you tell me your feelings.

Sender: That's right.

Receiver: Well, then, tell me more of what you like—so I don't feel like *all* I hear are complaints.

Sender: You would like me to tell you more of what I like so you don't feel that all you hear are complaints.

Receiver: That's right.

Sender: I'll try. And I need you to try to listen without hearing it as a putdown of you.

Receiver: You'll try. And you need me to try to listen without hearing it as a putdown of me.

Sender: Right.

Receiver: Well. Maybe I am too sensitive.

Sender: You think that maybe you're too sensitive.

Receiver: Yes.

Sender: Well. I'll try to let you know more of what I appreciate and that I love you. But I need you to be able to listen to me when something bothers me and not get angry.

Receiver: (Repeats.)

Sender: Yes.

Receiver: I'll try. Thanks for telling me. I didn't realize. (Hugs.)

We need to be able to teach our partner what pleases us and what distresses us. And as the partner, we need to be able to listen for information—not as a criticism of our being—and decide if and what we can (or want to) change for a better relationship. If all we hear is criticism, that is deflating and makes us strongly wonder if we are indeed lovable and good enough or why our partner would love us. But, if we can't listen to complaints directly—they may get "acted out" in another way, one more destructive to the relationship. On the other hand, if all we do is complain, maybe, as psychiatrist Daniel Casriel said, "If wherever you go, you smell shit, maybe there's a little stuck on the end of your nose—and you can just wipe it off! You can find anything you're looking for so you need to ask yourself, 'What are you looking for?' "

We need to hear from our partners more about what is good about us than what is missing. That is why we choose to share our lives. We do need to be able to ask for what we want and say what we don't want. But, if there is too much missing, maybe we shouldn't be together.

Or maybe there are things we really *do* need to and can change. Learning to give and to receive in a mutually loving relationship is a source of great joy.

PAIRS Exercise: Mind Reading

1. Write any assumptions you suspect you may be making about what your partner thinks and feels.
2. Write any assumptions you suspect your partner may be making of you.
3. Set a time to talk.
4. Ask *permission:* "Do I have permission to read your mind?"
5. State your assumption: "I think that you think that . . ."
6. Partner repeats the assumption using Empathic Shared Meaning.
7. When accurate, partner responds *with honesty.* You now have information that can guide your behavior and beliefs about what is truly there rather than allowing landmines of mis-

understanding to explode unexpectedly, leaving you or your partner shocked, victimized and painfully misunderstood.

In the next chapter, we will guide you in expressing resentment and disappointment in creative ways that build rather than destroy love.

Take a moment to write in your journal notebook about what you are beginning to realize.

9

The Art of Anger

■   ■   ■

*T*here are times when your partner does things that make you want to explode, logic and niceties be damned. You don't want to be nice. You don't want to be patient. You're tired of being reasonable. You don't want to figure out whether something set off an emotional allergy or if the way you feel is something you should bring up during the Daily Temperature Reading. You just want your partner to stop doing whatever it is he or she is doing: throwing underwear on the floor; changing plans at the last minute; belching at the table; talking during a movie. It may be that you had a lousy day and all your partner had to do in order to aggravate you was to breathe. Logic, psychology and facts make scant difference when we're in such a mood. This is when we are most likely to get into bitter fights.

Unfortunately, these are often the times we try to solve conflicts, not through logic or caring, but in anger, defense or intimidation. The only rules involve trying to win or destroy. We come up with solutions that feel right for the moment, but that aren't what we want at all, and we say things we later regret saying: "I wish you'd just drop dead." "Why don't you just pack your bags and go!" "If you don't shut up I won't go to the party with you!" and more. We make the mistake of acting on our feelings instead of honestly expressing them. Alternatively, we may try to avert unpleasantness by bottling up that rage. This causes us to distance ourselves from our partner (because we are still angry, even if we don't admit it), to let it *leak out* with nitpicking, nagging or sarcasm, or to get sick physically, emotionally or both.

Since avoiding anger is not only impossible, but as discussed earlier, unhealthy, how do we prevent it from destroying the pleasure of our relationships?

THE RITUAL OF RAGE

The late Dr. George Bach, author and director of his own center on relationships, believed that the only way to contend with anger was to confront it head on. He developed a series of rage release rituals to reduce the destructiveness (but not necessarily the intensity) of anger, thereby detoxifying an issue and freeing a couple to pursue logical solutions to it.

Many people who practice these rituals in PAIRS do not use them formally afterward. They're more like training wheels: exercises intended to make you more comfortable with anger—both your partner's and your own. However, others incorporate the basic principles of the exercises into the general conduct of their relationships.

These rituals can help you change your fighting style (see Chapter 5). If you are a Blamer, you can learn how to express your anger nondestructively without repressing it and you can learn how to accept someone else's anger without retaliating in kind. If you are a Placater, this exercise may be particularly daunting—and important.

- How does the idea of practicing these rage rituals feel?
- Does it seem silly? Intimidating? Unthinkable?
- What do you anticipate happening? Embarrassment? More distance? More pain?
- Does it make sense to you that getting angry at your partner, and vice versa, can enhance intimacy between you?

BLOWING UP

Rituals for rage release are basically blaming rituals—time-limited explosions of blaming done only with the listener's permission, in which you can yell, rant and rave—feeling the full intensity of your emotions (but you *do not* become violent or destroy anything).

These rituals won't work unless there is mutual goodwill. Each of you must trust that the other ultimately cares and wants the relationship to work. The goal of the rituals is to help you experience the air-clearing quality of the healthy release of rage and to see for yourself how it is possible to feel loving again toward the person you wanted to throttle five minutes earlier. One reason we avoid intense anger is that at a certain point we may experience it as a desire to hurt or get rid of the person with whom we are angry. Using the ritual, we learn that it is possible to express this level of rage in a controlled setting with the intention of getting back to love.

The key element of all the rage rituals is the granting of permission. It feels very different to me if I give you permission to explode and know that it is coming than if I experience your explosion as an ambush, for which my natural response would probably be to withdraw or counterattack. By agreeing to the ritual, I am acknowledging that the immediate problem here is not anything you say about me: The problem is the intensity of your rage, which I can help you deal with by agreeing to listen to it. If you are upset and you don't get it out of your system, nothing good is going to happen between us. My giving you permission means, "I'm not going to get even with you for expressing this anger. I am listening to help you get it out of your system because then we can get to a different understanding and feeling."

RITUAL I: THE VESUVIUS

The kids stuffed the toilet with three rolls of toilet paper and flushed it until two inches of water filled the bathroom and leaked through the kitchen ceiling and shorted out the lights; you spent three hours standing in line to get your car registered and were told you needed one more document and would have to come back again—and got a parking ticket for your trouble; your boss dressed you down in front of the staff for something your colleague did that you forgot to check. We often use the phrase "blow up" to describe the way we want to respond to such situations, many far worse and many far more trivial. The Vesuvius, named after the volcano, allows us to vent our rage about everything from the silly and annoying to the awful and the destructive.

This technique helps you to identify when your anger is approaching volcanic proportions, and to ritualize it so that the focus is on getting your anger out of your system. Your partner's role is simply to witness respectfully the expression of your anger as if it were an overwhelming natural phenomenon in which he or she is not a participant.

The underlying theme of this ritual is, "There are any number of things that I can't stand and I need someone to listen to me rage about them." It calls for no response from your partner except to listen. It carries no expectation of change.

If you want to let off steam, say something like, "I'm really about to explode. Can you listen to me for two minutes?" Any length of time your partner will agree to is okay, but two minutes can feel like a surprisingly long time to both the giver and receiver. If your partner says yes, all he or she does is listen with awe, as if watching a volcano explode—and let you know when your time is up. Your partner does not respond.

If your partner doesn't agree to the ritual, he or she may say, simply, "I can't listen now" (because it's inconvenient or because he or she doesn't feel up to it), "but I will this evening," or "I will listen within twenty-four hours." If it's intimacy your partner is after, he or she will be available to you within twenty-four hours, and you will do likewise when the occasion arises. However, if you are denied permission altogether, it is up to you to find nondestructive—even constructive—ways to let your feelings out (such as hitting a punching bag or a pillow, kneading bread, jogging vigorously, beating dust out of the sofa, throwing out old magazines or ripping out weeds).

When your partner is ready, just cut loose. Don't think too hard. Just let everything that bugs you come out. Do it loudly. Mean it.

"I left work exhausted today and just wanted to spend a half-hour on the subway winding down, reading. Two guys got on and turned up a radio. When I asked them to turn it down, they turned it up. I wanted to smash it to tiny bits. Hell, I wanted to smash *them* to tiny bits. I *hate* that. It's nasty and rude and they oughta be shot. When I got home, Mark hadn't bothered to move the garbage cans. What's the matter with him? Can't he even try to be a part of this family? And when I went upstairs to change, your socks and underwear were all over the place. What the hell's the matter with *you!* Don't you ever think of anybody else? On top of that, the robber barons at the garage said that the part they need will cost $159—plus another hundred to put it in. Why can't those idiots in Detroit make a car that lasts longer than an hour. No wonder nobody wants to buy American cars. They're *junk.*"

You can call people names, complain, nitpick, yell or scream, whether your anger is directed at your partner, your children (you will want to make sure they are out of the house or, if they are old enough, clued in on the rituals), coworkers, slow checkout clerks, bad politicians—whoever and whatever has gotten your goat. Give no thought to whether your complaints are legitimate or defensible. Ignore logic, manners and grace.

Your partner's job is to keep time and to listen—not to respond, apologize, defend or offer advice.

When you finish, your partner hugs you and thanks you for putting on such a good show and for getting this stuff out of your system directly instead of letting it infect your relationship.

The Vesuvius is useful for:

Training quiet or fight-phobic people to express their anger.
Teaching hot-tempered people how to manage their anger.
Helping the "listener" learn to hear outbursts of anger without taking them personally or counterattacking.
Clearing the air of unexpressed tension and grievances.

To the extent that you are the target of your partner's anger, the more you can distance yourself from the Vesuvius and view it as a spectacle, the easier it will be. Indeed, you may be able to distance yourself enough to see the comic aspects of this ritual, although this is by no means the time to laugh. Listen for information. There may be some things you don't know that you should be aware of. And regardless of whether you are hearing something for the first or the ninety-ninth time, try to empathize. Get a sense of how maddening the things being described really can be.

If, at the end of the ritual, your partner still feels angry and wants more time, it's okay to grant more time, but it's up to you.

RITUAL II: THE HAIRCUT

The Haircut is a blaming attack dealing specifically with some aspect of your partner's behavior. This ritual teaches you to focus on and express specifically what annoys you about your partner's behavior rather than experiencing and acting on a vague sense of irritation. The Haircut has the same ground rules as the Vesuvius: you must ask permission and set a time limit. You don't necessarily ask for a change in behavior: You clearly state a gripe about a particular thing that your partner does (or doesn't do) and tell your partner how this behavior made you feel. It might go like this:

He: I'm very angry at you and I'd like to give you a Haircut for two minutes. Is that okay?

She: All right. (If she refuses for now, she should try to set up an alternative time within the next twenty-four hours.)

He: I'm furious because when you went shopping last night, you brought the car back on empty. When I left for my meeting this morning, I had to stop for gas. I didn't allow time for that, you didn't tell me it was low on gas, and I was late. That was not a good way to come into the meeting and was totally avoidable! (Now he begins to get into it, reliving the anger he felt this morning. He starts to get louder, starts to wave his hands around.) I was embarrassed for being late and I was furious at you for not even considering that this is something you need to check. It was as if I didn't even count. I can't stand it when you do that. *Stop it!*

She (hugging him): Thanks for telling me what upset you.

He: Thanks for listening (hugging her back).

At the end of each of these anger rituals, the person who is listening thanks the person who is talking for expressing the anger or complaint. This may be difficult if you are feeling angry yourself or believe your partner's complaint is unjustified, but do it anyway. It's important for your partner to know that direct, honest expression of feelings is valued. You have the same opportunity any time you request it and your partner agrees.

It may make you more comfortable at first to practice these rituals by assuming roles—practicing either with your partner or with a friend and asking them to play your daughter, partner, boss or whomever. Don't make the mistake of thinking that you can take these rituals out into the world or to the office, however. They work only if both parties agree to use them and if both know what the rules are.

BELTLINES

Once you've become familiar with the rituals, the next time your partner blows up, you can consider saying, "That's a Vesuvius. Ask my permission so I can set myself to listen." Then it is up to your partner to ask permission to use a blaming ritual or to state clearly: "I have something on my chest, and I want you to listen to me." After your partner has dealt with the anger he or she will be better able to say to you in a nonthreatening way, "This thing that you do bothers me, and I would feel better if . . ."

Some people ask, How can you turn anger on and off like that? Well, you can, just the way you turn the plumbing on and off. You can learn to control when and where you dump your garbage; you can do the same with anger and blame. If you don't, and if you blame and criticize, throw tantrums and cry, or shut down and sulk, you are going to destroy your relationship.

These anger rituals are also helpful in establishing our "Beltlines" when we fight—topics, remarks or styles that we are particularly sensitive about and that feel "below the belt." During a Haircut, we may find that while we can accept our partner's anger fairly easily, when he or she brings up our shrill laugh, our paunch or some other self-perceived "defect" we are deeply hurt, angered or insulted. As we notice these, we should record them in our journal on a special Beltlines page and share them with our partner.

As you both learn to fight, you can learn to honor each other's Beltlines—without giving up the right to be assertive. We can be assertive without being deliberately hurtful or trying to score points; we can be assertive on behalf of the relationship without attacking our partners.

By keeping track of where our Beltlines are, we can decide for ourselves whether they should be adjusted. While most of us have "buttons" that we don't want our partners to push, some of us may have Beltlines that are far too high or too low to be constructive for a relationship.

Both problems are tied to self-esteem. If our Beltline is too low, we are allowing people to say almost anything they like about us. While some might view this as the virtue of extreme patience, it may also mean that we are unwilling to stand up for ourselves. We have a right to draw lines and to expect our partners to honor those lines. On the other hand, if our Beltlines are too high, it means we feel devastated by almost any sharp comment or any level of criticism. This can make it impossible for our partners to make any request for change or to discuss things that bother them. If they try to honor a Beltline that is up to our neck, they will end by stifling themselves, which will only hinder communication and force them to stuff down their anger.

Changing the Beltlines means working on raising self-esteem, specifically to adopt and believe in the positive statements discussed in Chapter 3. People who let their partners and others make whatever derisive comments they like need to focus on "I exist," which in this case means, "I am here and I deserve to be treated as a full-fledged human being, not as a doormat." They also need to remember that "I am entitled"—entitled to be treated lovingly and with respect. Someone with a high Beltline needs to remember the assertions "I am lovable" and "I am good enough." This translates into: Criticism does not discount me or my capabilities. It can provide important information that could help me and help my relationship.

For partners who have a number of "buttons" and who often see simple disagreements escalate into full-fledged firefights, discussing and negotiating Beltlines can be invaluable. Genuine efforts to express rage while being respectful of a partner's boundaries and sensitivities greatly enhances mutual trust. It is the first step toward handling conflict in a way that encourages intimacy—not alienation.

MAKING UP: THE DOGHOUSE RELEASE

The idea behind the anger rituals is to get beyond anger to love. It seems fitting to include here George Bach's apology-and-forgiveness ritual, which emphasizes the pleasures that we can experience once we have allowed an airing of grievances.

For most people, the hard part about fighting is learning to express and listen to grievances. Some people, however, have trouble ending a fight—either the offending party has trouble apologizing, or the offended party has trouble forgiving and letting go of a grudge. Fortunately, Dr. Bach has had the good sense to see that a sense of humor and an appeal to self-interest are often the best way out of a difficult situation. We thank him for the Doghouse Release.

The Doghouse Release is useful for getting someone "out of the doghouse" after he or she has been given a Haircut. It's a pleasure-oriented way of encouraging the angry partner to let go of his or her grudge.

If you feel you have suffered a specific injury or disappointment from your partner (that is, he or she is really in your doghouse), you may ask permission to give him a Haircut, and after you've given it, your partner may ask what he or she can do to get out of the doghouse. Whatever you specify must be pleasurable for you— the idea being to replace punishment and guilt for the offender with pleasure for the offended party. You may want a simple "I'm sorry," or you may want something more: a back rub, breakfast in bed or being taken to that movie you've been dying to see.

The Vesuvius, the Haircut, Beltline limits and the Doghouse Release are all techniques that help us understand how anger works and how to release it without contaminating our relationships. We are now ready for the next step: learning how to resolve some of the issues that provoke anger in the first place.

Take a moment to write in your journal notebook about what you are beginning to realize.

10

The Art of Fighting Fair

■　　　■　　　■

*P*ossibly the most helpful technique from George Bach's fight-training repertoire is a negotiating process called the Fair Fight for Change. This is a format for stating which behavior of your partner's bothers you and what behavior you would prefer in its place. Designed to replace pleading, ignoring, blaming and threatening, the Fair Fight is a structure for isolating and resolving problems. In many ways, it's not a fight at all. It's a negotiation. It's not against your partner. It's in behalf of a better relationship.

It's not always necessary to do a Fair Fight to settle a conflict. Sometimes all we need to do is exchange information, as with the Dialogue Guide, or in Empathic Shared Meaning. The value of the Fair Fight is that it forces both partners in a relationship to think through the specifics of any given issue, decide clearly what they want and enunciate it just as clearly to the other partner. Then they search for a mutually agreeable solution. You may fear asking for something that you think your partner will refuse to do, but in the long run it is important to know whether certain hopes and expectations are realistic or unrealistic, and whether you can find a way to have your wishes met.

BASIC STEPS OF A FAIR FIGHT FOR CHANGE

This is the basic format for the Fair Fight:

1. *Engagement:* Ask, "Will you engage in a Fair Fight for Change? (Ask permission.)

2. *Private Reflection:* Reflect on what you want from your partner, taking care to pick out and stick to one issue, and reflect on how you can word it. (You may want to refer to the Dialogue Guide to clarify the issue for yourself.)

3. *Complaint:* State your complaint clearly. (What specific behavior?)

4. *Feedback and Reward:* Using the Empathic Listening and Shared Meaning technique (see Chapter 7), receive feedback from your partner until it is clear to both of you that your complaint is understood. Show appreciation for being heard correctly.

5. *Private Reflection:* Reflect on options for change, even small ones.

6. *Request for Change:* Ask for what you want, being as specific as possible.

7. *Feedback and Reward:* Receive feedback from your partner. Show appreciation.

8. *Evocation:* Ask, "Are you willing to seek to arrive at a new contract?" Make provisions for evaluation and renegotiation. Responsibilities of each party should be clear.

9. *Partner's Private Reflection:* Reflect on options, considerations.

10. *Partner Response and Feedback:* Agree, disagree, state reservations and suggestions.

11. *Acceptance, Rejection or Modification:* Continue process to closure.

12. *Closure:* Close the fight. Show appreciation (hugs). Set time for re-evaluation.

In everyday life you won't always use every one of these steps, but when you are first learning this technique it will help you to follow them carefully, so you can internalize the principles, structure and logic of the ritual. The following is a detailed example of how a Fair Fight works. You will want to keep it nearby when you practice the technique in the exercise later in this chapter.

EXAMPLE: FAIR FIGHT FOR CHANGE

Ask permission and set aside time. Say to your partner, "I'd like to have a Fair Fight," and ask when would be a good time. Agree on a general time limit for the fight—half an hour to an hour and a half. Be sure that you're really ready to have a Fair Fight, and not simply looking to vent your anger. If you're full of feelings, get the emotions out first, using a Vesuvius or a Haircut, and then start the Fair Fight. Keep in mind that if things get touchy and you find yourself growing angry or upset, you may ask for permission to do a Vesuvius or Haircut or just to take a break. This is the time to use logic and not let it be overridden by out-of-control emotions that you can dump. Remember the Dialogue Guide: It can be used both to organize and to express your thoughts.

Sit opposite each other, holding hands, knees touching, and maintain direct eye contact—it's harder to misunderstand each other this way.

> *Maureen:*   Something has been bothering me and I would like to have a Fair Fight about it. Can we do it now or should I wait?
>
> *William:*   Now's as good a time as any. Go ahead. (They sit where they can face and touch each other.)

Reflect silently. Spend some time really thinking through specifically which behavior gripes you, what you want to do about it, and how you are going to word what you want to say. Reflect on how you can present your request so that your partner can best understand and not feel attacked.

> *Maureen:*   OK. Give me just a minute so I can be clear about this.

State your complaint. State specifically which behavior of your partner's is bothering you and describe your feelings about it ("It bothers me when . . ."). State your case as *your* case ("I . . ."), and not as blaming ("You . . ."). Stick to one complaint per Fair Fight. It's overwhelming to deal with more than one behavior change at a time. Start with small issues so that both of you can become accustomed to how the Fair Fight works.

Maureen: We agreed some time ago to try to talk every day. I'm very upset that we don't do it very often and that when we do, it's always because I suggest it. Even then, you often say you want to put it off. I think it's important because it helps us keep our relationship on an even keel. It bothers me a lot if that doesn't seem important to you.

Get feedback and thank your partner for listening. After you have presented your complaint, ask your partner to repeat to you what he or she has heard. You may want to state your complaint in two or three segments and have your partner repeat it back one piece at a time. If so, just make this clear by saying, "There's more," when you end the first segment. If your partner didn't hear accurately what you said or intended to say, make your statement again, adding whatever you need to add to make your meaning clear. Continue restating until your partner indicates that your message has been heard accurately.

This step may seem tedious, but it serves several functions—it slows the communication process so you both have time to think; it allows you to clarify areas in which there are misunderstandings; and it keeps you from presenting too much material at one time.

If you are receiving the complaint, your role is just to listen carefully and repeat faithfully (in your own words) what your partner has said—without editing, interpreting or rebutting, even if you find yourself getting angry because you think that what your partner said was inaccurate or unfair. The purpose of your feedback is to let your partner *know that you have heard his or her truth,* which may not be your truth. Later you can say, "I heard what you were saying, but the way it looked (felt) to me was . . ." If you initiated the Fair Fight, once your partner has given you accurate feedback, thank him or her, adding a touch or a kiss or hug to show your appreciation that your partner has listened carefully. Do this even if either of you is feeling angry.

> *William:* What you said isn't really fair. I—
>
> *Maureen:* You can reply later. Right now, I need you to follow the rules and make sure you heard me.
>
> *William:* You're right. I'm sorry. Let me try again. You're angry that we don't talk more often, even though we agreed to. You don't like being the only one to suggest doing it. It makes you think I don't care that much about our relationship.
>
> *Maureen:* That's right. Thank you. (She squeezes his hand and kisses him.)

Reflect silently. Think again: What specific behavior do you want your partner to change—where, when and how? What new behavior should replace the old?

> *Maureen:* Okay, let me think again for a second.

Make a specific request for change. State which specific behavior you would like your partner to adopt to replace the behavior you have complained about. ("What I am asking you to do is hang up your pajamas or put away your clothes and put your dirty socks in the hamper, when you've finished your shower or changed clothes.")

Be sure to ask for what you really want (and can live with) and be sure that what you ask for is reasonably within your partner's capacity to give. Be specific and don't overload.

> *Maureen:* I would like us to set a time each day to talk, even to do the Daily Temperature Reading, so that we do it without thinking or without my having to prod.

Get feedback and thank your partner. Ask your partner to repeat what you have asked for and express (verbally and with a hug) your appreciation for correct feedback. This is a "thank you for listening to me," not thanks for agreeing to change. Your partner may listen carefully and still refuse your request.

William: You would like us to talk and even do the Daily Temperature Reading.

Maureen: Right. But there was a more important part. Would you like me to repeat it?

William: That's okay, I remember. You would like to have a set time for doing it so we just do it automatically. You don't want to be the one to always bring it up. Right?

Maureen: Exactly. Thank you.

Ask for a response. "Can you do what I want?" or "Will you do that?"

Maureen: Will you agree to that?

Allow your partner to reflect. Here your partner considers, "Can I live with this change? Under what conditions would this change be acceptable to me?" A time-out may be a good idea here.

William: Can we stop? I want a few minutes to think about this.

Maureen: Sure.

Get response and give feedback. Your partner may (1) agree to make the change, (2) agree to some modification of it or attach conditions to it (it's only fair to set conditions if they are related to the request; don't start bartering by saying things like: "I'll do what you want if you stop doing such-and-such"), (3) ask that the decision be postponed until a later (specified) time or (4) refuse to make the change you requested. Your partner makes his or her response in manageable pieces, and you feed it back.

William: On the whole, I agree with you and what you want, but I would like to make some changes.

Maureen: Okay, I'm listening.

William: I think that the Daily Temperature Reading is a good idea. But I feel as if we touch on most of the elements throughout the day and prefer to do it that way. It feels more natural and less structured. There's more.

Maureen: You're willing to do the Daily Temperature Reading, but you would rather we just work it in with the rest of our day instead of setting aside a particular time for it.

William: That's right. I know that makes you crazy sometimes because you find it hard to raise complaints about me and the Daily Temperature Reading makes it easier for you. I need you to understand that sometimes I just forget or you remember to do it at times that are bad for me, like when I need to rush to work or just as we're going to bed. That's why I like the idea of setting a time. There's more.

Maureen: You think the format makes it easier for me to raise complaints. You also feel that I try to do the Daily Temperature Reading at times that aren't convenient or comfortable for you. Oh, and you sometimes just forget.

William: Right. I would like us to learn how to touch on all five areas of the Daily Temperature Reading during the natural course of the day. But until we learn to do that easily, I agree that we need to use a more structured format. So this is what I propose: that we set a time to do it in the early evening, either over dinner or while we are cleaning up. During the day, and when we first get home from work, we can touch on as many of the areas as we like and make sure that we cover them all at dinner. I would also like, twice a week, but not twice in a row, to be able to tell you I want to skip it when I am tired.

Maureen: You would like to do it over dinner or while we are cleaning up, and say twice a week that you would like to skip it.

William: Well, that's not quite right. I may not want to skip it twice a week. I might never do that, but I would like the option. Also, I really want us to make a conscious effort to work it into our ordinary conversations.

Maureen: You would like the option of not doing the Daily Temperature Reading twice a week. You also would like us to weave it into our day-to-day life, right?

William: Right. But remember, I said not twice in a row, because I don't think that's fair.
Maureen: You would like to be able to skip it twice a week, if you want, but not two days in a row.
William: Thanks. (He hugs her.)

Accept, reject or modify. After considering your partner's response, you either agree to it, reject it or say under what conditions you can do it, and get feedback. You repeat this negotiating process until you reach an agreement, reach an impasse or decide you want time to think about the issue before making an agreement. Often, you learn things from and about your partner that change the situation and want a day or two to let the new information settle and see if it has changed your views. If you have not reached agreement, schedule a time in the near future to discuss it. If you have agreed on something, you may want to set a time to discuss how the new arrangement is working out. If you are practicing the Fair Fight, this is where you would change roles.

Maureen: I like your suggestion, with one minor exception. I would prefer that we stick to doing it during dinner. I find it hard to concentrate while we are cleaning up, and we often turn on the television or radio then. I would hate to have to compete with all the distractions.
William: You would like us to do the Daily Temperature Reading during dinner.
Maureen: Right. Is that okay?
William: Fine. I'm willing and I agree to initiate it. But if I forget, I hope you will do it.

Close the fight. Conclude the Fair Fight with hugs and kisses and thanks for listening and discuss any practical details associated with carrying out whatever change you have negotiated. Your partner may ask for help or for reminders about the promised change, and you will certainly want to set a time (perhaps one or two weeks hence) to discuss how the change is working out.

Maureen: I'm glad we talked this out. It was starting to really upset me, especially because you always said you wanted to do this, but it seemed like we never got around to it. Thanks for doing this with me. (She hugs him.)

William: I'm glad you brought it up, because I suspected it was bugging you. By the way, I know you don't want to have to remind me all the time, so I'll make a deal with you. If you have to start it or bring it up twice in a row, I'll give you a fifteen-minute back rub?

Maureen: That's a deal. In fact, if you remember for a whole week, I'll give you the back rub, at least for the first two weeks. OK?

Since the agreement to hold a Fair Fight presumes basic goodwill on the part of both parties, chances are you will not get an outright and adamant "no" from your partner when you request a change. You may, of course, find that your partner can't or won't do exactly what you want—in which case you may negotiate a modification of the request ("I can't promise that I'll remember to change the toilet paper roll every time it's empty, but I will always keep another roll handy above the toilet"). You also may find that your partner is willing to honor your request on certain conditions ("I'll be glad to figure out a new balance in the checkbook each week if you'll agree not to make withdrawals without at least consulting me first"). Remember, we are looking for the arrangement that is most beneficial to the relationship: Bargaining for bargaining's sake is not constructive.

If you encounter a flat no, you may simply have to accept it—or you may find that with more information (on your side or your partner's) the issue looks different or more negotiable. Or perhaps it will look different to one or both of you at another time. Sometimes you will have to start with what you can do to change your own situation. You can't always expect your satisfaction to depend on changes that must emanate from your partner. Ed's idea of how to spend Sunday afternoon, for example, was to watch sports events on television; Carol accepted this but resented it, and wished that they could do things together on Sundays rather than watching someone else do them. Carol assumed that they must do things together on Sunday afternoon when Ed was more than willing to make sure they spent time together during other parts of the weekend and there were innumerable other things she could do, like go out with a friend or do something on her own while he watched television. Sometimes we simply have to explore creative alternatives.

Keep in mind that all of us have core issues. I call them "walking issues." These are not open for debate. These nonnegotiable issues are centered on desires so deep or values so intrinsic to our nature that we would be willing to "walk away" from the relationship rather than change our position. Some are social conventions and values that are so obvious that most of us take for granted that we share them as a couple: taboos against incest, violence, illegal behavior. Others are much more difficult and sometimes emerge only during the course of the relationship. These include the questions of having children, use of illegal drugs or alcohol, fidelity, honesty, who works outside the home, religious views and even political beliefs.

Never assume that someone shares your deepest values or expectations. It's not unknown for marriages to end in divorce because one partner simply expected that they would have children or that a child would be raised in a particular religion. While we have no obligation to change our views on core issues, we are obliged to make clear to our partner what our "walking issues" are.

PAIRS Exercise: Practicing the Fair Fight

This is your opportunity to use the Fair Fight. In PAIRS we do the Fair Fight in groups of four, with one couple fighting and one couple acting as coaches. The coaches make sure that the rules are followed, provide helpful observations and help you determine what you are really after and really trying to say during the "reflection steps." In lieu of having friends who would like to play such a role or take part in this exercise, practice the fight with this book in glancing distance. Also, consider using a tape recorder so you can evaluate your style. If you are single, pick an issue that has arisen in past relationships and think through, following these steps, how you might frame it and be willing to reconsider it.

Follow these instructions for the exercise.

First, choose a time to practice the Fair Fight and decide which of you will go first. Allow about an hour the first time, as you will want to consult the book to remind yourself of the ritual's structure.

Second, follow all the steps of the Fair Fight faithfully the first few times you practice it, even if it seems tedious to repeat everything.

Third, avoid monumental issues at the beginning. Start with small things. For example: "Please don't play with the baby just before dinner" (not, "Let's have a baby"); "This is where I would like to take a vacation this summer" (not, "Let's take separate vacations"); "I think the person who washes dishes should also clean off the stove and counter" (not, "I earn more money than you, so you should do all the housework"); "Please don't leave me alone all evening at your office parties" (not, "If you're ever unfaithful, we are history"). By practicing on small issues, you can concentrate on learning the structure and spirit of the Fair Fight.

Reviewing Your Fight

How different did this feel from the way you usually handle disagreements? Record in your journal your impressions of how your Fair Fight went. Did you follow the basic rules?

Did you ask permission? You may deal with conflict only if you both agree to do so at a time when you can pay full attention.

Did you set a specific time and time limit? Did you allow for time-outs?

Were you specific, reasonable and realistic? If your partner gets used to you exaggerating your grievances, you may find yourself being treated like the boy who cried wolf. When you really have something to say, he or she will not be listening.

Did you ask only for changes in behavior? You can't realistically expect changes in thoughts or feelings.

Did you stick to current issues? Don't dredge up all your old grievances.

Did you show respect? Did you avoid intentional hurt?

Were you able to relieve the fight with humor? Did you avoid sarcasm or teasing?

Did you show appreciation for being heard and understood? What did you say to try to accentuate the positive aspects of your relationship?

Did you monitor yourself during the fight? Were you aware of whether you were Leveling with your partner, or when you needed time out to think or deal with your emotions?

To better understand your fight style, each of you should score yourselves on the following chart. Don't just score your Fair Fight. If you had a fight recently, use the chart to analyze where and how things escalated into destructive patterns. If you have a fight in the future that does not feel fair (you almost certainly will; these new skills take time to adopt and we will not shed our old styles overnight), remember to review this chart again. By scoring your fights, you can spot the areas where both of you tend to get ensnared by historical emotional allergies and destructive fighting styles. Check off which styles you used, the negative or positive, in each category. Use a zero for categories where you used a neutral style.

Fight Style Profile

	Fair (+)	Unfair (−)	
Facial Expression	Open, responsive, reflective, interested, real	Closed, guarded, impassive, uninterested, masked	
Focus	Here and now, direct, specific to problem, one issue, to the point	Past, museum tour, generalizing, gunnysacking, throwing in the kitchen sink	
Communication	Clear, relevant, shared meaning, response, accurate feedback and empathy	No empathy, no response, one way, inaccurate or no feedback	
Reality	Information realistic, accurate, authentic	Distorted, fantasy, lies	

Fight Style Profile (cont.)

	Fair (+)	Unfair (−)	
Injury	Comments reasonable, fair, above the belt	Dirty, insulting, sarcastic, ridiculing, threatening, accusing, labeling, taunting, name calling, demeaning, laughing at, mind reading, psychoanalyzing, attributing thoughts and feelings to others, contempt, stonewalling, assuming	
Responsibility	Willing to recognize own contribution to the problem	Denying, ignoring own part	
Openness to Change	Willing to change	Rigid, unchanging	

Adapted from The Intimate Enemy *by George Bach and Peter Wyden.*

PAIRS Exercise: Do We Engage in Dirty Fighting?

You are fighting dirty when you use tactics that escalate conflict and reduce the likelihood of constructive solutions. To pinpoint the fair and unfair fight habits you have, you and your partner should make two lists in your journal: 1) fight tactics that *you* characteristically adopt in the midst of conflict or in the heat of anger, and 2) fight tactics that *your partner* adopts in such situations. Pick the tactics listed below that fit and write them down in each column; feel free to add any that are not on the list. Try to note at least one specific example for each tactic; it's an easier frame of reference for your partner when you share lists later.

Bullying (screaming, exploding, intimidating)
Pretending your partner is being unreasonable
Mind-reading or "psychoanalyzing" your partner

Switching the subject with counteraccusations (blaming) or diversions (distracting)

Bringing up more than one issue or complaint at a time (dumping your whole "gunnysack" of issues instead of sticking to one issue)

Name-calling

Playing the victim

Dragging your feet

Using "cold logic" to hide from emotional reality (computing)

Mimicking

Contempt

Sarcasm

Exaggeration (You always . . .)

Humiliating

Taunting

Ordering (Don't you dare leave until I'm finished)

Denying

Stonewalling (I'm not talking to you)

Withholding (I told you once, I'm not going to repeat myself)

Making excuses (I started calling you names because you made me so mad)

Playing the martyr

Other

Once your lists are complete, compare them. Ask your partner for clarification if you don't understand something on his or her list. More important, ask your partner to remind you the next time you begin to use dirty-fighting tactics and do the same with your partner. Do this without blame and as calmly as possible, with the understanding that these are destructive styles that simply have become bad habits. You may even want to use specifics from the list as an issue in a Fair Fight, explaining to your partner how his or her style affects you and how he or she could change it in a way that would make it easier for you to deal with conflict between you. If you are trying to build a relationship intentionally based on deliberate and loving actions, you will welcome an opportunity to eliminate meddlesome habits that sabotage the way you really feel about the person with whom you have chosen to share your life.

FINDING WHERE YOU ARE

The simplest and most powerful way to tell how well we are doing in a Fair Fight is to examine the way we feel once a fight is over. While reaching agreement on a potent issue can be a good sign, such a compromise doesn't mean much if one of you felt belittled or bullied in the process. Bad feelings after a fight indicate that our style is destructive and demands attention; feelings of greater closeness and clarity mean that you are taking the right tack.

The chart on page 135 lists signs of a constructive result of a fight and signs of a destructive result. Think about the last fight or argument you had with your partner. Examine the feelings you had afterward and ask your partner to do the same. Then discuss the styles each of you have that could be changed so as to make fights more constructive and less destructive.

MAKING THE PIECES FIT

During PAIRS, most couples are astounded to discover that they can talk about issues that have been contentious or ignored—in some cases for years—without destructive, knockdown, drag-out battles. Even when they cannot agree on a solution, many find that genuinely listening and being listened to has reduced the tension around subjects that once divided them sharply. Every couple uses these tools differently. Some people whose relationships were marked by constant outbursts and tantrums rely primarily on the rage-release rituals, discovering that once anger is drained off, they can discuss and resolve things without any other structure. Others, often those who were unhappy in their relationships but had a difficult time understanding (much less articulating) their unhappiness, grew intrigued with the Fair Fight, using it to express feelings and resolve arguments over everything from car-pooling to having a child. The Fair Fight structure forced them to isolate those specific behaviors that disappointed them and those that pleased them. It also helped them to learn together how to negotiate for what they needed.

Many PAIRS graduates eventually use these tools only for the toughest of problems. Instead, they incorporate into their day-to-day lives the basic principles of these rituals and the communication

Fight Results Profile

Constructive Result (+)	Destructive Result (−)
Importance Feel more important to partner	**Importance** Feel less important to partner
Influence Increased; feel heard and understood	**Influence** Decreased; feel misunderstood
Self-Worth Increased	**Self-Worth** Decreased
Resentment Relieved	**Resentment** Inhibited, suppressed, or increased
Hurt Decreased	**Hurt** Increased
Fear Decreased	**Fear** Increased
Trust Increased	**Trust** Decreased
Closeness Feel closer, more affectionate	**Closeness** Feel more distant
Reparation Hurts mended; willing to or did make up for mistakes or mistreatment	**Reparation** No attempt to make up for mistakes or hurt feelings
Forgiveness Able to forgive partner	**Grudge Holding** Desire to withhold, withdraw, distance or get even
Progress Progress made toward solution	**Progress** No progress toward solution

Adapted from The Intimate Enemy *by George Bach and Peter Wyden.*

techniques described earlier. Just as a hammer and nails are used to build a house that will keep us warm and that we can fill with things that bring us joy and comfort, these techniques are tools to help us build new and constructive ways to communicate with each other so we can build a lasting relationship filled with pleasure, closeness, excitement and trust. Such tools are not helpful when they are not used appropriately. All of the communication techniques used in PAIRS are based on a philosophy of fair and open communication, which is described in detail in the following twenty-two-point guide. You can consider this guide a Superhighway on the Relationship Road Map that can keep your car moving toward the side of pleasure.

TWENTY-TWO-POINT GUIDE TO UNDERSTANDING COMMUNICATION AND NEGOTIATING FOR CHANGE

Nothing is more frightening than being in a relationship in which you don't know what is going on—where hidden meanings and motives, contradictions, inconsistencies, and sheer irrelevance are apt to crop up at any time. The captain of a ship who is navigating an unknown channel at night, certain that there are jagged reefs but having no idea where they lie, is in much the same fix. The following simple guidelines for sound communication make sense whether you're dealing with your partner, your parents, your children or your friends.

1. *First, learn to listen:* Risk setting aside your point of view to understand and empathize (not agree or disagree) with your partner's viewpoint.
2. *Speak using the "I" position:* "I" statements deepen your understanding of yourself, take responsibility for your own attitudes, feelings and perceptions, and avoid assumptions regarding your partner's motives or beliefs.
3. *Actions speak louder than words:* Your nonverbal communication is more powerful than what you say; when they contradict each other, it's confusing. Expect that your actions will be attended to more than your words, so pay attention to your behavior.
4. *Be relevant as well as congruent:* Define in your own mind what is important and illustrate it by examples. Define what is unimportant and ignore it.
5. *Accentuate the positive:* Without being phony or unrealistic, try

to find the positive aspects in the situation or person (invariably there are some) and give them recognition in your message—that is, something that shows regard for your partner's worth.

6. *Be clear and specific:* Avoid vague terms and unclear expressions, which often create confusion and resentment—and request that your partner clarify as well.

7. *Be reasonable and realistic in your statements:* Avoid the amplification, coloration and exaggeration that can be legitimate and effective when relating a story or event but can become habit forming—and when it sneaks into a serious discussion it can cause havoc. Learn to listen to yourself as well as your partner.

8. *Test all your assumptions verbally:* No matter how "obvious" it might be to you or how "certain" you are about your partner's views on the topic, if the conversation is important, check it out explicitly. Listen for intent, not just the words (the music beneath the words).

9. *Each event can be seen from quite different points of view:* Realize that different viewpoints don't have to lead to arguments. If you allow yourself not to get uptight about them, they can lead to enlightening discussions.

10. *Recognize that your partner may be an expert on you and your behavior:* You're very important to him or her, a subject of endless observation and study, so listen to and consider what your partner has to say—each mood, gesture and tone might tell your partner something about your state that you haven't yet realized or admitted to yourself.

11. *Learn how to disagree without destructive arguments or trying to win:* Monitor and reduce the irritated, angry or complaining tones of voice that can turn a discussion into an argument—this can be easier if you form the habit of viewing your partner and his or her feelings, desires, self-concept and goals with empathy and even if (or especially when) you do not agree with him or her.

12. *Learn to bring up significant issues even if you fear that it will cause an upset:* The kind of "upset" that comes from the hypocrisy and repressed resentments of a phony truce is often worse.

13. *Choose an appropriate time and place to be open and honest about your feelings and needs:* Don't choose public places where embarrassment is probable.
14. *Use tact and timing:* Don't bring up important issues when there is neither time nor energy to resolve them. Request a time that will work for both of you and stick to it.
15. *Don't use unfair or dirty tactics:* Don't go for the jugular just for the joy of hurting—it can boomerang! In any case, don't:

Use the atom bomb: scream, explode or intimidate as a tactic
Pretend that your partner has made an unreasonable statement or request
Mind-read or "psychoanalyze" your partner or jump to conclusions
Switch the subject by using counter accusations or diversions
Bring up more than one issue or complaint at a time
Use the self-pitying "numbers game" ("Just look how often I've . . .")
Use impersonal logic to hide from emotional reality
Interrupt
Blame your partner for something he or she can't help or do anything about
Use humiliation, insults, rubbing-in old faults, comparing unfavorably
Use "crazy-making" tactics—trying to make partner doubt his or her senses, denying the obvious, being inconsistent or deliberately obtuse
Use sarcasm or ridicule
Use the "cold shoulder" treatment—silence, pouting, ignoring and so forth

16. *Accept all feelings and try to understand them:* You needn't accept upsetting actions but you should try to understand them.
17. *Be tactful, considerate and caring:* Show respect for your partner and his or her feelings through your language and behavior.
18. *Don't preach or lecture:* Ask questions instead—but make them honest (not prejudging or sarcastic) and be sure, first, that you *want* an honest answer.
19. *Don't use or fall for "excuses":* Face the music—don't use state-

ments that pretend to be explanations but really hide or disguise the real reasons. Don't play games or try to manipulate.

20. *Don't nag, yell or whine:* Like water on a rock, these can erode the best relationship.
21. *Learn when to use humor and when to be serious:* No destructive teasing.
22. **And, finally, *learn to listen*.**

Take a moment to write in your journal notebook about what you are beginning to realize.

11

Letting Go of Grudges

■　　　　■　　　　■

*T*he ability to let go of past hurts is probably the single most important relationship skill we can develop. Keeping someone on the hook for a past transgression can carry an immediate sense of gratification or power, but this *always* occurs at the expense of our relationship. It may feel good at the time because we are relieving the lingering resentment that is boiling within us. But the only way to restore harmony is to *remove* such a feeling, not just relieve it. No relationship can recover from serious disappointments and mature if one or both partners cannot find a way to let go of bitterness. You cannot trust or love your partner while you are, secretly or loudly, resentful of him or her.

Letting go of a grudge is something that we do for *ourselves*, not our partners. We do it not to make them feel better, but so we can enjoy the pleasures that are possible in the relationship.

DECIDING WHEN TO LET GO OF A GRUDGE

There are two points of caution that cannot be overemphasized:

First, it is important to understand that we are not talking about sweeping things under the rug or ignoring troubling behavior. We are talking about confronting problems as they come up and unearthing old wounds that have not been thoughtfully discussed by using some of the tools in this book (the Fair Fight, the Haircut and the Dialogue Guide, for example) and then disposing of them.

Second and even more important: There are things that some people find unforgivable. Whether you can forgive is something only you can decide. If letting go of a grudge feels impossible or even dangerous, it may be that you need to decide whether you should continue the relationship. Fidelity is a good example. Some people are able to forgive their partners for having an affair and get on with their lives. To others, infidelity is the ultimate act of betrayal in a marriage or partnership and destroys their ability to trust their partner forever; to them, letting go of their hurt and rage means condoning behavior that they find unacceptable or immoral. I am not advising anyone to do that. I am asking you to recognize the extreme difficulty that accompanies a relationship that is continued with someone you cannot forgive.

It also needs to be understood that apologies and reassurances are sometimes not enough for you to forgive; they must be accompanied by a clear, demonstrated ability to change. The most extreme example would be someone in a physically or emotionally abusive relationship. I would never suggest that someone in such a situation remain in or return to their partner on the basis of a tearful "I'm sorry" or heartfelt "It will never happen again." Never remain in an abusive relationship. Consider returning to an abuser only if he has received outside help and after she has clearly demonstrated—not just promised—a change in behavior and an ability to handle anger without taking it out on you (or your children or anyone else) physically or emotionally. It would be advisable to seek professional help in evaluating such a situation. Even if both of you are undergoing counseling, extreme caution on your part is necessary.

Remember that as important as relationships are to us, there are some that simply cost too much. There is no substitute for our judgment on when a relationship is extracting too high a price.

HUNTING DOWN THE GHOSTS

To let go of a grudge, we must first define exactly what that grudge is. It's good to remember the concept of emotional allergy here. Something that happens in the present may remind us of a painful event in the past. Since much of our emotional memory is buried in our subconscious, we may not readily remember that event, but we still will experience the emotions tied to it. Remember, emotions based on past events can feel *as if they just occurred.* This can cause us to blame someone in our *present* life for feelings we have in the *present* that actually stem from the *past.* If those feelings were especially hurtful, strong feelings of resentment may linger for days, weeks or even years, forming a grudge that we can't seem to let go of. For instance, someone who grew up with a father who chose to be away from home much of the time, coming home drunk late at night, might have a strong reaction any time his or her partner comes home late. So might someone who experienced an unexpected accident to or death of a loved one. I suggest that when you start exploring grudges you begin with the ones you have held on to the longest, regardless of whether the people involved are still in your life. As you consider what grudges you might hold, you might want to review the notes you took during the Museum Tour exercise in Chapter 2 or even do the exercise again.

- What grudges do you hold against your partner?
- Are they based on feelings of neglect? Of betrayal?
- Is there something your partner can do to help restore your feelings of trust?
- Do you get a sense of security from knowing there is something you can "hold over your partner's head"?
- Is it clear to you whether your grudges are based entirely on something your partner has done, or is your reaction based in part on past experiences?
- What is interfering with your relationship more: what your partner actually did, or your "elephant's memory" of past hurts?

PAIRS Exercise: The Letting Go of Grudges Letter

Dr. John Gray (author of *What You Feel, You Can Heal*) called this "The Love Letter." It may at first seem anything but that. It is a process of "unmasking," of peeling away the layers of difficult feelings that so often choke off our ability to experience more than fleeting feelings of caring, love, understanding and compassion.

Think of an issue in a relationship about which you have strong, upsetting feelings and about which you are holding a grudge. The first time you do this exercise, select someone other than your partner as the object of your anger, such as a parent, a child, a friend, a colleague or a boss. Now start a fresh page in your journal: You can title it "Everything I Needed to Say and Didn't." You won't actually be sending this letter. Following the format, start with "Anger and Blame" and, sticking with the same issue, complete as many of the sentence stems in each category as you can. For this exercise, you may either complete the sentence stems or write a letter that uses the sentence stems as a guide. You may want to read the sample letter at the end of this section before starting your own. Don't edit your feelings or try to be nice, reasonable or even rational. And don't bother to defend or explain your point of view—that is, don't intellectualize the issue. Most of us are very good at such rationalizing. What we're not very good at is dealing with the peculiar logic of emotions. Take this opportunity to release whatever pent-up anger, resentment or wounded pride may be preventing the flow of more tender or forgiving emotions. Treat this as an organized Haircut, on paper. Above all, do not leave the letter unfinished: Carry it through to the fifth and final category.

If you have chosen a good, strong grudge, you definitely won't have positive feelings at the beginning of your letter. In fact, the more upset you are, the better—as long as you make an honest effort to get in touch with and express all your feelings in each of the five categories.

1. ANGER AND BLAME

I resent . . .
I'm outraged by . . .
I'm fed up with . . .
I can't stand . . .

I hate . . .
I can't forgive you for . . .
I needed . . .

2. HURT AND SADNESS

I feel hurt by . . .
I feel sad when . . .
I am disappointed because . . .
I feel awful because . . .
I want . . .

3. FEAR AND INSECURITY

I am anxious because . . .
I am afraid that . . .
What scares me is . . .
I'm worried about . . .
I want . . .

4. GUILT AND RESPONSIBILITY

I regret . . .
I may be to blame for . . .
I feel sympathy for . . .
I didn't mean to . . .
Forgive me for . . .
I wish . . .

5. FORGIVENESS, UNDERSTANDING, DESIRE AND LOVE

I appreciate . . .
I realize . . .
I forgive . . .
I value . . .

I love . . .
I want . . .
I hope . . .

Review your finished letter carefully, making sure that it truly does express all your emotions on this issue. Review it also for balance. If it gets skimpier as it progresses (plenty of expression at the beginning but very little at the end) it may mean that you're fixated on anger; if it's fat in the middle but lean at both ends you may be stuck on your own fear and guilt; if it's bottom heavy, you may be glossing over your anger or pain. Work at it until you've been completely honest with yourself. By gauging the balance in each of the five sections, you can judge how well you've explored and how honestly you've acknowledged the entire range of your feelings.

SAMPLE LETTER

The following letter is an actual one that Dan, age thirty-five, wrote to his mother to help him let go of feelings that he realized *he was acting out in the present toward his wife.*

Dear Mama,

I love you, and because of that I'm writing this difficult letter. We've grown distant from one another over the past few years; we've begun to be polite. I don't want to be polite. I want to be difficult, irritating, honest and close.

This letter is about love, but it's going to start out with some hard words. Read on, Mama. Maybe you'll have some hard words for me. Very well, you get your turn, too. But read on, because there is a happy ending to be had here. I love you, but I have some complaints. Let's talk about anger. Do you remember how terrible I was at Lisa's wedding—how I was constantly seething all through that weekend and how the slightest irritation made me furious? That rage was directed at you, and that kind of episode has haunted me throughout my adult life (though, thank God, not that intensely).

You helped saddle me with this sickening, boiling rage,

because you taught me that anger was bad. If I dared to raise my voice it was "Don't talk that way to your mother!" Even when I obeyed you, you beat me down if I showed anger in the process. Do you remember the time you sent me to my room and I stamped my feet on the way up the stairs? You told me, "Come back down here and walk up those stairs properly." Damn you for controlling me and for denying me my feelings. I still haven't forgiven you for that.

The only kind of anger you permitted was Righteous Indignation, and that was the guise you inevitably put on your human rage. What a lesson to teach me! Here I am, a grown man, and if the dishes aren't done to my liking I become Elijah denouncing the depravities of Israel, Jesus clearing the moneychangers from the temple. Have you any idea how absurdly overbearing that is?

Yes, let's discuss religion. You never ceased to. Now don't get me wrong. In my heart I have no quarrel with the faith in which you raised me. The values of love, compassion, responsibility and reverence for the Divine have formed the basis of my own beliefs. But I do not thank you for trying to bully, cajole, and especially guilt-trip me into following your religion. By the time I was fifteen, I knew that your brand of Christianity was not for me. Why could you not extend to me the kind of religious tolerance that you taught me to have for others? Why the attempts at coercion? Why the ubiquitous, conspicuous tears? I didn't reject your faith to hurt you, I did so because it didn't fit me.

And then there's sex. When I was young, you were very open about the subject. But what a betrayal it was when I turned sixteen and you devoted yourself heart and soul to seeing that I didn't have sex. All of the decency and beauty of sexuality seemed to evaporate and it was all dire warnings, shame and tears. Especially tears.

Why? I was becoming a man. I was being as God made me. And, damn it, I was more responsible about it than a lot of forty-year-olds I know today. I was a responsible human being making responsible choices about my own personal life. But you would not let me be. Why am I so vehement? Because this was betrayal. After all your talk about love and human openness, after all your cant about sex being a divine blessing (which it is), you turned on me with all the tired old Puritan shit that you had said you rejected. Tolerance you might have had for others—even for yourself. You admitted that you had decided in your youth that you would not "die wondering" if you did not marry. But tolerance and respect for my sexual values and practices you would not grant.

Well, there it is, Mama. I guess it's all about control. "Be a good boy." "Be pure." "Don't be angry." And if I don't do what you tell me you will cry. Not just a little—the Big Tears. The I Was Such a Good Mother to My Special Little Boy and Now See How He's Breaking My Heart Tears.

The worst thing about this unresolved shit is that it makes it impossible for me to show all the good things I feel for you. And there is so much—so much I appreciate about you.

More than anything I appreciate that you taught me how to love. The world is full of people, especially men, who live in dread of caring for other human beings. I'm not that way.

I've certainly made a few mistakes in my choices of people, but it has always been easy and natural for me to open up my heart to family, friends and lovers. I learned that from you, because you have always been generous with your love for me, for Dad, for Ken and Lisa and their families and for others as well.

And you were never shy about showing that you need love, too. The fact that you can ask for a hug when you want one has taught me that it's okay for me to need love and the demonstration of love.

So I hate it that between us, of all people, there should be such a distance, such a conspiracy of politeness, keeping us apart. And I'm afraid that it could go on forever and one day one of us would look at the other's grave and wonder why we didn't say something more. I regret my own reluctance to speak up before; this is already very old news. I expect you to take some of the things I've said badly, and I even fear that you may freeze me out and say I'm being an awful, ungrateful son and too painful to deal with. I guess I can't believe you'd permit such a state to last forever, but I'm still afraid of a very bad scene. I'm afraid of your tears.

But not so afraid I won't send this to you.

Mother, I love you and I know you love me. I need for our love to finish growing up. I hope we can do that together. I think we can.

Dan

Note: Dan sent this letter to his mother. She called. He visited her. They talked for hours. They are now respectful, loving friends.

- Having written your letter, what are you feeling toward the recipient as compared to when you began?
- Do you find that you are any less angry, any more able to forgive, to let go of grudges?
- Are you any more able to think of useful solutions?
- Are you in touch with any more positive feelings toward the person you wrote to?

The point of the Letting Go of Grudges Letter is to provide a tool for exercising the full range of your emotions so that you can think more clearly, understand more deeply, let go of the past and more constructively seek solutions. Some couples in PAIRS use this technique when they are upset—with each other, a child, a parent, a close friend, a boss. It's useful for any situation that is persistent and in which you would like to see tension resolved or misunderstandings straightened out or to feel that your rights are not being trampled on or ignored. The beauty of it is that it requires no immediate cooperation from the recipient. It's something that you can do alone, for yourself, and quickly, in some cases writing just one line for each category. Here is an example:

To: Jim
From: Gail
(*Anger*) I hate it when you criticize my driving.
(*Hurt*) I feel hurt by your comments because I am at least as good a driver as you are.
(*Fear*) It makes me nervous now when you are with me when I

am in the car. I'm also afraid that you are really upset about something else and are using my driving as an outlet.

(*Responsibility*) I'm sorry if I have made it difficult for you to be more direct with me.

(*Forgiveness and desire*) I realize that you don't usually criticize me unfairly—just when we're in the car—and I really want your opinion about things concerning me. I hope we can find a way to make it easier for you to be more direct with me, and for me to be more accepting.

Few people in PAIRS ever send their letters (although a few carefully thought-out ones have been sent, generally for the good). The healing act of writing the letter is usually the primary benefit. By writing the letter above, for instance, Gail may have discovered why her driving was such an issue. She is now better equipped to explore this with Jim.

LETTING GO OF GRUDGES: LETTER 2

Now that you have some feel for how this letter works, think of an issue that you have with your partner, a resentment or grudge you've been holding, and write a similar letter to your partner. After you've fully reflected and written on all the categories, *write the letter you wish you could receive in return.*

You may want to share both letters with your partner, or you may feel that doing the exercise for yourself was enough. If you choose to show your letters to your partner, be sure you've completely finished them first. The idea of sharing them may cause you to censor or soften what you write, which would defeat the purpose. Write it for yourself and hold nothing back. After you have reviewed each letter, if there are things in it you would like your partner to know, you might want to do a more reasoned second draft (removing insults or swear words). If your partner is not reading this book with you, describe or show this chapter to your partner and explain that you have written a letter that you would like him or her to read. Ask your partner if he or she would like to write a similar letter. If you decide to exchange your letters, make sure you set aside at least half an hour to discuss each one. You may want to use the Empathic

Listening technique from Chapter 7 when you discuss these letters. Be sure to express your appreciation for being able to share your letter, and for letting your partner get any grudges off his or her chest as well.

- What grudges are you still holding?
- Are there any you'd like to let go of?
- How hard was it to write a letter to your partner?
- Did it change your feelings?
- Did it change your perceptions of your partner?
- Did you learn something about the way your feelings operate and how to monitor and deal with them?

PAIRS Exercise: Letting Yourself Off the Hook

Many of us are our own toughest critics. Some of us have a great capacity to forgive everyone almost anything, saving our harshest judgments for ourselves. This can be just as damaging as holding a grudge against our partner, sometimes even worse.

Try writing a Letting Go of Grudges Letter to yourself using the same categories outlined earlier. You might want to come back to this exercise after you read Chapters 14, 15, and 16, in which the parts of self are described, so that you can write it to one or several of your different "parts."

This may be just as important as writing your partner. It's very difficult to explore and enjoy a relationship with someone else if you can't do the same with yourself.

Such a letter might look like this:

I hate that I am such a Placater, that I am so afraid of some-one's anger.

I am hurt when anyone expresses disappointment or gets angry with me.

I am scared that their anger means there is something wrong with me.

I may be to blame for some of the anger because it has escalated while I have been trying to avoid it.

I realize that I am as powerful as anyone else and have the same right to draw limits as anyone who makes demands on me. I don't need someone else's approval to feel whole. I don't need to be devastated when someone gets angry. I am good enough. I don't need to be perfect.

I hope I can be more balanced in my life and less fearful of others' reactions.

The User Friendly Communications Skills Guide for Specific Situations below will help you to identify the PAIRS tools we have discussed that you might choose to use should you find yourself in certain situations. The tools are versatile; many are useful in clarifying your own thoughts as well as in communication with others.

User Friendly **Communication Skills Guide** for Specific Situations

	To Do by Yourself	To Do with a Partner	Use This PAIRS Tool
1.	Reflect on past hurts that may be affecting your relationship	Reflect on past hurts that may be affecting your relationship	Museum Tour
2.		Strengthen, develop habit of confiding, Leveling	Daily Temperature Reading
3.	Clarify own thoughts and feelings for yourself about an issue that upsets you	Describe to partner range of thoughts and feelings about an issue that upsets you	Dialogue Guide
4.		Determine whether an assumption you have about your partner is true	Mind-Reading Exercise

5.		Listen to and understand feelings, thoughts of other person	Empathic Listening Shared Meaning Dialogue Guide Mind-Reading Exercise
6.		Discharge intense anger	Haircut/Vesuvius Anger Rituals
7.	Reflect on what behaviors are intolerable, "below the belt" or "walking issues"	Let partner know what is intolerable	Beltlines Core Issues
8.	Reflect on what your issue is and how you can most clearly and succinctly express it	Negotiate and request for change	Fair Fight for Change
9.	Explore whether a specific action or incident can be forgiven		Unsent, Uncensored Letting Go of Grudges Letter
10.	Act to reach feelings of forgiveness	Let go of grudges and forgive	Dialogue Guide Leveling Style Fair Fight for Change Doghouse Release Letting Go of Grudges Letter

COMES THE DAWN

People who dread getting up in the morning because a new day portends something awful or dull are living their lives by looking at the past and expecting it to be the future. They are burdened by their own history. People who see each new day as containing its own surprises and opportunities for successes as well as failures have come to grips with their past and see it as a map of where they have been, not necessarily of where they are going.

The ability to forgive and move on is, in large part, the ability to stop fighting old battles that may have been lost and to dedicate yourself to fighting new ones that can transform the course of your life. By exploring and extracting the wisdom we need from the past, we can illuminate the present without contaminating it with the past.

Take a moment to write in your journal notebook about what you are beginning to realize.

Making the Invisible Visible

■   ■   ■

The danger is that we will . . . direct at this "thing" between us all the frustration and rage left over from our childhoods. Our mate, of course, will not usually understand where this fury comes from, and will apply his or her own interpretation to it, often an interpretation that is based on similar distortions arising from the past.

—Gus Napier,
The Fragile Bond

12

The Three-Generation Family Map: Tracing Your Emotional Roots

■   ■   ■

*T*here's an old story about a boy who, having grown up at the edge of a wide, turbulent river, spent his childhood learning to build rafts. When the boy reached manhood, he felled some trees, lashed them together, and riding his raft, he crossed to the far side of the river. Because he had spent so long working on the raft, he couldn't see leaving it behind when he reached dry land, so he lashed it to his shoulders and carried it with him, though all he came upon in his journeys were a few easily fordable streams and puddles. He rarely thought about the things he was missing out on because he was carrying the bulky raft—the trees he couldn't climb, vistas he couldn't see, people he couldn't get close to and races he couldn't run. He didn't even realize how heavy the raft was, because he had never known what it was like to be free of it.

It's amazing how many of us carry with us old, burdensome habits of thinking, feeling and behaving that influence virtually every decision we make and that limit our possibilities for enjoying life fully. Our rafts, though invisible, are just as limiting as the boy's. Instead of wood, they are constructed of attitudes and beliefs that were picked up and developed during a lifetime, shaped by our experiences and our observations. The chapters in this section are designed to explore the nature of and our need for the rafts that we carry around. Some of us might be dragging the *Queen Mary* behind us when all we really need is an inflatable dinghy. To help us keep what we need and to discard the rest, we will examine the ways that our personal history shaped our beliefs; the effects that that history has on our current lives, especially our relationships; and methods to change outdated attitudes and beliefs to ones that better fit our current beliefs and desires.

Obviously, not everything we believe in needs to be changed or discarded. But we are guided by many beliefs that we have never examined. It is only by drawing these from our "creature" brain that

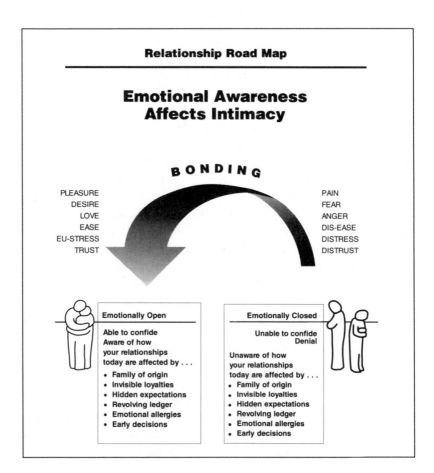

we can decide which are legitimate and helpful and which might be interfering with our capacity for intimacy.

The cost of doing otherwise is enormous. If we ignore our history, we still react to it, and in a relationship we often react to it in ways that hurt or alienate our partner, unknowingly.

THE REVOLVING LEDGER

To a large extent, our core expectations of intimate relationships are affected by all of our previous close relationships, whether with parents, siblings, former spouses, lovers or friends. To illustrate this dynamic, family psychiatrist Ivan Boszormenyi-Nagy developed the concept of the Revolving Ledger. Boszormenyi-Nagy's Ledger works like this: At certain periods in your life, important people, or even life itself, through events that affected you, ran up a series of debits or credits in terms of what you needed. Time passed. You walked through life's revolving door, and you hand the bill to whoever is there now. Therapists call this transference or displacement. In effect, your message to intimate others is: *I am owed by you everything that I didn't get before;* or *I will punish you for everything bad that happened to me before.*

Since the person to whom you hand the bill is unaware of the account books in your head, this makes for endless misunderstanding and disturbance. And these attitudes tend to be outside of your awareness, although they can be found through personal exploration. They also tend not to appear early in a relationship, but later on—when you are disappointed and discover that what you expected to happen isn't happening. You may find yourself thinking of your partner as the enemy, someone to hurt, get even with, punish—and because you don't recognize the Ledger as being behind why you act this way, you rationalize. You seek reasons to treat your partner as the enemy, when you are really just evening up the Ledger balance on someone else's account!

Here are some typical scenarios:

Mary told John after the third time he arrived home late that she was leaving him, even though they had a new baby. As she explored her history and that of her family, she realized that she was the third generation of women who'd been left by their husbands. This pattern had created in her an expectation of abandonment. She interpreted his tardiness as a signal that he was losing interest and getting ready to leave. She paid John back for this debt of abandonment by deciding that she would be the one to leave.

Mabel gets involved only with married men. This is the way her Ledger works: I'm competing with your wife as I did with my mother to prove that I am as desirable as or more desirable than she.

Jack is in love with Sheila, but she is growing angry with him because he won't commit to marriage. Jack seizes on her demands as pressure and as another reason that he is wary of marriage. As Jack tries to sort his own Ledger, he discovers that he is worried that Sheila will turn out to be a demanding nag, as he believed and his mother was. So his decision is: "I will withhold the very thing you want."

These examples involve extremely different expectations and debts. However, they are similar in at least one respect: Each person felt with certitude that he or she was acting in a positive manner for him- or herself. The creature brain was drawing deep satisfaction from paying back these debts, even though the intellectual neocortex might be questioning these actions and the pain they caused for all involved. It was only through examination of the creature part and the debts it was paying back, which were developed far in the past, that these people were able to see the effects of and change the Revolving Ledger they were presenting.

- Can you see what "balances" from your past you might be bringing forward now?
- Can you pinpoint the person from your past whom your partner may represent?

- Can you see what expectations you might be carrying on your Revolving Ledger?
- When you have arguments with your partner, does he or she tell you, "I'm not your mother" or "I'm not your father"?
- What effect does that have on you?
- Is it possible the dynamics your partner is referring to between the two of you are similar to those you had with your parents? Or your siblings?

THE THREE-GENERATION FAMILY MAP

To avoid the chaos that can be created by our Revolving Ledgers, we need to take a long look at how we accumulated our original set of debits and credits. This allows us to see the source of some of our attitudes and behaviors, which in turn gives us the ability to "reeducate" our creature brain, teaching it that things that once caused pain are now capable of bringing pleasure.

That's why I always ask couples to do a three-generation family map, or genogram. It isn't easy, but it's well worth the effort you put into it. If your family was large or complicated, this may at first sound like an overwhelming task. If so, simply do it a piece at a time—but do it, trusting that it will eventually be a key tool for understanding and improving your relationships.

Don't worry if your family was a mess, or if you didn't grow up in a conventional family situation. It doesn't matter even if the people who raised you weren't your biological parents—or weren't even family—they *were* your role models, and they did give you your sense of what relationships are like, and what you can expect of life. So adapt the principles outlined in this chapter to suit the "family" you did grow up with.

The family map I want you to do involves some data gathering. It goes back three generations, to the grandparent level. It also adds a few layers based on the kinds of observations family therapists traditionally elicit in order to gain insight into the emotional histories and family systems of their clients.

The family map was instrumental in saving the marriage of one couple who came to see me a few years ago. His mother was a member of a religious group who believed in positive thinking, so as a child he was taught to say only positive things, in order to create positive energy. In his wife's argumentative and superstitious but affectionate family, to say something good was to invite the Evil Eye—so she tended to discount positive things.

Because of the differences in their backgrounds (differences they had never discussed and of which they were largely unaware), their basic styles were in conflict. She would disparage things he felt should be praised, but he would never express how much this bothered him because that was against his family's rules. Then one day he announced that he was leaving. His wife was stunned: She'd had no idea he was upset. Getting their marriage back on track required a major adjustment of their attitudes about negative and positive comments. Fortunately, they were less defensive about these attitudes once their genogram helped them to place these attitudes in a cultural context.

You create more options for yourself by using the genogram to recover impressions, memories and associations. By bringing them all into awareness you can weigh each objectively and say to yourself, "This I want to keep, and this I want to let go of: this is useful to me, and this is no longer of use."

First, you will want to assemble the basic facts about your family in a visual format that makes it easier to perceive patterns. On the following pages are instructions for drawing your family map, as well as sample maps.

PAIRS Exercise: Constructing Your Family Map

Begin by gathering the materials you will need: a large sheet of paper (at least fourteen by twenty-four inches), a pen or pencils (two or more colors), a ruler and your journal.

In the center of the paper, draw a horizontal marriage line for your parents, with the symbols for each one (a square for males, a circle for females) attached at each end as shown in Illustration 1 on page 163. Write their names, birth dates and marriage date in the appropriate places. On the line itself, write your family name. If either parent is deceased, place an X in their symbol with the date of death and also note the cause of death. If there has been a

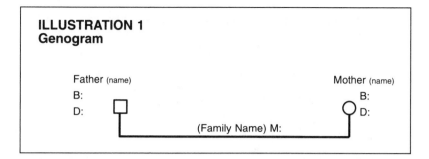

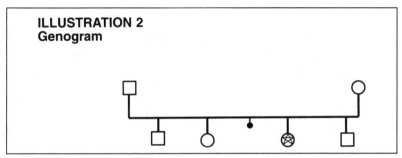

Example: The Star and three living siblings: an older brother, an older sister, and a younger brother. The darkened circle denotes miscarriage of a baby girl.

divorce, mark the date of separation or divorce with a double slash mark through the line.

Next, as shown in Illustration 2, draw vertical lines down for yourself and each of your siblings. Start at the left and make the symbol for a male or female, according to the order of birth. Leave enough space between symbols so that you can later add spouses (if necessary). Place a star in your symbol to denote that this is *your* map. Any miscarriages or abortions should be denoted by using the symbol key on page 167.

Fill in siblings' names and birth dates.

Follow Illustration 3 on page 164 and above each of your parents, draw a horizontal line with symbols for your grandparents, and add their names and dates.

Draw vertical lines down from the grandparents' marriage lines for each of their children as in Illustration 4 on page 164, being

ILLUSTRATION 3
Genogram

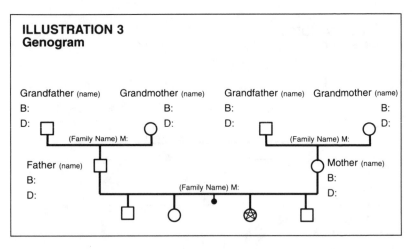

ILLUSTRATION 4
Genogram

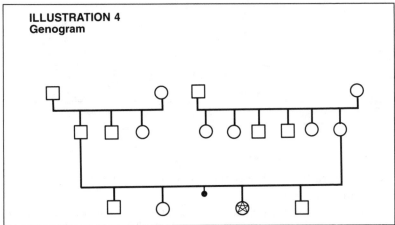

Example: The father of the Star is the oldest child of three and the mother is the youngest child of six.

sure that your parents appear in their proper order. Fill in proper symbols, names and dates.

What you now have is a picture of your closest blood relatives: parents, siblings, grandparents, aunts and uncles. As shown in Illustration 5 on page 165 now add your relatives by marriage and any additional blood relatives—your children, nieces, nephews, cousins. Beginning with you and your siblings, put in any spouses and their children. Remember to put the children in order of their birth from left to right and with the appropriate male or female symbol. Fill in names and dates. Use dotted horizontal lines to denote someone who is living with, but not married to another person.

If there have been multiple marriages as in Illustration 6 on page 166, be sure to show those by extending the marriage lines, showing any children of each marriage or those from previous marriages. Be sure to include the dates and symbols related to the beginnings and endings of each marriage.

If there were any nonrelatives who lived with your family, such as the nurse and boarder in Illustration 7 on page 166, indicate them on your map with a dotted line, indicating if possible their role in the family and their importance to you.

Congratulations! You have just completed your basic family map. Take a moment now to notice what you are already learning and record your reflections in your journal.

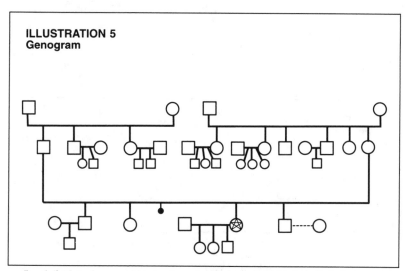

ILLUSTRATION 5
Genogram

Example (for clarity the names and dates have been omitted from this sample art): The Star's older brother is married with one son. Her older sister is not married. The Star is now married and has two daughters and a son. Her younger brother is unmarried and is living with a woman. Five of her aunts and uncles are married and have produced a total of eleven cousins (six boys, five girls).

Are you discovering . . .
- Some patterns in relationships you hadn't noticed before?
- That you are missing some important basic information about your family?
- Some significance to the dates of births, marriages or divorces—such as wartime or economic depression?

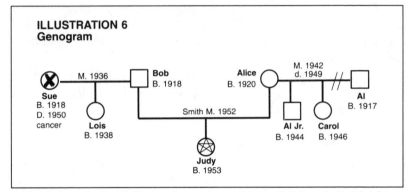

ILLUSTRATION 6
Genogram

Example: Judy is the only child of her parents' marriage, however, she has an older half-sister from her father's first marriage (he was a widower) and an older half-brother and half-sister from her mother's first marriage (she was divorced).

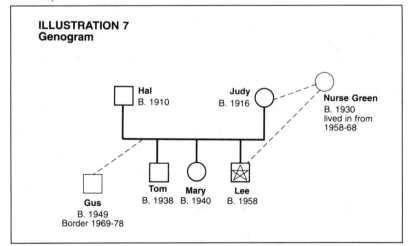

ILLUSTRATION 7
Genogram

Example: Lee was a "late" baby. His mother had a full-time career, so Nurse Green was hired to live with the family until Lee was ten years old. She was a surrogate mother to Lee. In 1969, a boarder took Nurse Green's room and became like an older brother to Lee.

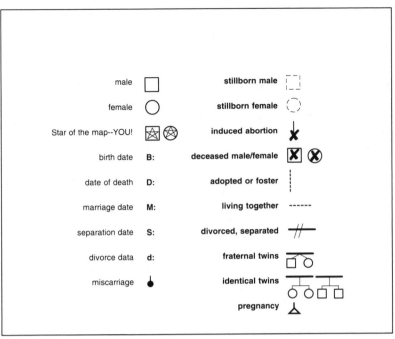

Use this symbol key for your Three-Generation Family Map.

ANALYZING YOUR FAMILY MAP

Now that you have created your family map, you are ready to deepen your understanding of the people and events shown on your map and to explore how the early influences of your family of origin affect your present relationships.

Look over your map and darken the symbols of those people who had special relationships to you, either in a positive or negative sense. Then write four or five adjectives describing what that person was like when you were a child, based on what you can remember (for example, funny, rigid, strict, kind, patient, flirtatious, religious, disapproving, distant, sympathetic, alcoholic, tyrannical). Assign, if you can, the appropriate stress communication style (Placater, Blamer, Computer, Distractor) to each person. Underline those qualities that had an impact on you.

(Eventually, you will want to reflect on how you are like these people and how you are different from them, which qualities you identified with or rebelled against, and which qualities they encouraged or discouraged in you. You and your partner will eventually share your maps to see how differences and similarities in your histories affect your life together today. It may also be useful to help each other as you go along, because you can bring to your partner's family map a knowing detachment: You benefit from knowing each other as intimates, yet to some extent you bring to your partner's childhood recollections the openmindedness of the outside observer.)

Draw a colored line connecting you to each person who was special to you, whether in a positive sense (use blue), or a negative sense (use black). Describe their impact on you and characterize your relationship with them as follows:

- A double line $=$ for especially close, positive relationships
- A triple line $\equiv$ denotes over-involved, overly dependent relationship
- A wavy line $\backsim$ indicates overt conflict and/or hostility
- A dotted line ⋯⋯ shows coolness or distance
- A triangle connection Δ indicates a relationship in which one person (can be different people at different times) is "odd man out" or is manipulated by the other two.

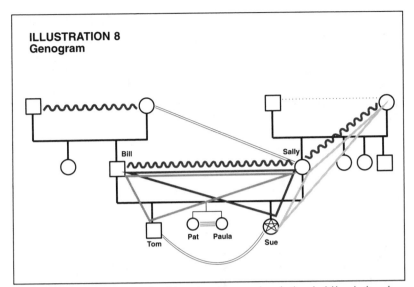

ILLUSTRATION 8
Genogram

Example: The Star, Sue, is in a triangle with her mother and her maternal grandmother, who dislike each other and use Sue to complain about each other. Sue is also triangled with her estranged mother and father—another conflicted relationship in which she tries to serve as referee. Her older brother, Tom, also gets pulled into a triangle with the parents; each tries to get him to take his or her side. As a result, Tom and Sue have developed a close relationship in which they rely on each other to clarify what's going on with their parents, as well as for mutual support.

The twins, Pat and Paula, have withdrawn into an intense, overly dependent, closed relationship with each other, partly to avoid getting pulled into their parents' feuds. Bill's parents also had an openly hostile relationship with many fights in front of the children. Sally's parents expressed their dislike of each other more through coolness and lack of interest. Sally has developed a close, sympathetic relationship with her mother-in-law.

Are you discovering . . .
- Characteristics you share with some family members?
- Who modeled your stress communication styles for you?
- What triangles you were drawn into and what effect they've had on you? Did you become the aggressive one, the shy one, the timid one, the peacemaker, the super-achiever?

Examine your map for patterns from generation to generation. Look for histories of alcoholism, drug abuse or other addictions, violence, desertion, broken or very conflicted relationships, infi-

delity, wild or tyrannical behavior, sexual abuse, repeated hospi-
talizations, family cut-offs (separations, feuds, disinheritances, lack
of contact) and so on. If you detect such patterns, how have they
affected you? Are they manifesting in some way in your own relationship, either by repeating themselves or by causing you to have
"allergic" reactions to any behavior that suggests one of these negative syndromes?

Are you discovering . . .
  • That you or somone else is the "Hero" who tried to hold
    the family together at the price of inner fear, stress and
    a need to control feelings?
  • That you learned to deny your feelings and needs because
    of the overwhelming needs of others in the family?
  • That you need to be an overachiever and yet feel guilty
    because you can't do more (in order to compensate for
    the stresses in the family)?

FILLING IN THE COLORFUL PARTS OF THE FAMILY TREE

Chances are you won't know the vital statistics about your aunts
and uncles and grandparents, but others in your family probably
will, and most people who keep track of family histories are pleased
to share the information they've collected over the years. When you
can't get precise information, write down what you and members
of your family can remember and indicate with question marks which
information is guesswork. Even the way they respond will tell you
something about your family.

Your family tree represents the bare bones of the family story—
the skeletal structure. You now need to fill in the colorful parts—
whatever you can find out about who the people in your family
were and what their lives were like. Ask other people in your
family:

- What was being in this family like for you?
- What were the members of our family like?
- What was your relationship with your parents and siblings?

- What was their idea of marriage?
- Knowing what you know now, how would you have changed things, if you could have?

One reason it pays to ask other people in your family to help you is that everyone has a different perspective; we don't all see everything. Bill, for example, grew up seeing his father as bitingly critical of him, so he never felt he was good enough in his father's eyes. When he asked his mother about it, however, he discovered that his father had been critical of everything and everyone. His grandfather had died when his father was seven. His father had to work hard all of his life and never had a chance to do the things he wanted to. He had just been a bitter person: His criticism had not been specific to Bill at all.

If you have aging relatives and would like to ask them questions, ask them now, before it's too late. Ask your grandparents and elderly parents, aunts and uncles what it was like when they came to this country, or growing up on a farm or whatever fits. How did they survive? Ask not only about what went on in the family, but also about what was going on in the world, because the history that is being made around us affects our behavior, as survivors of cataclysms such as the Holocaust or war know only too well. Then think how this has affected your behavior.

Sam, a thirty-five-year-old engineer, in PAIRS was particularly grateful to hear about how his grandmother had survived the Depression: "It helped me understand why I was such a cheapskate. I realized, 'Hey, I don't have to save every piece of string because there may be another depression.' Now I'll take a week off and go skiing. Before, I used to use tennis balls until there was no fuzz left on them. Now I buy a new can when I need it."

When you ask for help, encourage people to be realistic and avoid good-old-days nostalgia. Tell them that it is helpful to you to know both the "good" and the "bad" qualities and behavior patterns in the family. Your father's father, for example, may have been genial and relaxed when he met you in the balmy days of grandfatherhood, and your father may tell you he was hard but fair, but if an aunt tells you that he was tyrannical and was particularly hard on your father, you will have a better understanding of why your generally pleasant father occasionally behaved like a dictator on a rampage. Generally, try to focus on how the members of your family were when you or your parents were *children*, not how they are now, because people change and what you want to do is look at your *early* conditioning.

Take note of how members of your family react to your questions, because their responses will reveal much about family styles and attitudes. An engineer who charted his family emotional history told us that what he learned about his family was not nearly so important as his discovery that his mother was frank and responsive in answering his questions while his father said almost nothing—a pattern he had never noticed before and one that helped to explain why he himself had always been close-mouthed about personal matters. That awareness, and the realization that he preferred his mother's openness to his father's silence, created the atmosphere in which the engineer could and did change.

LOOKING FOR PATTERNS

In analyzing your family map, look at what you learned about the way a marriage or a life is or should be. What decisions did you make about what you wanted to be or not be and about what you wanted for yourself, as you watched your parents' marriage? For example, you may recall having a happy childhood, but if you never saw arguments between your parents, you may never have learned how to argue.

Shirley was an attractive woman of about average weight for her height, who was married to a fitness buff. Whenever she gained a pound or two, her husband would get on her back, telling her to eat this, not eat that, get more exercise and so on. She would agree to do so, but when he wasn't around she would indulge in little treats. Whenever he found out, he would be furious, and she would indulge all the more, secretly. Shirley had never had a serious weight problem, but as she made notes about the early part of her life she remembered that she had been slightly chubby as an eight- and nine-year-old and that her father had focused relentlessly on her diet—even when she got older and the chubbiness disappeared. The result of his nagging was that she had become a secret snacker on forbidden foods. Today even though Shirley didn't think she had a weight problem, she found herself eating rebelliously around her husband. When she realized that for the second time in her life she was reacting sneakily to a supernag, she confronted her husband directly. Telling him to get off her back was her solution. He then needed to figure out why her looking slender was so important to him. He found it related to his overweight mother, whom he hated for never having had time for him.

Often the patterns aren't immediately obvious. Sylvia was depressed and couldn't figure out why. When we talked about her family history, the answer became clear. Sylvia's mother had had a difficult life. Orphaned at eleven, married at seventeen and divorced at nineteen, she had lost her first child and only brother by the age of twenty-four. Then she had five children by a second husband, a weak man who was as drained of emotional resources as she. Sylvia, the oldest child, had effectively raised her brothers and sisters, and then had married young and raised her own children. Her first marriage had ended in divorce, and now, twelve years later, she had remarried. Her husband was a kind man with two children from a previous marriage, but she was tired of taking care of children. A part of her was saying, "When is it going to be my turn? When will I have a chance to do my own thing, not to always be taking care of someone else?" As a result of PAIRS, she came to understand that it was acceptable for her to want to get out from under. Finally able to talk to her husband about her feelings of depletion, she was surprised when he suggested that she go away for a week or two by herself. Time to herself, she realized, was a gift to which she was entitled. It had never occurred to her to ask for it.

You would be surprised how many people grow up thinking that, like Sylvia, they must *always* play a certain role—caretaker, provider, victim, rescuer, troubleshooter, cheerer-upper, or whatever—and simply do not realize that that role is not intrinsic to their personality and can be relaxed from time to time or even abandoned.

Like Sylvia, you will want to think about early messages to you that affected:

Your self-esteem: your view of yourself and whether you were acceptable and lovable. What did you feel you had to do in order to be loved, accepted or cared for—or were love, acceptance and caring given without qualification?

Your rules for living: what you feel it is important to do or to avoid doing in life

What you feel you can safely reveal of yourself to another person, what you cannot reveal, and what and how you communicate when you feel threatened in some way

How did you believe you were supposed to handle feelings of anger, fear, pain, pleasure, love, trust and disappointment? What about the feelings and attitudes that often don't get talked about in families: jealousy, envy, guilt, sexuality, possessiveness, power and control, competition and carrying grudges?

You may have learned that you were not supposed to be envious or jealous, so that if you were you couldn't tell anybody—except that maybe it came out as feeling that you hated the whole world. What did you learn about power? For example, if you grew up with a violent father and a long-suffering mother and thus saw power as being divided between a victim and victimizer, you may have decided that you always had to be in control or you would suffer. If we have to choose between being a victim or a victimizer, we generally choose the latter. And what about pleasure? Some people feel guilty about pleasure: How can I be happy when everybody else is so sad? And for some people pleasure is dangerous, either because it was dangerous when they were small, or because they are afraid that it will be taken away.

What did you learn about competition? Was competition part of family life and something you learned to live with comfortably? Or did you grow up in a family where there were only winners and losers, so that if you weren't the best you were nothing? How does that affect your current relationship? If you decide that you are not the best, and if that sends your self-worth to zero, does that mean that you aren't able to confide in your partner anymore? Maybe you learned that you were not supposed to admit that you were hurt or afraid or envious, or felt bad about losing or hated the winners.

TRIANGLES AND OTHER RELATIONSHIPS

As you do your family map, explore not only how people related to *you*, but also how they related to *each other*. The relationships you witnessed in your childhood became your models, whether positive or negative. You may have decided that you never wanted the kind of relationship your parents had, or you may have copied your parents in some areas and rebelled against them in others. On the other hand, you may have taken as your model a favorite aunt or uncle.

You also have been influenced by relationship triangles. You had a relationship with your father and a relationship with your mother, but you also were part of a triangle with them. If you look at your diagram, you can see an almost unlimited number of triangles, and in each you may have played a different role. The triangle of you, your sister and your father may have been quite different from the triangle of you, your sister and your mother. It is important to consider how you learned to deal with triangles, because that is how you learned to deal with jealousy, envy, possessiveness, rivalry and competitiveness, feeling special and feeling left out. What was it like for you when a one-to-one relationship became a triangle or a group?

As you study your chart, certain things should pop out. For example, if your sister was the perfect, overachieving Shirley Temple to your laid-back Mediocre Student, you may be allergic to any gesture of your spouse's that seems the least bit condescending. Or if you, as the oldest child, were expected to behave perfectly, while the bratty but beloved baby of the family got away with murder, you may see red whenever your spouse slacks off a little bit.

The lessons we carry with us from early experiences with triangles can be subtle and not always easy to detect in our adult pattern of relationships. Jennifer, at thirty-four, was the attractive wife of a philandering, politically powerful husband who refused to share the task of raising their five children and expected her to accept his schedule, needs and behavior unquestioningly. She dared not complain, for she feared his temper—but she felt like a doormat, and wondered vaguely why people like her husband always pleased themselves at her expense. Work on her family map revealed that as the younger of two daughters, Jennifer had learned early on to win the love and approval of her parents by avoiding the behavior for which she heard her older sister being criticized. By walking the straight and narrow, she had won out in the competition with her sister for their parents' approval, but she also had gained the undying enmity of her sister (with whom she knew she could never win in a head-on struggle). And the script of "good one" that worked in the triangle with her sister made her a loser in her marriage. She had never learned to make demands for herself, to argue for more equitable or loving treatment, or even to explore her sexuality— she didn't know what she needed in bed. Ignorant both sexually and in terms of dealing head-on with conflict, she now felt confused and depressed. It took work for her to realize that being the "good one" was not an ingrained part of her personality but something she had *learned*, and that in order to get what she needed as an adult she would have to modify her self-image and the behavior that flowed from it.

THE IMPORTANCE OF BIRTH ORDER

You and your partner may want to think about how your birth order or your status as an only child affected the development of your personality and your expectations. There seem to be certain patterns: First and only children are typically responsible decision-makers who easily take leadership and assume they know what is right (or feel guilty if things are wrong); youngest children tend to let others take the initiative (though if the oldest child is involved in an intense triangle with the parents, the functional positions of the siblings are sometimes reversed). Only children often have trouble sharing and sometimes fail to consider other people's feelings the way they might have if they'd grown up with siblings.

This all has direct relevance to the roles played out in intimate relationships. For example, in the marriage of an "oldest" child (of whichever sex) and a "youngest" child, the lines of power will be fairly predictable—the "oldest" child will tend to take the lead and the "youngest" child will tend to follow. Most family therapists agree that the marriage of two oldest children tends to produce conflict, and marriage of two youngest children tends to produce indecision, and the marriage of an oldest brother of sisters and a youngest sister of brothers is often fairly harmonious.

CUT-OFFS

Find out if there were cut-offs in the family—divorces, separations, feuds, a grandfather who disinherited his son, a rift between sisters, an uncle who left home and broke off all communication with his parents. Often when there is a cut-off in your family's past, and particularly if there were cut-offs in *your* life, they could be affecting your relationships today.

Whether it's through death or through emotional or geographical distancing, you can think of a cut-off as being like an amputation—in which the flow that normally goes through a limb is blocked, and scar tissue forms, and what pain is felt is felt in the phantom limb. When a relationship is cut off, the energy that was meant to flow toward it can't go there anymore. The flow either is diverted, is frozen or dries up. When an important relationship ends, and whatever feelings you had tied up in that person get suspended—perhaps so you can avoid experiencing pain or anger and the feelings of loss—your ability to be emotionally open and trusting in future relationships may be severely limited. Alternatively, if you are cut off from expressing your feelings about an important relationship in an open, direct and healthy way, the energy and feelings tied up in that first relationship may be displaced onto any future relationship that evokes the *memory* of the cut-off relationship. The unresolved and unexpressed feelings will seek out a person or situation that gives them a channel for expression and may leak out in inappropriate ways.

Recognizing cut-offs in your own life can help you end the pattern of displacement. Jason, for example, was the eldest son of a mother who was proud of her son's athletic achievements but who showed him little affection. When he was crippled in an automobile accident at age sixteen, she was so upset that she had his sister care for him. When she realized that he could no longer compete athletically, she distanced even more, showing the least support for him at the very time when he needed it most. He toughed it out and left home as soon as he could—but he hated her and never had anything to do with her again. Eventually he married Chris, who was enormously supportive, but who needed a lot of affection and reassurance herself—which he could never give her. He resented her neediness. He punished her for his mother's cold withdrawal and for his not allowing himself to acknowledge personal need.

It is not easy to resolve problems associated with painful emotional cut-offs. They can play havoc with your life together as a couple, until you recognize them for what they are and make appropriate changes.

INVISIBLE LOYALTIES

Attached to Boszormenyi-Nagy's theory of the Revolving Ledger is his concept of the Invisible Loyalties that carry over from one generation to the next—the feelings of *entitlement* and *indebtedness* ("who owes whom") that accrue in a family over the generations, whether we acknowledge them or not. We see this at work in the child who deeply resents her father but who instinctively defends him when he is criticized by someone else. We see it in the adopted son who feels strong bonds of loyalty to the natural mother whom one might expect him to have written off for abandoning him. We see it in the "parentified" good child who feels obligated to make up for deficits in the parenting of battling or alcoholic parents and who feels responsible for saving the family from destruction. We see it in the split loyalties that tear apart children of embattled divorces (the child often feeling compelled to stay with the parent who is being "left behind"). We see it in national loyalties, religious loyalties, ethnic loyalties.

Filial loyalty runs deep in all of us. It is difficult for a parent to destroy the fund of trust from which the child's feeling of indebtedness arises. We feel this loyalty most strongly when we try to maintain a connection with our aging parents, however difficult they are. We may experience it in more covert forms, too, which are often unhealthy and may entail legacies from earlier generations: the artistic son who buries his creative longing because the family legacy is success in business; the scapegoat child on whom the parents dump the family legacy of badness instead of dumping it on themselves or each other; the family outcast who, by rigidly maintaining a position of opposition to the family, holds the rest of the family together at his or her expense. The legacy of expectations, in other words, may entitle us to certain things, but it may also bind or imprison us. With awareness, we increase our options.

Whether we are aware of it or not, our behavior is greatly affected by the *family* ledger of entitlement and indebtedness. Tracing the deficits, restoring trust, and finding healthy ways to make loyalty payments on our family accounts is not always easy, but to deny the ledger—to "forget the past and get on with the present"—is to blind ourselves to the practical implications of our human tendency to maintain the balance owing and owed.

NOTHING IS WRITTEN IN CONCRETE

When you and your partner have finished your charts, compare them and discuss what you have each learned in the process. Don't criticize or judge. We're inviting you to be detectives, uncovering what you were conditioned to be and to expect in your own family of origin. There's the classic story about the woman whose husband loved roast beef rare. Every time she bought a roast, she would cut it in half and roast both halves—which always came out well-done because they were such small pieces. He always complained and wanted to know why she had to cut it in half. She said, "Well, my mother did it that way." Finally, he said, "Why don't you find out why your mother did it that way?" So she asked her mother, and it turned out that *her* mother had had a very small oven and that the only way to get the roast in was to cut it in half.

Our learning in the past enabled us to survive. But often we no longer need to be that way. We must look to the past to illuminate the present. It can contaminate our present because we tend either to perpetuate the past or to decide that we hated the way it was, so we vow to do the opposite. Either way we are controlled by the past, allowing it to cause problems in the present.

We are adaptable. The lessons we learn as children allowed us to adapt to our childhood reality. The function of the genogram is to *map* that childhood reality so that we can see which of its many lessons no longer apply. This process frees us to adapt our behavior more happily to our relationships today.

Take a moment to write in your journal notebook about what you are beginning to realize.

13

Arriving at Maturity

■   ■   ■

When we think of maturity, we tend to consider it as a chronological process—we expect to be a certain way when we arrive at a certain age. We don't think about the process of change that we have to go through to get from one level of maturity to another. Nor do we consider the difficulties that such changes can pose.

Psychiatrist Roger Gould describes the adult's journey to maturity in his book *Transformations*. He sees maturing as a process of "letting go" as much as one of "growing up." He believes that we carry many constraints placed on us in childhood—constraints that were necessary and that protected us—into our adulthood. Maturing, then, is the gradual process of letting go of these restraints. And, as we shed them, we often experience a confusing sense of ambivalence, pain or even grief.

We often like to believe that we are mature simply by virtue of being adult—and rather young adults at that. But Gould believes we haven't really matured until we have experienced many of these periods of confusion and arrived at a fuller sense of our own integrity and destiny—the genuine life of "inner directedness." That often doesn't happen until we are in our forties or fifties.

The pain and grief that occurs as we pass from one stage to

another is caused largely by an unconscious battle being waged within us—our emotional need to retain some of our childhood assumptions ("Mom and Dad will always be there to protect me") versus the need to become independent (moving away to pursue your own goals and dreams, such as education, a career or a loving relationship).

Gould believes we should see such periods as a kind of rite of passage, a positive sign that we are developing and growing. And instead of just succumbing to feelings of pain or confusion, we now have an opportunity to examine their source.

Briefly, Gould characterizes the various stages of growth that we all experience and the characteristics that mark them in this way:

- Ages 1 to 15, when our childhood assumptions, rules, fantasies, dreams and irrationalities are developed, largely conditioned by our awe of the "power" and "size" of the adults around us ("Adults have all the answers" or "Someone else has to show me the way"). This reference point stays with us for much of our adult lives as, in our competitive society, we tend to judge ourselves and others in terms of rank, status and money.
- Ages 16 to 22, the transition period during which we leave our parents' and caretakers' world.
- Ages 23 to 28, when the theme is basically, "I'm nobody's baby now," and we are preoccupied with careers and family roles.
- Ages 28 to 34, when, often experiencing discontent and an urgent need to "do" something with our lives, we begin to open up to our unique qualities, values, and inner resources. At this ("What's it all about, Alfie?") stage, we start to question the validity of criteria of "power" and "size."
- Ages 34 to 45, the midlife decade, when we begin to make solid contact with, and act upon, our inner sense of meaning and purpose. Progressively, we become freer to determine and control our own lives.

LEVELS OF EMOTIONAL MATURITY

Sustaining a loving relationship depends very much on both partners' having achieved a level of emotional maturity at which they are genuinely capable of *mutual* concern, of consciously choosing to be there for your partner and to allow your partner to be there for you. This has nothing to do with chronological age, because emotionally we can be stuck at any age. Most people have no sense at all of the emotional age of the people with whom we choose to become intimate. It emerges only when we are sharing our lives. And it has nothing to do with how we or they handle a work situation. People who are extremely competent in their careers may behave like emotional infants at home.

In getting to know each other with an eye toward starting a long-term intimate relationship, we might keep these categories in mind. And we might consider them in how we interact with our partners at home now.

EMOTIONAL STAGES OF DEVELOPMENT

Chronological adults who remain *emotionally infants* are basically *self-centered*. They expect to be taken care of and to get what they want when they want it, without having to give in return. They know *only what they need*, see others primarily as *objects* to meet their needs and are incapable of empathizing with the needs of others. In their personal relationships, they tend to be tyrants.

Chronological adults who behave like *emotional children* tend to be obedient, passive, placaters, appeasers or covertly rebellious. They say in effect, "Tell me what to do," and expect to have their needs met in return without really having to spell them out. They assume that they will be taken care of if they do what is expected of them. When they are disappointed, they *act out* their feelings, often in covert or devious ways, such as lying, stealing, manipulation, foot dragging, deception, blaming, sarcasm, withholding, daydreaming and withdrawing. They are not verbally honest about their discontent, nor can they negotiate openly for what they want.

Chronological adults who are *emotional adolescents* are stuck at the stage of working through dependence-versus-independence. They are still asserting their own right to decide for themselves, so their position is, *"Don't tell me what to do."* Feeling that any expression of others' feelings or needs is an attempt to *control* and exert power over them, they reject them. They see meeting them as being reduced to a child. They tend to see others' pain, disappointment or requests as *manipulations* intended to control them, and defend against them by *withholding the very thing their partners want.* If you say "I'd like flowers for my birthday," such a person may well bring you a card or nothing at all. He or she will wait until the last minute to meet your requests or will ignore them altogether, finding reasons why they are irrational. He or she cannot give you what you want without feeling diminished, and feeling a loss of independence.

Only at the *adult* level of emotional maturity are we capable of empathizing with our partner's thoughts, feelings and needs, capable of mutual concern, and self-sufficient enough to be responsible for revealing our own. Only at this level can we sustain a loving relationship, giving and receiving love.

Achieving an adult level of maturity requires a sense of your own worth and respect for the same in your partner. Otherwise you may efface yourself so much that your needs don't get met; you may be so arrogantly overbearing that you ignore the needs of your partner; you may need so much reassurance that it becomes a burden to your partner.

How do you become more mature if you sense that you have in yourself an emotional infant, child or adolescent? That's what awareness and working on "self" is all about, whether it's on your own or in therapy. We will speak more of this in the chapters that follow.

OUR NATURAL CHILD

Becoming an adult doesn't mean forgetting how to be a child. All our lives we need to keep alive the energy of the natural child within us. Certainly many of the characteristics that are important to intimacy are qualities that we began with as children:

Curiosity	Responsiveness
Imagination	Receptiveness to new ideas
Playfulness	Honesty
Spontaneity	Eagerness to learn
Open-mindedness	Ability to feel the full range of
Willingness to experiment and	our emotions
take risks	Above all, the need to love and
Flexibility	be loved
Humor	
Energy	

Our inner child is a wellspring of energy. It is the source of our deepest feelings and greatest joys, of our ability to explore the world and be excited about what we find. It is also the source of our greatest limitations. Our child is quick to feel abandoned, hurt, terrified, overwhelmed, helpless and in need of rescue. We shouldn't try to dismiss our inner child, but neither should we put our child in charge when it's important to have an accurate perception of adult reality or when we must take someone else's needs and feelings into consideration.

One of the gifts of being an adult is that we have the power to take better care of our "child" than our parents did. As an adult, we have power that we never had as a child: power to earn our own money and to decide how to spend it, to come and go as we choose, to leave if we're threatened, to speak up for ourselves, to ask for help from reliable sources, to decide what sources *are* reliable and to develop the resources to help *ourselves*.

Becoming an emotional adult is not easy, and it's not necessary to be one all the time. But you need to be aware of and have control over the "states" that you are in. You need to be in your emotionally adult state to handle conflict constructively. On the other hand, be aware of the pleasure for you in intimacy when you can be in a trusting, playful, confiding, affectionate child state with your partner. It is a fun and powerful way of recharging your batteries. A good relationship also creates a wondrous opportunity for your natural child to be expressed. If your natural child was unable, while you were growing up, to express complaints ("don't whine") and be creative ("be practical" or "grow up") or was otherwise stifled, you and your partner can create together an atmosphere that permits these things. Many of us may feel as if we were cheated out of happiness while growing up. We can bemoan the loss of those years and endure the pain endlessly, but we don't have to. We have the power to create a happy childhood for ourselves now—regardless of our age.

To do so, we need to be aware of when we are, consciously or subconsciously, under old parental or authority-based rules that may need to be re-examined, such as those concerning sexual pleasure or not thinking of yourself (always be polite, never interrupt). Otherwise, you may never be heard! Be aware of when you need to be in your adult problem-solving mode, processing information. When serious matters are at hand, and when it is important to solve problems nondestructively and with full awareness of current reality, it's important that you put your emotional adult in charge.

PAIRS Exercise: Being A Loving Parent to Your Inner Child

Sit quietly, take a few deep breaths and allow your body to relax. Imagine yourself as a child in one of your favorite childhood places. It could be outdoors, in your room, at a friend's—any place where you felt happy and playful, or lonely, or worried. See yourself as the adult you now are. As an adult, approach your inner child of the past and invite your child to take your hand. Allow your child to lead you where he or she would like to take you, perhaps to show you something or to play a game, or to take a walk. Do this. Then, in your imagination, take your child of the past on your lap and invite him or her to tell you how things are. Listen, as your child tells you of the hurts, of the fears, of the scared times, of the upsetting things that have happened. Ask your child to tell you of whatever he or she has needed from mother or father or siblings (or from anyone else and hasn't had.)

Then allow yourself to soothe your child, to lovingly explain the things he or she needs to know, such as that it's natural to be afraid of the dark, that your child is lovable just the way he or she is, that he or she doesn't have to measure up or compete with others, that you will guide and protect your child and offer whatever he or she needs. You as an adult can deeply understand your child's needs and feelings and can lovingly respond to them, explaining what needs to be explained and using your resources to find whatever else is needed. Take the time to reflect on those things your inner child holds in heart and mind and how you can now respond, with the knowledge, skills and strengths you have as an adult. Reflect on what your child needed to know and didn't, needed to have happen that didn't, and think of how you can respond to that now, for yourself. Say to your child all the loving and tender things he or she needed to hear and didn't, and then, hold him or her to your heart and then gently say good-bye for now.

Now, being aware of the child of the past part of you, write in your journal what your child was feeling and what she or he told you. Write your responses. Write how it felt for you to be back in touch with this part of yourself, back at a time in your life when you had very little power, limited knowledge and many needs and feelings. Write what you wanted and needed and didn't receive. Recall any decisions you made at that time that may still be affecting you now, such as "Don't trust anyone, don't need anyone," "Don't count on anyone" or "Don't stand out" or "I can't compete." Think of what different decisions you can make now. Write your reflections in your journal. Later on, share what this was like for you, as well as any specific recollections and any new understandings you have, with your partner. Appreciate yourself for all you have had to learn and to overcome to reach this day and time.

REFLECTIONS

The experiences we had and the decisions we made as small and powerless children still operate in our lives today. As long as we live we may keep repeating the patterns established in childhood. But it is also true that insight at any age can free us to revise old decisions and to not need to sing the same sad songs again.

And now, prepare yourself for one more journal exercise, one that can be profound, poignant, enlightening, that encompasses not only what happened to you in your childhood, but also what has happened to you since then, in friendships, love relationships and life experiences. The following exercise is designed to help you gain a perspective on these.

PAIRS Exercise: Time/Life Dimension

Allow yourself an hour or more. And allow yourself to return to this later as new thoughts and memories prompt you. This important PAIRS exercise is adapted from the work of depth psychologist Ira Progoff, who studied turning points in the lives of creative people. It covers five critical areas: the significant time periods that your life divides into; the meaningful events that occurred during each of those periods; the people who were important to you in each period; the emotional impact upon you of these people and events, and the decisions you made as a consequence. The chart below presents a sample suggested structure for this.

Period	Events	People	Emotional Impact	Decision

Be prepared for this to be a significant experience in recollecting and reconnecting to lost and perhaps long forgotten events in your life, events that in many ways have determined your life patterns and your own invisible script.

Now start a new page in your journal and head it Time/Life Dimension. Take a deep breath and prepare to begin.

We begin the work of drawing your life into focus with the *now* moment of your life. But *now* is more than a moment. It includes the most recent part of the past that is a meaningful factor in the present. This forms the period that is the *now* of your life, your most recent relevant past as it moves into the present. For each

person, this elastic *now* has a different content and a different duration. It may be measured by a love relationship or the loss of one.
It may be measured by work, by a move, by a change in the circumstances of your life. This present moment may cover a short
period or a longer one. Whatever its duration, whatever its content,
whether pleasant or painful, this is the unit of time, the period with
which you begin writing in your journal.

Begin by closing your eyes, relaxing and quietly, inwardly, allowing yourself to feel the movement of your life. Ask yourself,
"Where am I now in my life?" Allow yourself to inwardly feel the
movement of your life as it has been taking shape in this present
period. Do not think of your life, but "feel it." Feel the inner movement of your recent experiences without judgment or censorship.

As you are feeling into this recent period of your life, a picture,
a simile or a metaphor may come to you. "It has been like climbing
a mountain, or being on an express train, or being in the eye of a
storm." This period has been like a . . . As a picture or a metaphor
comes to you, write it in your journal.

Allow yourself now to reflect. When did this period start? Is
there a particular event with which it began? Allow yourself to
reconstruct the outlines of this period. What memories come? Were
there events involving relationships, or work, or inner experiences?
Were there illnesses? Were there losses?

As you note this recent period, allow yourself to reflect on the
events and on the people who affected your life in this period. Who
were the people who were important or meaningful to you, whether
fulfilling or frustrating? Note them. What events were important to
you during this period? Note them briefly. As you allow yourself to
reflect more fully on this period, think of the emotional impact on
you during this time of the significant people and events, and decisions you made during this time: decisions about life, about love,
about trust, about relationships, about needing, about goals, about
hopes for yourself. Jot down the thoughts that come to you.

And now, having positioned yourself in this most recent period
of your life, allow yourself to reflect on the period before that and
the people and events that were significant to you during that previous period and their impact on you and decisions you made based
on your life experience, your learning at that time. Briefly note what
comes to you.

Allow yourself to reflect now on the still earlier periods of your life, going back in time to your beginnings. What were the marker events that set off each period? Was there a move, a disruption, a new stage of activity, a beginning or an end, a change, a loss? What possibilities opened for you? What alternatives presented themselves? What critical decisions were made or left unmade? What did you learn? What were the decisions?

Look particularly at the steppingstones in your life, the transition periods when you made decisions and set new goals. Write about early family conflicts and stresses; extraordinary events and changes; about your earliest memories; about your happiest ("peak") and most tragic experiences, and about key experiences related to school, work, career. Who were significant nonfamily members, mentors and models outside of the family? Who betrayed you or felt like your enemy? How did that affect you? What was the impact of siblings on you? What were the effects of losses such as the death of a parent or other significant figure? Who was particularly helpful or kind to you?

Briefly describe the nature of whatever memories come to you. What were you like at different ages? What was the feeling tone for different periods? When did you make decisions about the way life and you were "supposed to be" or about how you would deal with anger, disappointment, pain, fear, love?

Some questions you might explore are: What events caused you to circumscribe, conceal or reveal certain feelings? What incidents stand out as having affected your attitudes about trust, power, control, affection and sex? What incidents led you to feel guilty or ashamed or humiliated? What were special moments of pride and glory? When were you happy; when desolate? When secure and insecure? About what? What were the losses you experienced as a result of deaths or of people leaving or moving away? Were there other losses such as pets dying, being fired or losing your home from fire or flood?

Write a brief description of each incident you recall and its impact on you—how it influenced your feelings about yourself, others or life in general and how it may have changed the direction or quality of your life, beliefs or values.

Allow yourself to reflect quietly on the passage of your life, unraveling the past time units of your life at whatever pace feels comfortable. Reflect and write.

And now, at this moment, allow yourself a message of appreciation for you, for all of the learning you have done and trials you have had to overcome to be the person you are today. Appreciate yourself, and be aware that in knowing where you have been and where you are now, you can make new choices where the old ones no longer fit. You can use your resources of mind and heart and body, to substitute new learnings and to gain new wisdom.

In the following chapters, we will guide you in thought-provoking and insightful ways of discovering more of your unique resources.

Take a moment to write in your journal notebook about what you are beginning to realize.

14

Your Inner Cast of Characters

■   ■   ■

Of all the things I have asked you to do so far, this unusual exercise is perhaps the most fascinating. It provides a new view of your own complexity, along with ways to gain new understanding of your partner. Finally, it suggests ways to find more harmony both within yourself and with your partner. It offers humor, whimsy, a language and a new vocabulary.

> The human mind is very much like a ship where the sailors have mutinied and have locked the captain and the navigator in the cabin. Each sailor believes himself free to steer the ship as he pleases. First one sailor and then another takes over the helm, while the ship travels on a random and erratic course . . . these sailors cannot agree on a goal and, even if they could, they do not know how to navigate the ship to reach it. The task of the individual is to quell this mutiny and release the navigator and captain. Only then is he free to choose a goal and steer a direct course to reach it.
>
> (Plato's *Republic*)

Imagine yourself as the Captain of the ship that Plato saw all of us guiding. On this ship, you have a motley crew. This crew is your Inner Cast of Characters, or the various parts of yourself that emerge in different situations. It is crucial to know who your crew members are. Why? Because at any point in time, if you are tired and want to take a nap and you turn the wheel over to one of your crew, you may not end up where you intended to go. You may have been heading for the Bahamas, but if you turned the wheel over to a crew member who is a Goof-Off, you may find yourself grounded in Baltimore. If you turned it over to your Rebel, you may find yourself in a tidal wave, smashed against the rocks. If you turned it over to your adventurous Explorer, you may find yourself headed for the Amazon. Your ability to captain your ship depends upon assuming a leadership role in acknowledging and orchestrating your various parts. Then you can choose your course and choose to call upon the parts who are best qualified to get the job done.

Another way to understand this is to think of yourself as a many-faceted crystal, with each tiny facet catching the light in different situations. You may be an Autocrat at the office, a Dictator in an argument, a Mother Hubbard with children, an anxious Child in private, Ernest Hemingway or Virginia Woolf at the typewriter, Danny Kaye at a party, a sexy Cleopatra in the bedroom, and a mystical St. Augustine in prayer.

It is useful and fun to label your major "parts" with handy references to famous personalities. Quite rich images are conveyed when we speak of different sides of ourselves as Godzilla or Rambo or James Bond or Machiavelli. And it would be difficult to misunderstand what is meant if we speak of my Joan of Arc, my John Wayne, my Florence Nightingale, my Rhett Butler or my Scarlett O'Hara. We instinctively fall into these personality grooves in response to the demands or opportunities around us. Our partners, often highly sensitive to our moods, may pick up on subtle signs before we're even aware that we're into our outraged Spoiled Brat, long-suffering Martyr, Cutie Pie, absent-minded Professor, scatter-brained Clown, or miserable Grouch.

The impact of each of our parts on our relationships can be profound. Every part, mood or attitude that we present to our partners provokes a response. We then respond to their response, starting unpredictable chain reactions between our parts. If we are unaware of which part was in charge at a certain time, it can lead us onto the rocks without either of us knowing how we got there.

An example of this was provided by Harold and Dorothy, who came to PAIRS after twelve years of an unfulfilling, rather joyless marriage. They had three children, ages four, seven, and eleven. They described the following situation.

When Harold came home from the office overwhelmed by business problems, all he wanted was loving and nurturing, a chance to forget work for a while. It was as if the part of Harold that walked through the front door was Tiny Tim—a scared little kid in a cold, hostile world. The instant that Dorothy saw that part of Harold, his body language, the look on his face, her Chicken Little button was pushed. In effect, the sky was falling because if Harold was worried, Dorothy was even more worried. When this happened, Harold (getting the opposite of what he needed) invariably became angry and withdrew into his isolated Trappist Monk part, making Dorothy even more frantic. Typically, days and even weeks would go by before they recovered equilibrium.

In PAIRS, they were able to identify their parts and diagram how and when this happened as well as what each of them felt. As they labeled their parts (which I will ask you to do later in this chapter), they were able to see the patterns of interaction and find ways to break the vicious cycle.

Dorothy, who had a solid Nurturing Mother part, realized that if she shifted into this mode when he came home, Harold could then replenish his strength and be available to allay her need for attention and calming. She was able to deliberately choose to switch gears. This simple exercise offered them a strategy to resolve a painful impasse. It also offered a language that allowed them to define the once undefinable and to negotiate issues that were long nothing but a muddle.

With surprising ease and even a sense of discovery, we can begin to identify parts of ourselves that are activated under different circumstances. Some parts likely will be in conflict. How many of us have found ourselves screaming in anger at someone, saying things so hurtful that some part of us can't believe we are actually saying them? How many of us have a Walter Mitty preoccupied with fantasies that intrude on our daily grind? How many of us have a

Little Engine That Could that keeps us steadily on the daily grind?

Some parts rarely come into the light. It's these submerged parts, hidden in the shadows, that often cause trouble in a relationship. Keeping them down takes a lot of energy. Eventually, the parts that are hidden or on hold tend to come crashing out anyway, as if to say "When is it my turn?" When a part of you that has been repressed finally insists, "Now! I want my turn now!" it tends to choose its own time for doing so. It can push everything and everyone else aside, and you may not feel as if you have much control over what's going on. This is the phenomenon writer Gail Sheehy described in her landmark book *Passages*, when people make abrupt, shocking or disrupting changes in their lives: It's as if their formerly repressed parts were saying, "I want my turn *now*!"

When Anita left her financially successful husband, Jim, and five children to live in a one-room efficiency, complete a degree, and pursue a career as a teacher, no one understood how she could possibly do that. What she said was: "I married at seventeen. I never dated anyone except Jim. We met when I was twelve and he was fourteen. I've never known any other life but that of a daughter, a wife to Jim, and a mother to my children. There's got to be more to life than that. I can't live that way anymore."

It's as if unlived parts of Anita had been on hold, waiting for Anita to experience them, to pursue her own interests and new relationships. Those parts became so pressing, they overturned her entire life.

Following a spectacular, joyful twenty-fifth wedding anniversary celebration, Jonathan calmly told his wife he was leaving. He wanted the opportunity to experience other women, other sexual relationships, before he was too old. Their relationship was the only one he had ever known. He had been a responsible husband, father, provider. Now he wanted to be free to explore his sexuality elsewhere. His Don Juan and Warren Beatty parts were saying "I want my turn *now!*" Janet was shocked. She had never dreamed this side of him existed. She had thought he was content. He had been an avid gardener, an active handyman, an attentive father and husband.

In PAIRS, we have a Suppressed Parts exercise (developed by Virginia Satir) that illustrates the power of our hidden parts. We invite participants to identify the parts they feel good about and those they don't. Then, we have class members each represent a part, with the ones that are being suppressed kneeling on all fours and actually being sat upon by the others. When the suppressed parts get restless (as they always do), they overturn the entire arrangement. Only when they can stand up and speak for what they, too, want and need is there a chance for coordination and harmony within the group.

Our parts are both interconnected and autonomous. They, at different times, can compete for control, interact in turn, form alliances and even, at times, go to war with each other. Many of our parts owe their development to our early family life. How often the voices in our heads sound like Mom or Dad—and how often we have other sides of us that disagree with or even do battle with Mom or Dad, selves that developed in our history as oppositional.

This was the case with Kent and Lila. When they decided to marry, after a long and loving courtship, they experienced a marked shift in their relationship. Suddenly, everything Lila asked of Kent was met with a lack of interest or with resentment; even a few hours of time together for a movie or a drive on the weekend were begrudged. Eventually, they both questioned their commitment. But, because they remembered the pleasures they had found previously with each other, they chose to take PAIRS.

In class, Kent realized that as an only son with a widowed mother, he felt controlled by his mother's needs and guilty whenever he didn't do whatever she wanted. He even felt guilty about doing anything for himself, except working hard. He worked overwhelmingly long hours. He further realized that in committing himself to marriage, a part of him anticipated that he would be controlled by Lila's desires, as he had been by his mother's. He headed this off by bringing out his Rebel, who was resistant to virtually anything Lila wanted. He started avoiding her. She experienced this as unloving, felt rejected and found herself in conflict within herself. She fought hard not to become a whining, complaining Blamer or to bring out her Independent Feminist part, a part that didn't need anyone and would leave the relationship.

When Kent brought out his Detective side, he was aware of how his history (his hidden expectations, his joyless and loveless decisions) was destroying the love he had felt for Lila. In identifying the parts of himself that developed out of his childhood history, he found himself able to see the difference between his mother and

Lila. They were very different. He was able to restore the Romantic Lover who found joy in their relationship. And Lila was able to reclaim Cleopatra.

Angry and fearful parts are sides that people often try to keep hidden, as they worry that they will be seen as immature or childish. Sometimes the angry parts stay denied and hidden, but then leak out as the Don Juan who tries to seduce every woman he meets; the Walter Mitty who secretly dreams of abandoning the family and setting out alone for Alaska; the Rambo who rages at every driver who inadvertently cuts in front of him and insults waiters or waitresses on any pretext; the Camille who fends off gloom and despair with constant illness.

We suppress or ignore these parts because we believe they are somehow dangerous to us. We're afraid we may lose control, embarrass ourselves, become violent. We're scared that we may actually leave for Alaska and never want to come back to a much-loved family. Scared we'll actually act out our sexual fantasies. We're scared that if we acknowledge these parts they will destroy us.

Virginia Satir told a story of a man who kept a pack of wild dogs penned up. He rarely fed them and whenever he walked past their pen, he would curse at them. One day, they got loose, and they ate him up! Another man, who also kept a pack of dogs, talked to them, fed them, told them he cared about them. One day, they got loose. They ran around, but they didn't eat him (or anyone else).

PAIRS Exercise: Naming Your Inner Cast of Characters

I'm going to invite you to become aware of and to choose names for your own Inner Cast of Characters. This is a fun and powerful way to see how different aspects of yourself emerge in daily life. You probably will have no trouble coming up with six or seven right off the bat. Consider how you act in various situations: at play, at work, under stress, at rest, when you feel confident, when you feel loving and sexy, when you are sure you're nothing but a loser, when you are embarrassed, when you are angry. Try to spot specific attitudes and give them names, such as "A Good Wife Never Screams at Her Husband" or "Save It for a Rainy Day." If a particular attitude was learned from a certain person, you might choose to use that person's name. For instance, Harry had a part that acted as a constant critic, telling him that no matter what he did, it wouldn't be good enough. As he explored the voice, he realized that his father had been critical of his every move and had never praised him for any of his accomplishments. He labeled that part Big Ralph.

Over the course of several days, add more parts as you listen to your various inner voices commenting on day-to-day events. Different seasons, holidays and family reunions can be big "parts evokers." Some PAIRS alumni add to their lists for years, adjusting them as their awareness grows and as they change.

Do this exercise with a sense of whimsy, of impishness, even of exaggeration. The most common PAIRS reactions to this exercise are hilarious appreciation of the often comic aptness of the titles we give to the Parts, excitement at the discovery of how they reinforce or provoke each other and affect our relationships, and a sense of liberation that comes from realizing that so many of the parts we have hidden or masked can be revealed, understood, and accepted.

The following is a beginning list of character names and descriptive adjectives. Do any of the names fit any of your Inner Cast of Characters? Add others that have meaning for you and change any of the names on the list to ones that fit more precisely. Your list can include names of well-known figures, actors or actresses (living or dead), historical or literary figures, comic strip characters, political figures or figures that have personal meaning for you. Write them down on the chart that follows the list with adjectives that fit and remarks describing how frequently they emerge and how you feel about them.

Acceptor	Pays any price to be loved, accepts mistreatment, tries hard to please
Adventurer	Risk taker, enjoys trying new things, explorer
Albert Schweitzer	"Reverence for life," philosopher, scientist, healer
Alexis Carrington	Vindictive, power-hungry bitch, overbearing

Amelia Earhart	Courageous pilot, explorer, persevering, determined
Angel	Never makes waves, good beyond belief
Archie Bunker	Crude, insensitive boor
Barbie Doll	Vain, superficial
Belittler	Turns your dreams and accomplishments to ashes, discourages you from trying new things
Betty Crocker	Homemaker, putterer, cook
Betty Friedan	Feminist, ambitious, hardworking, a leader
Bill Cosby	Witty, hilarious, good-natured, performer
Blamer	Critical, nit-picker, sarcastic, accusing, judging
Blaze Starr	Sexy
Boy Scout	Does good deeds, helpful
Brady Bunch	Loving father
Brat	Whiny, complaining, always wants own way
Brown Nose	Seeks attention, approval
Burt Reynolds	Risk taker, roguish, sexy
Bulldog	Tenacious, stubborn, determined, persevering
Bumbler	Clumsy, incompetent, never gets anything right
Captain Ahab	Driven, punitive
Caretaker	Helpful, nurturing
Charlie Chaplin	Funny, playful
Chicken Little	Alarmist, shrill, anxious
Chopin	Anguished, vulnerable, brooding, romantic, genius
Cinderella	Martyr, victim, awaits Prince Charming
Cleopatra	Ultimate sexiness, manipulative
Comforter	Reassures you, helps you take care of yourself and get over things and move on
Curious George	Curious about everything, nosy
Dick Van Dyke	Fatherly, charming, humorous

Distractor	Irrelevant, changes subject, avoids issues
Doctor Jekyll/Mr. Hyde	Dual personality, evil, dangerous
Don Juan	Seducer, "World's Greatest Lover," vain, womanizing
Don Knotts	Guilty, insecure
Doubting Thomas	Cynical, questioning
Dreamer	Creative, imaginative, helps you see things in new ways
Droopy	Self-pitying, down in the dumps, gloomy
Eileen Garrett	Mystic, psychic
Eleanor Roosevelt	Humanitarian, leader, organizer, nurturing
Elizabeth Barrett Browning	Poet, romantic lover
Fan	Believes in you, cheers you on, compliments you
Felix Unger	Perfectionist
Florence Nightingale	Caring, healing, nurturing, service
Frightened Child	Cowering, timid, suspicious, needy
Frog Prince	Ugly on surface but a prince underneath
Gandhi	Self-sacrificing, fighter for justice peacefully
George Burns	Wiseacre, showman, loves attention and laughter
Gloomy Gus	Negative, depressed
Godzilla	Raging, uncontrolled fury, intimidating
Go-Getter	Gets things done, helps you to realize your goals, sees that you accomplish what you set out to do
Golden Retriever	Eager to please, confused, irrelevant, loving
Good Buddy	Companion, confidant, sympathetic, defends you against critics and enemies
Goof-Off	Persuasive arguments for never accomplishing what you could

Hamlet	Brooding, tragic, victim, depressed
Harry Homeowner	Fixes everything, a tinkerer, handy
Natural Child	Playful, imaginative, spontaneous
Hedda Hopper	Notorious gossip, meddlesome
Hell's Angel	Born to be wild, outlaw, rebel
Hercules	Strong, independent, can do anything
Hero	Rescuer, strong, powerful
Howard Hughes	Controlling, rigid, powerful, pathological
Imelda Marcos	Materialistic, greedy
Jane Fonda	Fitness enthusiast, priority on health and looks
Jesus	Savior, healing, mystic, loving
Jimmy Stewart	Wise, compassionate
John the Baptist	Martyr, articulate, self-sacrificing, a zealot
Judge	Judgmental, critical, rigid, perfectionist
Judith Viorst	Insightful humor and wisdom
Julie Andrews	Musical, actress, performer, ingenue, pretty, innocent
Katharine Hepburn	Aloof, aristocratic, proud, skeptical, unforgiving
Knife Twister	Reminds you of every wrongdoing, creates anxiety
Lady Macbeth	Vindictive, controlling, jealous
Leonardo Da Vinci	Creative genius, inventor
Little Miss Muffet	Timid, fearful
Little Orphan Annie	Vulnerable, innocent, trusting, needy
Little Prince(ss)	Spoiled, royalty
Little Red Riding Hood	Trusting, innocent
Lord Byron	Romantic poet
Lost Child	Hurt, wounded, helpless
Louisa May Alcott	Writer, solitary, loves children
Love Crusher	Doubts anyone's love, fears rejection, rejects
Machiavelli	Sly, shrewd, conniving, strategist, manipulator

Madame Butterfly	Naive, innocent, trusting, tragic
Madame LaFarge	Judging, sentencing, ruthless, heartless
Mama Cass	Self-indulgent, performer, lusty
Marie Curie	Scientist, seeker of truth, perfectionist
Marilyn Monroe	Seductive, sexy, kittenish
Martina Navratilova	Winner, athletic, competitive, number one
Martyr	Victim, long-suffering
Mary Tyler Moore	Positive, cheerful, optimistic
Mascot	Funny, positive, optimistic, cheerful
Mata Hari	Sexy, manipulative, spy
Michelangelo	Artistic, creative
Mick Jagger	Lewd, exhibitionist
Miss Ellie	Worried, intrusive
Mommie Dearest	Mean parent, vengeful, blaming, nasty
Mother Hen	Fretful, fusses
Mother Teresa	Caring, compassionate, kind, helpful
Mr. Peepers	Cowering, fearful
Mr. Rogers	Gentle, sharing
Mrs. Brady	Cheerfully domestic
Mussolini	Pompous, posturing, a fascist dictator
Nana	Sensual abandon, earthy, sexy
Nancy Drew	Playful, curious, explorer, friendly, loyal
Napoleon	Power-hungry, dictator
Narcissus	Temperamental, self-centered
Natalie Wood	Eager, naive, youthful, innocent, loving
Native American	Mystic, nature lover
Nerd	Bookish, academic, naive
Oliver Twist	Bereft, abandoned, unloved
Optimist	Thinks positively, avoids getting bogged down in gloom
Overindulger	Everything in excess—food, drink, drugs, spending
Ozzie and Harriet	Supportive, loving parents

Pandora	Troublemaker, provocative
Pessimist	Voice of doom and gloom, expects the worst
Peter Pan	Eternally youthful, free spirit
Pit Viper	Vicious, lethal
Pope	Judgmental, critical, pretentious, dictatorial
Professor Higgins	Controlling, attempting to sculpt another person
Queen	Imperious, calculating, regal
Rebel	Oppositional, contrary, rebellious
Rejector	Price of love is too high, won't allow self to love anyone
Rhett Butler	Powerful, charming, sexy, a gambler, wheeler-dealer
Rockefeller	Wealthy, controlling, powerful
Santa Claus	Hearty, generous
Scapegoat	Victim
Scaredy Cat	Afraid of everything, keeps you anxious
Scarlett O'Hara	Vain, superficial, charming, jealous, conniving
Scrooge	Greedy, penny-pinching, bitter, cynical
Siddhartha	Spiritual seeker
Sigmund Freud	Insightful, analytic, profound, wise
Sleeping Beauty	Passively awaits her prince to bring her to life
Slippery Dan	Confused, con artist, manipulative
Solomon	Wise, mediator, problem solver, regal
Spoiler	Pleasure stealer, takes the fun out of everything
Super(wo)man	Can do anything, miracle worker, rescuer, risk-taker
Tank McNamara	Clumsy, inarticulate
Tarzan	Primitive, manly, adventurous
Thomas Edison	Inventive, creative, curious
Thoreau	Contemplative, nature lover, philosopher, mystic

Three-Toed Sloth	Lazy, sleeps endlessly, does nothing, indolent
Torquemada	Cruel, dictatorial, ruthless
Ugly Duckling	Misfit
Voice of Reason	Level-headed, common sense, helps make wise choices
Walt Whitman	Poet, loves life, mystic, unafraid
Walter Mitty	Dreamer, lives in fantasy
Whiz Kid	Bright, innovative, evokes envy
Witch	Sarcastic, biting, angry, aloof
Workaholic	Works endlessly, joyless
Zeus	Omnipotent, rules by intimidation and lightning bolts

MY INNER CAST OF CHARACTERS

Descriptive Adjectives	Name of Character	When It Tends to Emerge	Like or Dislike

Who Are You?

Many couples find it helpful and interesting to work together as they draw up their inner cast of characters. If you are working with a partner, you can turn this exercise into a game by having your partner sit opposite you with a pen and paper and in a dispassionate, calm manner, ask you "Who are you?" repeatedly, writing down each response as you offer it.

Each time, think of a way you would describe yourself, such as:

Who are you?	I am hardworking.
Who are you?	I am caring.
Who are you?	I am playful.
Who are you?	I am a good and loyal friend.
Who are you?	I am a loner.
Who are you?	I am a poet.
Who are you?	I am naive.
Who are you?	I am competent.

If you are working alone, you write down each description yourself. If with a partner, your partner writes each one down. At the end, if you wish, you can invite your partner to add any specific qualities he or she is aware of that you may have left out. Add them to the list.

Now, for each set of adjectives, choose a character that can represent that part of you. Try to be as honest as possible with yourself.

In the days ahead, add other adjectives or names of characters to your list. Do it without being judgmental about them. Some of your parts may have negative connotations. It is important to know that every part of you has at its core a need or desire that was originally good. We all start out needing to be loved, cared for, protected and wanted, to survive and to grow.

Take a moment to write in your journal notebook about what you are beginning to realize.

15

Taking Charge: Arranging the Cast

■   ■   ■

*N*ow that you have identified your Inner Cast and given them names, we are going to look at which go well together, which are in conflict, which sabotage and which you can use at special times. The point of this exercise is to Empower you as the Captain to coordinate your parts.

Accepting your parts doesn't mean using negative parts in a negative way; it means accepting their existence in us. By concealing or imposing a negative judgment on a part, we keep it from being useful to us.

Parts that cannot express themselves directly tend to get expressed in rigid or distorted ways. If we don't acknowledge jealousy or envy, for instance, we may get angry and withdraw or become oppositional, which doesn't resolve the problem. If we can be sympathetic to the underlying needs our parts have (such as the need for safety or the need to have our own accomplishments), we can find a whole new resource in ourselves. Once you accept those parts that express such aspects as jealousy, vengeance, bitterness, sneakiness, manipulation and deception, they won't ambush you and make things go awry. You want to get to a point where you can look at your parts and say, "I own you, and this is how I want you to behave next time."

Taking charge means sorting things out. Talk to your parts and have them talk to each other. What are your parts telling you about the needs they have?

Look at your list. Which parts do you see as "ally" voices and which as "enemy" voices? Which parts take precedence? Do the voices speak in turn or is there chaos? Is it a democratic process or is there a dictator who controls everyone? Which are on hold? Which are a source of worry? Which parts are the most reliable? Which cause you the greatest surprises? Which cause the greatest trouble? Which would you like to develop?

Just like people, they tend to operate in cliques, teaming up with each other in particular situations. Once we can recognize who is there, we choose how we can best accommodate them.

Milton, a college professor, came to PAIRS after he and his wife had separated. It was his second marriage. While each hoped for a better relationship, they clearly were at a terrible impasse. Milton offered to identify and describe his parts, stating that he knew he had parts that were difficult, critical, pessimistic. These were the parts he identified:

Torquemada	Dictatorial, sadistic, ruthless
Judge	Judgmental, critical, dictatorial
Sting	Confused, a con artist
Walter Mitty	Dreamer, imaginative
Orphan	Bereft, abandoned, unloved
Sigmund Freud	Profound, insightful
Mick Jagger	Exhibitionist
Robert Young	A loving father
Chopin	Anguished, vulnerable
Johnny Carson	Socially charming
Madame LaFarge	Driven, punitive, vindictive, heartless
Natalie Wood	Eager, innocent, naive

In PAIRS, we invite class members to act out each of the parts of a person as if they were meeting at a party and to divide into natural groupings. Virginia Satir, who developed this exercise, called it the Parts Party.

As the class played out Milton's parts, it was clear that powerful, negative parts were in coalition and took precedence over the softer, gentler, more needy, more loving, more creative parts of Milton. As the parts arranged themselves in rows, Torquemada, the Judge and Madame LaFarge came out powerfully in the front, with the Sting and Mick Jagger on the sides, not far behind. In the row behind them were Johnny Carson, Sigmund Freud and Robert Young, and in the farthest row, the last and least heard from were the gentle dreamer Walter Mitty, the poignant Orphan, anguished Chopin, and eager, naive Natalie Wood.

It was not difficult to see the problems Milton had in his marriage. His wife, who was in the class, nodded in recognition at these groupings, seeing what she indeed experienced in her relationship with Milton.

Then we asked Milton to choose to arrange his parts in a different order, one that he would prefer. He chose to place the powerful coalition of Torquemada, the Judge and Madame LaFarge in the rear rank, to be called upon as protection *only if needed*. He chose to place the loving, charming, needy, vulnerable parts in the front.

As he arranged the parts, Torquemada left the rear rank and marched up to the front of the group, as though to take command. At this, Milton laughed, recognizing that no matter how he tries to subdue his Torquemada, the pompous ruler always seemed to wind up right in front.

At the end of his Parts Party, I reached out to hug him and found I was hugging a rigid, guarded, distant stranger. I said, "I want to hug the Orphan." Instantly, I felt Milton relax and felt him hug me warmly back. He was able to choose to shift his parts. All it had taken was awareness and the willingness to make a conscious choice.

Sometimes, we discover embryonic parts in our personalities that would be useful to develop more fully. Psychologist Ira Progoff speaks of the "seed model of growth," referring to the concept that each of us has an entire range of capacities that can be developed, but some of them are in seedling stages. When I developed my own list of parts, they included:

Elizabeth Barrett Browning	Romantic poet, writer
Richard Rodgers	Musician, composer
Mother Hubbard	Nurturing, devoted mother
Natalie Wood	Trusting, loving, innocent
Simone de Beauvoir	Philosopher, writer, feminist
Albert Schweitzer	Humanitarian, nature lover, scientist, mystic
Bulldog	Stubborn, persevering, hard-working, tenacious
Camille	Tired, sick

I found that I had many caring, creative and hard-working sides. I had no part that was *carefree* or that could just have fun, cool down an argument or let go of grudges. In some deep crevice of my being, I would remember upsetting things forever.

When I realized this, I was able to deliberately develop a fun-loving "let bygones be bygones" Goldie Hawn part to help me enjoy life more and get over grudges. Goldie has been enormously helpful to me in relieving stress and *keeping a sense of balance*, especially when I am inundated with problems, either my own or those of others. I can bring in the Albert Schweitzer or Simone de Beauvoir sides to decide if the problem is very important, or if it's okay to let it go. But things Simone once would have analyzed to death or that the Bulldog would have pursued relentlessly, I now decide are just not that important. I can laugh more, change subjects, even take vacations—I don't always have to work so hard or be so serious. This is particularly wonderful because I can share it with Morris, who has a very large Imp in him who can be playful and carefree. This further encourages my Goldie part to come out and play.

The danger of not learning to develop fun-loving or easygoing parts is that the overly serious or even destructive parts can insist on running things, usually driving them right into the ground. One such story came from Al, a depressed man in his late forties who came to me saying that no relationship had ever worked out for him. He described the following: "When a relationship isn't going well, I bring in a part of me I call the Axe Man. He chops down, destroys and gets rid of everything to do with that relationship. Then the Hit Man comes in. He says to the Axe Man, 'Stop chopping. Stop destroying. You lived without this [relationship] before. You can do it again. Stop!' and the Axe Man stops chopping. Then

I bring in the Concrete Man. And he pours concrete over the whole thing."

At this point, intrigued with the vivid imagery, I asked, "And then what happens?"

"And then I drag it behind me for the rest of my life," he said.

All of your parts are *potential resources*, with both advantages and disadvantages. Your Procrastinator or Three-Toed Sloth enables you to relax, take time out, turn off your energy at the end of a stressful day. However, it would be a real drag if your Sloth was in charge while you were threatened and you had to move quickly and make rapid decisions. You have to figure out what the part's *positive function* is meant to be. Sarcasm, for instance, can serve as humor and insight. Similarly, self-pity can be transformed into compassion, naivete into wonder, servility into thankfulness, mania into excitement, bitchiness or grumbling into power, fear into courage, restlessness into vitality and exploring, inertia or escapism into peace, depression into joy, prejudice into loyalty, jealousy into ambition, blaming into problem solving, suspiciousness and hostility into openness, cunning into intelligence, guilt and overapologizing into empathy and sensitivity, aggression into creative energy.

Look back at your list of parts. In your journal, write what you think the positive need of each has been—for example, love, power, survival, protection, creativity, energy release, pleasure. Make a special effort to stretch your imagination in seeking the positive intent behind parts you consider negative.

Now, on a new page in your journal, I'd like you to arrange your parts starting with the way you feel they are placed now. Do it as you might arrange a "Family Portrait," with the most frequently present or the most powerful in the front.

Pay particular attention to the parts that seem to interfere with your ability to do or enjoy things. If you like to write but never find the time, what voice is telling the Writer that he doesn't deserve the time or have the ability? If you never speak up at staff meetings, even though you have many ideas, what part is telling the Innovator to keep quiet? If you feel lonely in a relationship, what parts are saying to your Lover or your Playful Child that your partner cannot be trusted or is boring? If you are in an abusive or unhealthy relationship, what part is telling you that you can't or shouldn't leave?

If you snap at or constantly criticize your partner, what part is hurt by or angry at him or her, but is too reticent to bring the problem up directly? If you feel out of shape, what part is telling your Fitness Buff to watch television instead of taking a long walk?

Once you've assembled your parts, begin to think about how you might like to rearrange them. How might certain parts support one another? Think about ways to give your favorite and most important parts the most prominence and support. Don't stop arranging until you are satisfied with where every part is placed. Use two principles in rearranging them:

1. Move to the front those parts that you wish to empower, and move further back those you wish to be less important in your life.
2. Move next to each other those parts that you want to have support or modify each other, either by strengthening each other's qualities or offsetting each other's overbearing aspects.

As you consider your new arrangement, which parts do you see being the most likely to try to force things back to their original state? Which parts will be most satisfied with their new roles and work to keep their place in your psyche? Which parts will be in charge of monitoring your new crew and making the appropriate changes as you grow and change?

The following is how Don described the split-second interaction of his parts, as well as the rearrangements he made.

Vaudeville Showman	Loves to clown in the spotlight
Rambo	Rages
Good Little Boy	Seeks to please
Thoreau	Contemplative, loves long walks in the woods
Anxious Child	Fears loss and abandonment
Lone Eagle	Thrives on independence, solitude, freedom
Spunky Kid	Loves to play, sometimes rough

| Chief Justice | Source of perfect knowledge, assessor of all he surveys |
| Handyman | Loves to work with his hands |

"If someone criticizes me, the Good Little Boy gets upset, because he feels that he hasn't done his job properly. He calls on the Chief Justice for support. The Chief Justice quietly but sternly explains to the critic why the critic is wrong, asks just what the matter is with him anyway, and announces that if he is going to go around criticizing people, he'd better get his own house in order first.

"If Mary, my wife, says she is going out with some friends for the evening, my Anxious Child starts to worry that she wants to spend time away from me because she doesn't love me anymore. My Anxious Child talks to the Good Little Boy, who nudges the Handyman and says, 'Gee, tonight was the night I was going to help you finish staining that old rocking chair.' When Mary says we will have to work on the chair on Sunday because she's already promised her friends that she would meet them, Anxious Child tugs on Rambo's sleeve. Rambo becomes enraged that someone has hurt his good little friend and raids his arsenal for every weapon at his disposal: 'Christ, I wish you would quit wasting so much money eating those fancy dinners with your fat friends. We can't pay our bills or have a night out because you always spend so much time

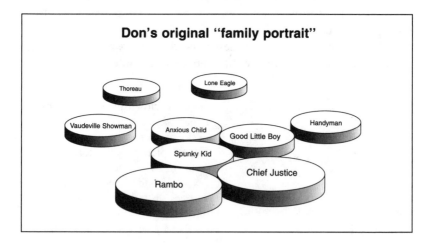

Don's original "family portrait"

and money away from home. Besides, it would be nice if you did something around the house for a change. I'm sick of having to do everything here.'

"If sometime later Mary spends the evening doting on me, the Anxious Child might get nervous again, worrying why she's being so nice. The Spunky Kid might feel that someone is out to trap and smother him. Lone Eagle and Thoreau get together and decide that this is the perfect time to go for a long walk and look at the stars, *alone*. Maybe with vengeful Rambo's approval, 'Now I'm not here for you!' "

Don's parts emerge in a Family Portrait with his most powerful protecting his most defenseless and vulnerable parts. Rambo and the Chief Justice are in front, with the Good Little Boy, the Spunky Kid and the Anxious Child in the center, and the more fun-loving and creative ones pushed to the back or side (Vaudeville Showman, Lone Eagle, Thoreau). If this Family Portrait remains this way, it undoubtedly won't be long before Mary complains that he appears angry, critical or distant all the time and that she can't take much more or she will respond with similar behavior. And that fairly well destroys any chance of intimacy. If Don wants an intimate relation-ship, *he needs to find ways to modify or rearrange his parts.*

This is his story: "My parents divorced when I was six. My father moved out of state. My mother died suddenly when I was twelve. I went to live with my father. He had remarried and had other children. I always felt like an outsider. It seemed the only time I was recognized at all was when I did chores around the house or helped my father with carpentry (birth of the Handyman). And then he usually pointed out that I had screwed things up. Sometimes I'd relieve tension by clowning. It got me in trouble at school (the Vaudeville Showman) but my friends enjoyed it. I joined the Army at eighteen. The family acted as if I couldn't leave soon enough."

As Don talked, he realized that while Rambo raged at the people who had left him, he had never grieved over his mother's death, the loss of his home, or his father's lack of interest. The Anxious Child had always had the capacity to grieve, but feared that the pain would be overwhelming. With Rambo's courage, perhaps now he could face and experience that pain. He also realized that as much as he loved to work with his hands, the projects he worked on always seemed to be what someone else wanted. And if the Anxious Child felt somehow threatened and distrustful, he would call on Lone Eagle or Thoreau and get away by himself.

By exploring how his parts cooperated and conspired, Don also saw how they failed one another. By maintaining distance, either through anger or isolation, the Anxious Child and Lone Eagle, who *feared abandonment and loss of love*, virtually ensured that Don could not sustain a loving relationship.

This is how he chose to *rearrange* his portrait and find a new balance for his Parts:

"I would put the Anxious Child in the middle row. Right next to him is the Chief Justice, reminding him of his real desire: to be loved. The Chief Justice can also act as an arbitrator, determining when there is real danger or reason to distrust. In turn, the Anxious Child, who knows about pain, can help the Chief Justice learn compassion and empathy and turn judgmental criticism into helpful insights. On the Anxious Child's other side is the Good Little Boy who can help him to nurture himself and the people in his life by putting him in touch with what he wants, not just what he fears. The Anxious Child can help keep the Good Little Boy from going overboard in trying to please others, reminding him that he has needs that deserve to be fulfilled.

"Rambo and the Spunky Kid are next in line, with Rambo slightly to the back so his size and strength don't obscure the others. These parts help me to take risks and be assertive. The Spunky Kid's love of life and rambunctiousness can help the Good Little Boy have more fun, not just do things to please others. Rambo can be on hand to protect the Good Little Boy from giving away the store. The Good Little Boy and the Anxious Child can mellow Rambo, offering him compassion, concern and fun and help him harness his rage as power needed to bring about change. Spunky Kid can team up with Rambo to help me keep my body in shape.

"In the front, I place contemplative, spiritual Thoreau, along with the fun-loving Vaudeville Showman. Arm in arm, they can prevent each other from being too remote or too outrageous. The Handyman can be on one side and Lone Eagle on the other. The Handyman can now be free to make what pleases me instead of others. He is my creative side. Lone Eagle is my ability to recharge, to restore my strength, to find the quiet I need to solve problems

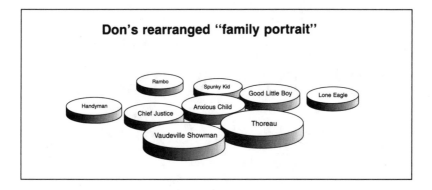

Don's rearranged "family portrait"

or penetrate the meaning of things or to be alone without being lonely."

Don's arrangement is not a static one. It will change day in and day out as circumstances change. He may choose to reveal his Anxious Child to Mary at times, but not to his boss. He may go for long periods with Lone Eagle in the back row and Rambo and Spunky Kid in the front. But what doesn't change is Don's greater ability to keep his life *on a path of his own choosing.*

In the next chapter, we will look at the rich, complex interaction of the parts of a couple.

Take a moment to write in your journal notebook about what you are beginning to realize.

16

The Dance We Dance:
Parts of a Couple

■   ■   ■

What happens when you and your partner bring all of your Inner Cast of Characters together? If each of you have ten or more parts, that's at least twenty characters wandering around in your relationship, demanding space and attention. Anyone would have to feel crowded at times. Exploring how your mutual casts of characters interact will help you understand how periods of tension, conflict, emptiness, joy and calm come and go.

Writer Michael Ventura eloquently describes pairings that occur early in a relationship and then some surprises later on:

> My tough street kid is romancing your honky-tonk angel. I am your homeless waif and you are my loving mother. I am your lost father and you are my doting daughter. I am your worshiper and you are my goddess. I am your god and you are my priestess. . . .
>
> But what happens when the Little Boy inside him is looking for the Mommy inside her and finds instead on this particular night a sharp-toothed Analyst dissecting his guts? When the Little Girl inside her is looking for the Daddy inside him, and

finds instead a Pagan Worshipper who wants a Goddess to lay with.

When our dreams begin to turn into nightmares, our understanding of our Inner Cast of Characters offers us a useful new way to think about what is happening and what we can do about it.

Dina, a red-haired, attractive mother of three school-aged youngsters, identified one of her parts as Mommy Dearest, a side that would suddenly develop an intense, raging hatred of her children and become vindictive and intimidating. The one part of her husband that could bring Dina out of her Mommy Dearest part was his Lawn Boy, easygoing, accommodating, relaxed, seductive. But if he was into his Three-Toed Sloth (lazing on the sofa), her anger would quickly escalate into a screaming fight with him or the children.

Sharing their Inner Cast of Characters made it clear how Eric could help Dina at such times. She, in turn, was able to offer Eric the same kind of help. When he was being his overworked, perfectionist Horatio Alger, her sexy Cleopatra could help him to switch gears and unwind.

Gloria shared in PAIRS that when she was concentrating hard on a project, she shifted into a part that her husband, Norm, labeled the Bulldog—tenacious, ferocious, stubborn and persevering. She needed to be this way to get the job done. In this mode, she was not to be disturbed.

When Norm wanted her attention, the two parts he used that would unfailingly reach her were his Golden Retriever—eagerly wagging a nonexistent tail and seeking affection—and his Hurt Child, needy and somewhat pathetic. Either one would elicit Gloria's laughing Playmate. Norm's knowing that he could always reach her this way when he wanted to enabled her to work as intensely as she did without threatening their relationship. And, in naming their parts, they had a vocabulary they could always turn to with humor.

Exercise: Sharing, Pairing, and Comparing
Many couples who have been unhappy together find this PAIRS exercise particularly helpful. It gives them insight and a language to break long-established, destructive patterns. It also has been im-

mensely helpful to many who have been unable to sustain lasting relationships or who have had difficulties with trust, sharing and sustaining love.

Finally, this exercise is one of the most hilarious in PAIRS. In the course itself we do this exercise as a group, with class members acting out the various parts of each couple. In doing this at home as a focused exploration with a partner, using paper and pencil, you need to use your spontaneity, whimsy and imagination to let yourself go—using the language of the Inner Cast of Characters.

Set aside at least an hour for this Sharing, Pairing and Comparing parts exercise. You are going to each need your list of parts, a large sheet of newsprint or poster board and marking pens, preferably in two colors. Find a quiet, comfortable place to sit together. Bring a relaxed, humorous, accepting tone to this conversation.

STEP ONE:
First, each of you should look over your own list of parts to be sure it best represents you as you see yourself.

STEP TWO:
Now, exchange lists with your partner. Each of you read the other's list, examining it to see if it makes sense, if you have any questions about the parts that were chosen. Ask questions to clarify what each part represents. If your partner has significant parts that you feel have been left out, suggest adding them. Share with each other why you think these parts should be added. Often your partner sees sides of you that you may not have recognized and vice versa. Be open to suggestions. Look over the list of possible parts in Chapter 14 for names of parts to add.

STEP THREE:
Take back your own completed list. Now, assign a number to each of your parts, starting with one and numbering your list consecutively. Your partner does the same with his or her list.

STEP FOUR:
Using the large sheet of newsprint or poster board, take a colored marker and print your list of parts with their accompanying numbers and descriptive adjectives on one side of the sheet with your partner

doing the same, writing his or her list with the other colored marker on the other side of the sheet. Your lists of parts with their numbers now appear opposite each other, as shown below.

YOUR PARTS (ADJECTIVES)	PARTNER'S PARTS (ADJECTIVES)
1.	1.
2.	2.
3.	3.
Etc.	Etc.

The parts do not have to appear in any particular order, just so long as each has a number.

The following is a sample of Kent and Lila's parts lists and their chosen descriptions:

KENT'S PARTS	LILA'S PARTS
1. The Father—responsible, loving, compassionate	1. Thoreau—nature lover
2. The Doctor—fixes problems	2. Marie Curie—seeker of truth
3. The Indian—nature lover	3. Amelia Earhart—explorer, stubborn, persevering
4. Don Juan—world's greatest lover	4. Mama Cass—self-indulgent
5. Narcissus—very, very vain	5. Charlie Chaplin—funny, playful
6. Last of the Mohicans—righteous, judgmental	6. Sigmund Freud—insightful, wise, analytical
7. Felix Unger—perfectionist	7. Blaze Starr—sexy
8. Mr. Rogers—gentle, sharing	8. Michelangelo—artistic
9. Lewis and Clark—explorer	9. Madame Butterfly—naive, innocent, loving
10. Imelda Marcos—materialistic	10. Lord Byron—romantic, poetic
11. Howard Hughes—private, controlling, rigid	11. Superwoman—can do anything, risk taking, hard working

12. Thomas Edison—inventive, creative, curious

13. James Bond—detective, manipulative, seductive

12. Walter Mitty—dreamer

13. Mother Teresa—caring, compassionate, kind, helpful

Can you see as you look at their parts which may be in conflict, which get along well with each other?

STEP FIVE:

Now you are going to play by the numbers. You are going to look for winning combinations of numbers—those that can open the treasure chest—as well as those that "jam the safe" so it is unlikely that it will open at all. You also will match those parts that can coexist or cooperate and those that operate independently of each other. You are looking for *relationship patterns*.

Starting with your parts numbered one, discuss how they get along with each other. Mark your decision by a code next to each part. A star ★ might mean that these two parts have an excellent relationship, a check ✓ means good or okay, an × means not good, a zero ∅ means disaster. Go down your lists of parts, discussing how each numbered part gets along with each of your partner's same-numbered parts.

For example, Kent's number-one part is the Father, who probably would get along with Lila's number one, Thoreau, as well as with all of her parts except perhaps self-indulgent Mama Cass, of whom the responsible Father might be critical. On the other hand, he probably would be wonderful with Mother Teresa, unless his fathering is more for his own family and not for all of humanity, in which case there could be conflict.

Their number-two parts—the Doctor and Marie Curie—could undoubtedly find much to talk about, as one is a fixer of problems and the other a scientist who seeks answers. So that can be an excellent combination, a source of pleasure between them.

STEP SIX:

Now, when you get to parts that are in conflict with each other, discuss which other parts might be brought in to defuse the situation, or whether time out might be needed.

For example, if Kent's Doctor gets paired with Lila's Amelia Earhart, it is likely Amelia will feel constantly annoyed and pestered, because she can resolve her own problems. Kent and Lila might decide that Kent's Mr. Rogers might enjoy Amelia more, able to watch and revel in her self-sufficiency. When Lila's indulgent Mama Cass and Kent's materialistic Imelda Marcos show up, they might want to make sure that her Sigmund Freud and his Last of the Mohicans are close at hand to make sure that they really want to add that two thousand dollars on their VISA card for a quick trip to the Caribbean.

As you go through your mutual lists of parts, ask yourselves these questions:

1. Which parts antagonize each other and when? Which supportive parts can we bring in that might help (by providing wisdom, tact, humor, nurturing)?
2. When I am in my _____ part, what does it generally mean about my state, needs, and feelings? How have you typically responded to me?
3. When I am in that part, what is it that I actually need or want or don't need or want from you? How can you provide it?
4. What parts need separateness? What parts need to be encouraged? How?

Often, only common sense is needed to select the behavior or response that would detoxify the interactions between parts. Sometimes, however, the parts reflect basic beliefs that require more fundamental changes. If you encounter what seems to be a stone wall in certain areas, do not attempt to force resolution. Make a note of it in your journal and consider the tools you've learned to negotiate further.

Don't forget to focus on the positives as well as the negatives. With your partner, discuss these questions:

1. Which of your partner's parts bring you special pleasure and joy? What seems to activate them? How can you invite those parts in more often?

For instance, if his childlike, kittenish part gives you special pleasure, and it seems to occur with significant frequency when you make a bowl of popcorn to eat while watching the tube—well, it doesn't take an Einstein to figure out how to entice that part into action.

2. Which of your parts give your partner special pleasure and what brings them out? How can your partner evoke those parts in you more often? How can you make it easier for him or her to do so?

3. What other as-yet-unlinked parts can you both bring together for greater pleasure? For example, you appreciate his sober, thoughtful side (the time he needs for occasional introspection) and he enjoys your "nesting" side (the quiet pleasure you get from knitting). Perhaps, in the past, those Parts haven't been in sync. Instead, there's been competition for each other's attention at awkward times. Perhaps, rather than going off alone to claim these parts, you can enjoy quiet nesting and thinking time together.

Finally, don't limit this to a paper-and-pencil exercise. Let the concept of parts be part of your dialogue. Continue to use the parts concept with each other playfully, humorously, or in serious problem-solving discussions. The habit of self-awareness gives you the power to *choose* how to act rather than acting by rote. Tensions may lessen; everyday life can appear to be more of a smorgasbord than an obstacle course.

Continue to make choices for yourself as Captain of your ship and crew, so that you don't find yourself in Baltimore instead of the Bahamas, if the Bahamas is really where you'd like to be.

Take a moment to write in your journal notebook about what you are beginning to realize.

SECTION IV

Pleasuring

■   ■   ■

Without caring context, sexual intimacy is
just seduction, exploitation, manipulation,
depersonalization, a cushion against loneliness, a thrill, a duty, a diversion, a habit, a
way to burn up calories. It becomes an arena
in which to act out everything from aggression and anxiety to power and punishment—everything but love and sexual
pleasure.

—*George Bach and Laura Torbet,*
A Time for Caring

17

Encouraging Pleasure

■　　　■　　　■

We choose to be together, to make a commitment, because we take pleasure in one another. If a relationship loses its luster and we begin to feel alone, or even to feel tormented, it is because, somehow, the pleasure between us has dissipated or disappeared.

Much of marital counseling, and indeed much of PAIRS, concentrates on the things that we do that interfere with or block that pleasure—the fight styles that create confusion instead of harmony; the harsh disappointment we experience when one of our hidden expectations is not met; the chaos caused when one of our suppressed parts seizes the wheel and lands us on a reef. Even without these hidden barriers, the challenges to keeping pleasure alive are many.

For many of us it is growing harder every day to draw pleasure from our relationships. Between work, children, growing economic pressure and a society that provides entertainment and diversion at the push of a button, pleasure between two people can easily be squeezed out. If we are to be anchored on the pleasure side of the Relationship Road Map, pleasure needs to be carefully cultivated.

Pleasure between intimates, like a Japanese garden, has many components that all need attention. A successful Japanese gardener draws together all the elements of nature—water, rock, wood and

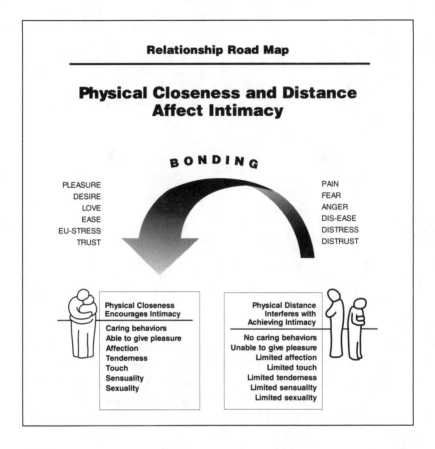

Relationship Road Map

Physical Closeness and Distance Affect Intimacy

BONDING

PLEASURE	PAIN
DESIRE	FEAR
LOVE	ANGER
EASE	DIS-EASE
EU-STRESS	DISTRESS
TRUST	DISTRUST

Physical Closeness Encourages Intimacy

Caring behaviors
Able to give pleasure
Affection
Tenderness
Touch
Sensuality
Sexuality

Physical Distance Interferes with Achieving Intimacy

No caring behaviors
Unable to give pleasure
Limited affection
Limited touch
Limited tenderness
Limited sensuality
Limited sexuality

plants—to create a spiritual atmosphere of serenity and unity. When two people create that same spiritual quality between them, we call it love and romance. That sense of unity arrives only when our whole being—the primitive brain, the creature brain and the intellectual brain—is in a state of deep, satisfying pleasure.

These three "brains" experience pleasure when their separate needs are met. So our challenge as a couple is to address the needs of each.

The most primitive part of our brain needs to feel safe. By doing the exercises in the first three sections of this book, we help create this sense of safety by reconditioning the primitive brain, teaching it that situations (like being close) that may have once been dangerous are safe now. The primitive brain is very physical. Dr. Harville Hendrix, author of *Getting the Love You Want*, believes that this sense of safety is greatly enhanced when we do physical things together so that our primitive selves get to know and feel joy with one another. He suggests having a "fun list" of physical things that stimulate this part of ourselves, such as wrestling, tickling or otherwise roughhousing together, as well as taking time for the sensual (with sex and massages) and to be active (exercising together). All these activities bring comfort to the primitive self and make it feel less defensive.

The creature brain needs to feel nurtured and cared for. It is drawn to things that make it feel good emotionally. Loving touch, comforting, loving words and generous gestures are among the things that bring the creature brain pleasure. We can add here as well fun, excitement, laughter and play, sensuality and sex.

The intellectual brain seems to have three chief and distinct needs. First, it needs to be able to make sense of things. For it to be content, it needs to feel as if things are in order. Second, it needs to be challenged and exercised, just like our bodies. It loves recreation, stimulation through books, movies, the arts and conversation. Third, it needs to rest and relax. This is the part that governs us during much of the day and grows weary. It looks to find safety for the primitive part and pleasure for the creature part so it can occasionally turn the reins of the self over to them and take time off from thinking.

- Do you make time for pleasure in your relationship, or do you feel as if fun things always need to be put on hold until all of your work and responsibilities are completed?
- Do your fun activities include your partner?
- Do those activities address the needs of all three parts of your "triune brain," or just one or two of them?

PAIRS Exercise: Caring Behavior

We need to think about what gives us pleasure. Many people are surprised to find that they are so used to thinking about what pleases their partner, or being irritated about things they wish their partner would or wouldn't do, that they have trouble actually pinpointing what would make them feel more content.

The point of this exercise is, first, to make a list of the little things that your partner does or could do to give you pleasure, delight you, excite you, make you happy, make your life better. Write the list on a piece of paper that you can pin up in the bathroom, put on the refrigerator or keep some place where you both have access to it.

Be specific. Don't say "I want you to love me." Indicate which behavior(s) tell you that you are loved. Your partner may feel that going to work, earning a living and bringing home a paycheck is showing love, when what makes you feel loved is a phone call every afternoon, a warm embrace when you arrive home or leave in the morning, and perhaps flowers now and then.

Don't censor yourself as you prepare your list. Write down the first things that come to your mind. List at least twelve things, but don't limit yourself. And if you think of something a few days later, add it. If you have difficulty thinking of behavior that gives you pleasure, think of things that happened when you were dating or in your courtship—and things that you always wished would happen but perhaps didn't.

Here are some caring behaviors others have listed:

I FEEL CARED ABOUT (OR I LOVE IT) WHEN YOU:

Give me a massage (not *only* as a prelude to sex)
Give me a bath and wash my hair
Initiate sex
Ask me about my work or how I'm feeling or how my day went and really want to know
Plan an evening out instead of my planning it
Kiss me good-bye in the morning
Hold my hand in the movies
Put your arm around my shoulder or your hand on the back of my neck

Rub my head or play with my hair

Do one of "my" chores (for example, make dinner, wash the
dishes, mow the lawn)

Open the door for me

Exercise with me

Are nice to my mother (friends, and so forth)

Call me during the day

Give me loving notes

Bring me flowers on my birthday and our anniversary

Hold me in the morning before we get up

Bring me coffee in bed

Secretly arrange to have the children stay at a friend's house for
the night.

You might include a section for special circumstances:

When I am sick, I love it when you . . .

When I am tired, I love it when you . . .

When I am worried, I love it when you . . .

When I am afraid, I love it when you . . .

When I am unhappy, I love it when you . . .

For celebrations, I love it when you . . .

When you have finished your lists, exchange them, or put them
up where your partner can read them. Then, during the next seven
days, try to do at least three things on your partner's list each day.
For these seven days, you don't need to do more than three. Avoid
the temptation of turning this into a competition. Enjoy what you
can give as well as what you receive.

As an added delight, have a surprise list wherein you can spon-
taneously surprise your partner with things you've privately noted
he or she would like. And add to the list activities that are exuberant,
playful and fun to do with each other, and do them!

At the end of each day, acknowledge what you noticed that your
partner did. Point out what you did that he or she didn't notice.
At the end of the week, sit down and talk about whether the caring
behavior made a difference in how you felt toward each other. The
growth of love often involves a reciprocal exchange of pleasure: it's
human nature to seek out pleasure, and it's human nature to want

to be noticed for the positive things we've done. Caring behavior, nurtured and appreciated, helps create the atmosphere in which pleasure and love can thrive.

CARING BEHAVIOR LIST

Name _____   _____ Did it today

(partner's name)

1										
2.										
3.										
4.										
5.										
6.										
7.										
8.										
9.										
10.										
11.										
12.										

INSTRUCTIONS

1. List twelve or more specific behaviors that your partner could perform that make you feel cared about, special, important.
2. Post the list where it can be seen each day.
3. Perform at least three caring behaviors from your partner's list each day.
4. Review both lists each night:
   a. On your list put the date in a box beside each behavior your partner performed that day and thank your partner for the caring you received.

b. With your partner's list, note if there were positive behaviors you performed that your partner didn't notice or mark and, if so, gently call attention to them.

5. *Enjoy!*

Because pleasure is essential to any healthy relationship, this is one of the most crucial exercises in PAIRS. If you find yourself balking or withholding, you need to take the risk and go ahead and include these caring behaviors in your daily regimen anyway. You also need to explore what is behind these feelings. Many of us have a large Rebel part or are stuck in our adolescent stage of maturity. We deeply resist being told or asked to do something. Use the parts exercises and the other exercises for the self to learn how to remove these barriers.

Take a moment to write in your journal notebook about what you are beginning to realize.

18

Bonding

■　　　　■　　　　■

Of all the qualities we seek from an intimate relationship, the most elusive is a feeling of wholeness. We expect, without really knowing how, that our partner will make us feel complete in soul. We often experience this sense of unity in the physical and emotional passion of sex, but many of us find this all too fleeting.

If we continue to seek this sense of wholeness only through sex and still find emptiness, our sex life can become thin because we expect too much from it. The path I have found to the spiritual realm that can be known only as a couple is through bonding—physical closeness between two people who are emotionally open with each other.

Many of us have never experienced the pleasure of adult bonding because we learned early in life that our need for closeness was a source of pain and rejection rather than pleasure. Perhaps childhood experiences convinced us that it wasn't safe to confide in anyone, that no one wanted to know what we thought or felt and that our lives would be safe only when we were controlled, controlling, productive, and competent—not giving, close or loving. Many of us see bonding as potential bondage. We are so worried about losing our freedom that we never attain the depth of fulfillment that comes from true closeness.

Some of us may have experienced bonding briefly and then lost it. Often we are scared off by such internal warnings as, "It won't last," or "You can't count on others," or "Don't set yourself up for heartbreak," or "There'll be too high a price to pay." If any of this sounds familiar, it's important for you to begin to dissolve the defenses you have built against closeness. You may be living in a fortress you once needed but no longer do, so that now it may have become your prison.

One of the key problems that brings couples to therapy is an apparent difference in sexual desire. Often the husband complains that his wife is either uninterested or not as interested as he in sex. The wife's counter complaint is usually that closeness always has to end in sex, so that she often keeps her distance because even though she feels affectionate she might not feel like making love. Often one or both of them will say how lonely they feel, even when they are together, or how empty they feel after lovemaking.

For couples like this, sex has often become a substitute for bonding as well as a defense against closeness. Once couples learn to recognize the difference between their sexual needs and their need for bonding and begin experiencing the pleasure of bonding regularly (at bedtime, perhaps, or first thing in the morning), it is amazing how often discrepancies between their sexual needs tend to even out.

SOME BENEFITS OF BONDING

Bonding can be effective in alleviating anxiety since it allows feelings to surface that for one reason or another have been repressed. Many couples know just by holding each other whether their partner is hurting or feels drained and needs to be held and healed, the way a parched plant needs to be watered. One PAIRS participant said that bonding with her husband was like "hugging each other against the cruel world. I used to associate snuggling more with sex or affection. Now I think of it more as a physical sanctuary we have created."

Lloyd is an architect who troubleshoots everything from complex design problems to petty office squabbles all day. He describes bonding as a powerful antidote to stress. The child of a distant father and an unpredictable, alcoholic mother, he experienced his early home life as painful and anxiety producing.

"It churned me up inside and made me really needy, but there was nowhere to go to get those needs met. I entered adult life with a terrible deficit. And (like many children of alcoholics) I'm a caretaker. I'm inclined to give all day, and am not real good at receiving, even when it's offered. I wish I operated in such a way that I came home all pumped up by the experiences of the day, but I don't: By the end of the day I am empty—I almost feel an emptiness in my chest.

"Bonding has become particularly important to me, because it's one area where I've acquired the ability to take in a big way. When Evelyn and I lie together, with our arms around each other, her head on my chest and her legs draped over mine, it's as if I literally experience a direct transmission of warming energy from her; it comes in like a salve, transforming and very healing. It's when the need is acute—particularly when I'm stressed out and have a lot of anxiety—that that kind of feeling is very dramatic. Other times, it's like warm milk. I'll awaken in the middle of the night worrying about an office problem and bonding will put me back to sleep. It brings on a deep sense of security and peacefulness."

The bonding has changed the way Lloyd relates to his children:

"I followed my mother's pattern of looking to children for comfort and physical contact to meet my own needs. Increasingly I take bonding into my marriage relationship where it belongs. Now my focus can be on responding to my children when they need it and not when I need it. I can be the parent treating them like children, instead of being the child looking to them to be my parent—to make up for the parents who weren't there when I needed physical and psychological support, to make up for the vacuum."

When our creature self is content and relaxed, when we feel calm, safe and connected with our partner, our thinking is no longer colored by panic, rage, doubt or torment and we are free to think clearly and creatively.

Holding each other first and talking later is a wonderful strategy for reducing the frequency, intensity and destructiveness of fights.

When we try to deal with an emotional situation "rationally," we often say things we don't mean and later regret having said. By lying together closely and accepting each other, anger and all, couples are far more likely to discover the hurt that almost always underlies withdrawal or angry explosions and can avoid letting an upsetting episode escalate and become even more hurtful. Bonding is often most effective with highly verbal individuals for whom words have become an elaborate defense against feelings, a way almost of talking emotions to death.

Bonding is particularly effective in helping us become aware of preverbal memories—memories that often have to do with physical fears (of being abandoned, for example, or shaken, or beaten, or neglected) or early deprivation of loving, trusting closeness. For this reason, when two people first begin to bond, they may find themselves uncovering and needing to express a real backlog of emotions based on past history. What may appear to be an emotional overreaction to a current situation is often simply the surfacing of an overload of unexpressed feelings from childhood or previous difficult experiences.

Once we understand our own emotional histories, feelings about which we might once have gotten defensive are suddenly less threatening, and bonding with each other becomes increasingly a source of pleasure. It can be addictive, too—in a positive way—which is what lasting love is all about.

PAIRS Exercise: Bonding

Find a quiet time and place to lie down together in a total-body cuddling position. You can lie down side by side facing each other and nestle together spoon-fashion or lie with one partner on top. Hold your partner as you would hold a beloved, trusted teddy bear. Allow yourself to relax. Let your feelings surface, whatever they are—trust or distrust, need, fear or pleasure in closeness. Allow yourself to feel them and in some brief way let your partner know what you are feeling: "I feel really good," for example, or "I feel upset." Allow your partner to continue holding you as you experience your feelings, trusting your partner to hold on and just be there for you. Allow your sense of separate identities to dissolve. Do this for ten minutes or more.

Now reverse it. You be the teddy bear for your partner. Just hold each other for pleasure, for closeness, for comfort. Stay this way as long as you can, allowing whatever feelings are there to surface.

If something makes it difficult for you to lie closely with your partner like this, think about what it may be, share your awareness with your partner and keep holding on. Do this until you achieve a feeling of peacefulness, of greater calm and relaxation. When you do, savor it. Allow yourself to take it in and experience it fully. This is what bonding is about.

Because this exercise is indeed the heart of intimacy, there may be a lot of difficult emotions surrounding bonding. If your partner seems reluctant or uncomfortable, do not nag or pressure him or her. If your partner seems unwilling to talk about this reluctance, consider seeking professional help for both of you, or at least for yourself, to deal with the disappointment.

Write about your feelings in your journal. Were your feelings during bonding positive or negative? Did you feel peaceful and loving, or did you experience anxiety, pain or anger? Were you able to express your feelings freely? Was it easy for you to take this "time out"? Did you feel connected to your partner? Did you feel your partner responding? Is this something you would like to do regularly?

Many couples choose to start and end the day with bonding. They say that without it the day is missing something—the pleasure they give to and get from each other.

A BIOLOGICAL NEED

The need for bonding is a basic part of our biological heritage *from infancy on*. The inability to fill this need gives rise to many symptoms—including depression, illness, anxiety, tension and feelings of emptiness, loneliness, helplessness and despair, the by-products of a society that highly values self-sufficiency and being "cool."

Encouraged by our culture to deny or conceal our feelings and our need for closeness, many of us try to fill the void with such psychic painkillers as drugs, alcohol, food and sex. We often immerse ourselves in our work, children, home, church or good deeds—or act out our dissatisfaction through rebellion, antisocial behavior or violence. Yet the feeling of incompleteness lingers. Our emotional distress and isolation may reveal themselves in such physical symptoms as migraines, hypertension, muscle spasms and ulcers.

People who are starved for bonding often feel tense and unhappy, but they can rarely pinpoint the cause of their discomfort, except that they do not feel a sense of belonging, of being at home with themselves or others.

Some people who are starved for bonding show no apparent symptoms. Often they have shut down emotionally. Perhaps they chose (usually at a very early age) to settle for feeling empty or neutral rather than continue to experience hurt or deprivation. They feel nothing, much the way someone who has not eaten for four or five days finally stops feeling hunger pangs. They don't realize that you can continue to starve after you have stopped feeling hungry.

Many of us who are fearful of physical and emotional closeness find pets a safe outlet for our affectional needs; for people living alone they are sometimes the only outlet. Indeed, pets play an enormously important role in many of our lives and may be especially important to the emotional development of children. Pets aren't as capable as we are of learning emotional and physical inhibition, and as they openly present their needs for closeness and affection, they often allow us to meet our own needs with a freedom many of us will not allow with another person.

EARLY CONDITIONING

For many couples, developing the ability to sustain emotional closeness means unlearning early conditioning that has colored their beliefs about the acceptability of feeling such emotions as pain, fear and anger, as well as the more positive emotions of pleasure and love. Sex-based differences in our conditioning often cause us to misread each other's cues for closeness. And many people are so unaware of their need for physical and emotional connection that they are doomed to a frustration they can't even identify.

This is often especially true of men, who are frequently conditioned to control or hide their feelings or needs for closeness—all too often from themselves as well as others. Whereas women tend to have more problems accepting and expressing feelings of anger, men are more likely to have trouble accepting and expressing feelings of pain, fear and the need for love—although plenty of men also have trouble with anger. Many men need to learn that a woman's tears are not necessarily manipulative, nor do they necessarily signify pain. Many women, conditioned to suppress anger or fear, cry tears of rage, frustration or even panic. The most loving thing a man can do in this case is to put away his own defenses and encourage his partner to let out her feelings. Both men and women are usually surprised to learn that an angry explosion in a man often hides fear or pain. Once couples understand the interplay of their individual conditioning, their response to each other's behavior quickly becomes more supportive.

Conditioning also affects our attitudes about physical closeness. Many fathers stop hugging their pubescent daughters. Males are generally conditioned earlier than females not to expect physical closeness, to feel that cuddling or needing to be close to another person is not acceptable or manly.

Body contact sports offer boys one acceptable way to be close to people as they are growing up. Sports offer a kind of camaraderie, as well as backslapping and wrestling that may satisfy part of their natural skin hunger. (Judging from the number of pleasure receptors in our skin, nature seems to have intended that we experience the pleasure of touch often.) Then, in adolescence, boys learn that sex is an acceptable way to want to be close to females, and sex becomes a way to fulfill their need for bonding. Affection, closeness, sensuality and sexuality all get rolled into one act, and for many people the sex gets so mixed up with performance ("Am I good enough?") and competition ("Will he [or she] prefer others?") that it's hard to relax and just take in the nourishment that comes from being physically close to each other.

PAIRS Exercise: Affection—Your Family Models

Caring, tenderness and affection may be shown in three basic ways:

Physically: by touching, caressing, patting and other gestures
Verbally: with words and tones of affection
By Deeds: by actions, deeds or special effort to please

In any family, affection may be conveyed in some ways and not others—through hugs, say, rather than in words. Affection may be conveyed through cookie-baking sessions, bedtime backrubs and hours spent playing games together.

How was affection shown in your family? Write about it in your journal and fill in the following chart (check one or more):

	Physically	Verbally	By Deeds or Action
Father showed affection for mother			
Father showed affection for me			
Mother showed affection for father			
Mother showed affection for me			
I show affection for my partner			
My partner shows affection for me			

Was there a difference in the affection your mother and father showed you and what they showed to your siblings or to each other? How did that affect you?

- I would like to be able to show more affection for my partner by . . .
- What blocks me is . . .
- I wish my partner would show more affection for me by . . .

> • One moment of affection with my partner that stands out
> vividly in my memory is . . .

Think about what you have written in your journal. What patterns do you see unfolding? Does your partner show affection one way and you another? Do either of you end up feeling unloved because you show affection in different ways or amounts?

When you have both completed this exercise, sit down together and compare notes. Which emotions do each of you experience but not express? Do you know why? Can your partner do anything to make it easier for you to express the feelings you have difficulty expressing but would like to be able to share?

If you have difficulty comparing notes about this exercise, consider making some insights part of your Daily Temperature Reading: "I realize that I don't tell you about . . ." "I could more easily talk about these feelings if you . . ." (wouldn't advise, judge, correct, discuss, laugh and so forth).

Under stress, we may need more bonding than usual.

Jerry, for example, had a serious and unexpected business loss, and he feared that his entire career and financial investment might go up in smoke. He spent an entire weekend bonding with his wife, Lila, who held and nurtured him while he woefully expressed his doubts and fears. At the end of the weekend, he found he could think clearly enough to return to the office and call a meeting of his staff. There he conducted himself with such poise and control that the catastrophe was averted. When he asked his wife if she was upset by his need over the weekend, she laughed and said, "Well, if it went on for years I might need a short break, but I'm glad I could be there for you."

BONDING AND SEX

Being held or holding may lead to sexual arousal and as such it is a part of foreplay. Or it may be the expression of our deepest nonsexual longings. It is now recognized that these are needs that exist early in life and throughout life. In a compatible marriage, nonsexual as well as sexual desires—childlike as well as more adult needs—are gratified.

Set aside time for bonding that you agree in advance will not be specifically sexual. The main reason for this is to *help you appreciate the difference between sex and bonding*. If it is clear to both bonding partners that there will be no sex, neither partner need be preoccupied with worries about whether they will be able to perform, whether they will seduce or be seduced or control or be controlled by the other.

TAKING PLEASURE IN EACH OTHER

Taking pleasure in each other is a habit that some couples have to acquire. Some people enjoy the pleasures of closeness only as caretakers: They can "give" closeness, if it serves a caretaking function, but they can't seek closeness for themselves. Others do everything they think they "should" do and then wait for closeness to be "given" to them, like the pat on the head they hoped for when they were good little girls and boys.

In a way this is to be expected. As children we are dependent on our parents to satisfy our needs, and parents often attach a lot of conditions to meeting those needs. If, as children, we routinely greeted father, exhausted and grumpy after a hard day at the office, with displays of affection, we may have been ignored or, at best, given a brief and perfunctory pat or kiss. The message received loud and clear in such a situation is that it's "wrong" or "painful" to express affection and stupid to expect a warm response. Thus, the concept of taking pleasure is foreign to many of us. We don't realize how it feels when someone we love reaches out and holds us because we are a pleasure to them. Perhaps we do not realize that this can be a pleasure, or perhaps we're afraid of rejection or of seeming to be selfish. We're so busy being self-effacing and noble and doing good deeds that we don't realize that *taking pleasure in our partner is the very thing our partner needs from us—that bonding is a gift we give each other*. We need to experience that we can each be a genuine pleasure to the other.

Take a moment to write in your journal notebook about what you are beginning to realize.

19

Sexuality: Beyond Fantasy and Friction

■   ■   ■

$\mathscr{B}$onding helps us achieve wholeness as a couple through depth and serenity, rocking and comforting us as if we were in a boat on gentle waters. Sexuality leads us there through passion, lust, desire and intensity, as if we were shooting down a hill on a toboggan.

Our male or female sexual essence is expressed in all of our emotional, intellectual, physical and fantasy experiences and responses and relationships—in all the ways in which we take and give comfort, pleasure, challenge, meaning and stimulation to those of the same as well as the opposite sex. Our sexuality embraces our need for affection, closeness, touching, communication, sharing, relating—in short, our need for "being"—as well as our need for release of the neural and physiological tensions accumulated during sexual arousal.

PAIRS Exercise: How Satisfactory is Your Sex Life?

All too often, we expect sex to take care of itself. We often are anxious about discussing our sex lives with our partners because we fear it is inappropriate or somehow will detract from the mystery. This silence, as well as other attitudes we have about sex, only prevents us from gaining knowledge about our individual tastes and desires that can deepen our sex lives. This exercise is designed to help you evaluate your sex life, chiefly geared to making it easier for you to talk with your partner about anything either of you experiences as a sexual problem in your relationship.

Write the numbers 1 to 42, corresponding to the items below, in your journal. Next to each number, indicate your level of satisfaction with that aspect of your sexual life by writing a score next to it—with a high of 5 for very satisfied and a low of 1 for very unsatisfied. If you find that giving a high or low score to a particular aspect of your sex life makes you feel awkward, embarrassed, uncomfortable, shy, fearful, guilty, inadequate, indignant, proud, sexy and so forth, make note of this in your journal—but score it honestly anyway.

Remember, the scores are 5 for very satisfied, 4 for somewhat satisfied, 3 for neither satisfied nor dissatisfied, 2 for somewhat unsatisfied, and 1 for very unsatisfied.

1. How we decide to have sex
2. How often I initiate sex
3. How often partner initiates sex
4. How often we engage in sex
5. Partner's way of initiating sex
6. My way of initiating sex
7. Partner's way of saying "no" to sex
8. Setting in which we engage in sex
9. My level of interest in sex
10. My partner's level of interest
11. Time of day we engage in sex
12. The degree of privacy we have
13. Method of birth control we use
14. How my body looks
15. How my partner's body looks
16. Cleanliness and aroma of partner's body
17. Time and attention given to foreplay and buildup of passion
18. Variety of foreplay
19. Partner's knowledge of my erogenous zones
20. My knowledge of my partner's erogenous zones
21. Time spent in intercourse

22. Partner's intensity of passion
23. My intensity of passion
24. Position(s) used in intercourse
25. Degree of sexual experimentation
26. Frequency of my orgasms
27. Frequency of my partner's orgasms
28. My degree of fulfillment from foreplay
29. My degree of fulfillment from orgasm
30. My degree of fulfillment from afterglow
31. My partner's apparent sexual fulfillment
32. Amount and style of affection partner shows before sex is initiated
33. Amount and style of affection partner shows before climax
34. Amount and style of affection partner shows after climax
35. Amount of affection I show before sex is initiated
36. Amount of affection I show before climax
37. Amount of affection I show after climax
38. Amount of nonsexual affection
39. Ease with which we discuss sex
40. Our sexual compatibility in terms of level of mutual desire
41. Our sexual compatibility in terms of kind of sex we enjoy
42. Our sexual compatibility in terms of desire for sexual variety

Go through your list now and count the number of 5s, 4s, 3s, 2s, and 1s you scored. There is nothing scientific about this, and there is no point, really, in coming up with a grand total. What you want is a general sense of how satisfied you are and a feeling for the areas in which you are not so satisfied. If you give yourself all 3s, and are quite happy with your sex life, you've won half the battle. Problems arise either when your level of dissatisfaction is relatively high, or when there is a marked discrepancy between your scores and your partner's. If more than a third of your scores are 1s and 2s, or if one of you is experiencing all 3s, 4s and 5s and the other is experiencing quite a few 1s and 2s, you have some work to do. Take heart, however: You can begin that work here by identifying the areas of your dissatisfaction. In this chapter you will discover some tools that many others have found helpful in raising their level of sexual satisfaction.

Do you think your scores are very different from the scores your partner is recording? Can you detect a pattern in your scoring? Are you unsatisfied with the preliminaries to sex, for example, or with the degree of variety and experimentation, or with the amount of affection shown or what? Are there items on this list that belong on an *Issues* page of your journal? Can you think of a specific request for change that might turn a low score into a higher score? If you write "1" next to "The degree of privacy we have," for example, can you think of ways to assure more privacy—perhaps installing a lock on the bedroom door; teaching your children to respect your need for occasional privacy away from them (training them to honor a "Do Not Disturb" sign); hiring a babysitter to take the children out of the house now and then, so you aren't distracted by their presence nearby; purchasing a telephone answering machine, or at least a telephone on which you can turn off the bell?

MYTHS AND FALLACIES ABOUT SEX

One of the best ways to increase sexual pleasure is to discover and discard many of the myths and fallacies about what constitutes good sex, inherited family attitudes that cast a shadow on your pleasure and stresses that prevent us from experiencing the full range of sexual intimacy.

There is an almost endless list of myths about sexual behavior and functions. It may be useful to focus on just a few myths that seem curiously prevalent even among sexually aware moderns. * Confusion and myths are inevitable, of course, in a society that permits its youngsters to be exposed to two such basic and contradictory messages as "Sex is dirty!" and "Save it for the one you love!" Even the recent sexual enlightenment movement is giving rise to equally harmful fallacies.

Male expertise. Some people still believe that the male is inherently endowed with special sexual knowledge and capability: that he instinctively knows what the female wants or needs and should be the guide and instructor. Essentially, this makes him responsible for the quality of the couple's sexual performance. This also makes it improper for the female to take the initiative or to be sexually sophisticated and expressive. That we can all agree intellectually that

For a more complete list, read Male Sexuality by Bernie Zilbergeld.

this is absurd doesn't obliterate the emotional impact (the male's sense of insecurity and the female's sense of guilt) when the female proves to have more sexual imagination or practical skills.

Orgasm. The idea that intercourse is best only when there is simultaneous orgasm is a relatively recent fixation. No doubt when orgasm is simultaneous by coincidence or design it heightens mutual satisfaction, and there's no reason why a couple that prefers it shouldn't strive for it. But many aspects of the male and female arousal patterns make simultaneous orgasm a relative rarity—and it's absurd to straitjacket the full expression of sexual feelings with such a mechanical detail. You can make it important, just as you can make it important not to step on sidewalk cracks, but you can lose a lot of the joy of sex in the process.

Performance. The sexual liberation movement has tended, perhaps understandably, to result in an inordinate emphasis on sex as physical skills and athletic prowess—on dexterity, technique and the number of orgasms, rather than on the quality of what goes on between the two partners. By and large, during the dark ages of "unmentionable sex," technique was so thoroughly ignored that the current emphasis on it was inevitable and is, in many respects, healthy. But the pendulum seems to have swung too far. Focus on technique removes the participants from all the other elements that a total sexual experience should contain: the spontaneity, the exploring and childish fun, the unprogrammed tenderness and the genuine sharing of each other's pleasure that can come only with total immersion of "self" and "other" in the moment. Technique also tends to result in excessive genital focus—ignoring the fact that your partner's *entire* body is a rich field of insatiable sensual and sexual responsiveness and gratification. You can have an orgasm and lousy sex; by the same token, you can have a memorable sexual experience without an orgasm.

Spontaneity. While we should be spontaneous during sex, we needn't be spontaneous *about* sex. We carefully plan dinner parties, work schedules and almost everything else in our daily routine—but we're cavalier about setting aside time for one of the most important aspects of our lives. This is no doubt partly due to the understandable feeling that planned sex may be somewhat mechanical, but it needn't be. While we should never downgrade the fortuitous "nooner," we owe it to ourselves to be sure that we create plenty of time and optimum circumstances for sex "dates" with our partner.

Stereotyping. One of the most deep-rooted and harmful fallacies is the assumption that all people get turned on sexually in much the same way—that is, in the way *you* do. Even more harmful is the assumption that, if they don't, they *ought* to—because that's the "normal" way. There *is* no "normal" way; we're all quite idiosyncratic in the ways in which we get aroused. We'll go into this in more detail in the exercises in this chapter, but the basic point is that each one of us is responsible for getting in touch with what it is that actually turns us on. This is apt to require considerable self-examination (physical, emotional and intellectual) and honesty, for it's a topic most of us have ignored—either because it seemed silly (our turn-ons were obvious) or because it was threatening (our turn-ons seemed embarrassing or "abnormal"). And, finally, it may take some courage—because it is also our responsibility to communicate our wants and needs to our partner. The evidence seems quite clear: Most poor sex stems from poor communication, from misunderstanding of what one's mate actually wants—*not* from unwillingness or inability to give it.

THE EFFECT OF FAMILY ATTITUDES

Sex often functions as a barometer, reflecting general strengths and weaknesses in a couple's interactions. It may also serve as a dumping ground for issues that haven't been worked out elsewhere— whether they have to do with failure, boredom, monotony, power, performance, pleasure, intimacy, anger or anxiety. The woman who rebuffs her partner may be trying, passively, to redress an imbalance of power in other areas of the relationship. When a couple gets into a pattern of one partner demanding and the other partner withholding, the problem is rarely sexual at its base.

The following sentence completions, from Dr. Nathaniel Branden's guide, *If You Could Hear What I Cannot Say*, can be useful in increasing self-understanding about intimacy. If you compare responses with your partner, they can make you both aware of areas in which sensitivities may linger. In your journal, complete these sentences:

Mother gave me the sense that my body was . . .
Mother gave me the sense that sex was . . .
Mother gave me a view of men as . . .
Mother gave me a view of women as . . .
Mother gave me the sense that love was . . .
One of the unspoken messages I got from my mother about love
   was . . .
When my mother touched or held me, I felt . . .
Father gave me the sense that my body was . . .
Father gave me the sense that sex was . . .
Father gave me a view of men as . . .
Father gave me a view of women as . . .
Father gave me the sense that love was . . .
One of the unspoken messages I got from my father about love
   was . . .
When my father touched or held me, I felt . . .
I am becoming aware . . .
I am beginning to suspect . . .

Sex is a subject so many parents feel uncomfortable discussing
with their children that you shouldn't be surprised if it's hard for
you to get a fix on your sexual attitudes, even with this exercise.

Discuss your journal writings with each other, and explore as
openly as you can any aspects of sex or sensuality about which you
feel inhibited, sensitive or inadequate. It may help if you can see
the humor in some of your hang-ups. When asked which ghosts
were in the bedroom with her, for example, one PAIRS participant
who had compared herself unfavorably with every movie star from
Marilyn Monroe on responded, "The cameramen from Metro-Gold-
wyn-Mayer."

While you are reviewing the ghosts in your bedroom, think
about how you deal with issues of assertion and control. If you
didn't get much past the infant stage of emotional development in
this connection, you may approach sex with the "I want what I want
when I want it" attitude. This won't work for very long. If you got
stuck in the good-girl or good-boy stage, you may assume that if
you are obedient and helpful your partner will reward you with
great pleasures. The trouble is, your partner can't read your mind

any more easily in bed than elsewhere, so you may not be happy with what you get.

If you got sidetracked in the adolescent stage of development, you most likely have a problem with power. *"Don't tell me what to do"* *is lethal in the bedroom.* The adolescent is saying, "If you tell me what you want, I feel it's an attempt to control me, to treat me like a child. The minute you tell me what will give you pleasure, that's the last thing in the world I will give you." Sexual pleasure deteriorates into a power struggle with no winners.

You can assume that stress is one of the enemies in your bedroom if more than a couple of the following seem familiar to you:

Sex sometimes seems like more trouble than it's worth.

Household chores and office responsibilities get in the way of sex.

You think about these responsibilities while you are making love.

You feel guilty taking time for sex.

You feel imposed upon when your partner shows an interest in lovemaking.

You get impatient when your partner takes too long to become aroused or reach a climax.

You feel that physical pleasure is a waste of time.

You get restless when sex lasts too long.

You make love when you are tired.

You fail to reserve special time for sexual rendezvous.

We all feel too much pressure some of the time, but if you suspect that the pressures in your life are chronic, you may have to make a special effort to spend less time tending your garden and take more time to smell the roses.

Don't expect your partner to guess what pleases you. Figure out for yourself what stimulates and satisfies you and ask for it, or take it. It's not enough to give and receive—we also have to be able to speak up or reach out on our own behalf and take. Ideally, sexual love will be a flow of this give and take—but it has to go both ways in order to keep desire alive.

THE ENEMIES OF SEX

The greatest enemies of sex are:

Lack of time and failure to schedule pleasure in our lives. Are you spending all your time earning money for the holiday and forgetting to take the holiday (or as psychiatrist Dan Casriel used to say, spending all of your time cleaning the barn and forgetting to ride the pony)? If you are putting all of your energy into work and social engagements and failing to reserve time to take pleasure in each other, sit down right now and make a commitment to spend at least one evening a week alone together. Make occasional dates for sex, and vary the timing and setting of your sexual dates.

Remember that sex requires energy. Don't expect your partner to be eager for lovemaking if he or she is ill or tired. Schedule sex for your peak, not your off-peak, energy hours. Don't delay it until bedtime, if you are usually ready then to collapse with fatigue. You'll probably feel a lot friskier earlier in the evening, first thing in the morning or on a Saturday afternoon.

One or both partners' lack of desire or an imbalance between their frequency of desire. Many times lack of desire has emotional roots. Indifference and boredom are often simply a disguise for unexpressed anger and resentment over unresolved issues and grievances. The upsetting emotions associated with stress can also short-circuit desire so that we aren't as responsive as we should be. Chronic stress about such issues as work, money or health can seriously undermine sexual desire.

Sometimes the feelings that inhibit desire are conscious, sometimes unconscious. We may be inhibited because we dislike or mistrust our partner, for example, or are fearful of pregnancy, infertility, pain or being judged (anxiety about sexual performance is a common killer of desire). Or we may unconsciously fear punishment, losing control or the deeper commitment that the sexual encounter implies. When such fears run deep, therapy may be called for.

The misuse of sex—for example, to manipulate or exploit, as a bargaining tool or a weapon, to relieve anxiety or as a substitute for bonding and affection. Because sex is such a powerful part of a couple's bond it is tempting to use sex for leverage or to withhold it to get even or to avoid feeling controlled, particularly if it is the only weapon you feel you have. In the long run, the misuse of sex will backfire by diminishing an important avenue of pleasure, and may ultimately destroy sex for both partners.

Ignorance and misinformation, often reinforced by the belief that talking about sex robs it of spontaneity and romance. Underlying much sexual dissatisfaction is the inappropriate belief, "If you loved me, you would know what I want without my having to tell you." Men and women are so different sexually that in this area more than most others it is simply folly to expect your partner to read your mind. It is important to let your partner know what gives you pleasure and to take heed of your partner's desires in your love-making. Unrealistic expectations also play havoc with many couples' sex lives. One of the things we'll ask you to do in this chapter is to begin identifying and communicating your sexual expectations.

PAIRS Exercise: A Guided Face Caress

This face and head massage is a wonderful restorative. You can also use it to teach each other what feels good for you—where you like a firm, deep stroke and where a lighter one, and where you prefer not to be touched at all. Many of us assume, often incorrectly, that our partner will like the same things we do. Use this exercise initially to discover your own and your partner's preferences, and use it thereafter as a gift of pleasure.

Allow ten minutes to half an hour for this exercise. Dim the lights, turn on soft music and have your partner lie on a mat or bed in front of you, with his or her head harbored between your legs. For back support, lean against a wall or the headboard of the bed.

Place both of your hands along the curve of your partner's jaw, one hand on each side, cradling the head gently. Slowly yet firmly stroke the jaw, feeling its structure and the warmth and texture of your partner's skin. Close your eyes for a moment and imagine that you are a blind person whose only way of knowing your partner's face is to explore it with your fingers.

Pacing yourself to the music, slowly move up your partner's face, touching and feeling each part of it with your fingertips, exploring it as if it were a map on which you are going to trace every road. Move your fingers upward from the cheekbones, gliding toward the temples, those little indentations in the sides of the head where all of the nerve endings meet. Place your middle finger there and hold it gently but firmly in place for a moment—this relieves tension. Then make slow small circles in the temple area.

Moving to the center of your partner's forehead, place both hands along the forehead, with the little fingers between eyebrows and the other fingers spanning the forehead. Flatten your fingers and quietly hold the forehead between your two hands. This is a very calming position. Slowly trace the lines across the forehead from the inner part of the eyebrow all the way out to the ear, stopping to trace firm circles around the temples. Move your fingers down behind the ears to the base of the neck, making firm circles around the bone structure behind your partner's ears as you go.

Using both hands, make firm circles behind the neck, going as far behind the neck as you can to where all the nerve endings are. Move slowly and using your entire hand, squeeze the muscles behind the neck, then move down to squeeze the shoulders firmly. Stroke down the large shoulder muscle, then squeeze it. Flowing with the music, sweep your hands over the shoulders, down the arms, and away from the body area—as if you were sweeping all of the tension out of your partner's body. Do this three or four times.

Now place your fingers back on your partner's forehead and trace the lines on it gently, making little circles every time you get to an indentation. With your fingertips, trace every line of the face, the bone structure around the eye sockets, a line above the eye sockets and the rims below the eye sockets. Trace down the sides of the nose where the sinuses are, move your fingers in a large circle up the sides of the nose, around the eyebrows and the cheekbones.

Now circle the crevices and indentations of the ears with your fingers, three or four times. Gently place your hands over the ears and keep them there for five or ten seconds. Circle the ears again.

Trace the lips with two fingers, the cleft beneath the nose, and the cleft down the middle of the chin. Leave no part of the face untouched. Gently tap the face with your fingertips in tiny dotlike movements.

Now slide your hands up the sides of the face and run your fingertips through the hair and scalp, firmly rotating the skin in circles around the top, back and sides of the head. Massage all of the nerve endings in the scalp; they carry a great deal of tension.

Using your fingers, stroke down the back of the neck and out onto the shoulders, carrying the tension from the scalp to the large shoulder muscles. Grip the shoulders again, then repeat those long sweeping motions down past the elbows, sweeping the tension out of your partner's body.

If you were the one getting the massage, tell your partner how it felt, and which parts of the face caress felt particularly pleasurable. Then return the favor, giving your partner the same kind of face massage and finding out how it felt. Write in your journal about how it felt to be both giver and receiver of pleasure.

AROUSAL

Sexual arousal is more subtle than the erotic fondling with which it is usually associated. People differ greatly in how they are aroused and in how their passion is heightened. These different preferences aren't good or bad. They just are. And it is your responsibility to learn what they are for you, and to be comfortable enough with them to be able to talk about or show them to your partner.

Our largest organ for receiving sexual pleasure is the skin and the chief instruments for giving pleasure are the hands and mouth. The sensitive use of your hands, mouth and tongue on your partner's body can evoke a level of sensuality and eroticism that far surpass the intensity of genital sex alone. It is important to take time to find out which parts of our partner's body are especially erotic. Many people don't know that fingers and toes in a warm mouth can be an intensely erotic experience. For some, the breast area is highly sensitive to touch, kissing or sucking; for others less so. (Incidentally, the nipple area is as sensitive for some men as it is for some women.)

The abdominal area is full of nerve endings and also responds to different kinds of touch—from the light tracing of fingernails to massage and tonguing. The insides of the elbows and the backs of the knees can be very sensitive to stroking, kissing or licking, and for many people, sensitive caressing of the ears with the lips and tongue can be erotic enough to cause orgasm. Caressing, kissing and tonguing different parts of the neck can be equally erotic. It is essential that you take the time to learn how to use your mouth, tongue, fingers and hands to give sensual pleasure to your partner.

Different people are turned on by different things during sex.

Some like to talk ("dirty" or otherwise), others prefer allowing the silent creature part of themselves to take over. Some like soft music and incense; some want the lights high, low or off; some like to savor sensations quietly, others to abandon themselves totally, thrashing and screaming; some delight in the "animal" aspects of their sexual passions while others experience an almost spiritual loss of ego boundaries during sex and can feel ecstatic, as if merging with the infinite. Almost everyone finds that sex can relieve anxiety and tension and restore a sense of peace and tranquility.

The variety of things that turn people on sexually is amazing. Couples have listed such sexual turn-ons as:

Feeling the warmth of the sun	Hearing what my partner likes
A romantic setting (or just	about me
being away from home)	Slow hands and an easy touch
An appointment for a sexual	Showering together
date	Good muscle tone
Surreptitious fondling of erotic	Dancing
areas in public places	Spontaneity
A nice fragrance	A sense of humor
Certain specific clothes (or	Even anger
nudity)	

Fantasy is an important source of erotic arousal. Many people believe that they are being unfaithful if they think of anything or anybody other than their partner in lovemaking, but sexual fantasies are entirely private, unless you choose to share them. For many people the ability to fantasize erotic events (which they don't necessarily want to happen) is crucial to their ability to reach climax. Many who have been unable to achieve sexual release previously have found that sexual fantasy has enabled them to be orgasmic.

Fantasies range from the mundane to the fantastic. Couples have listed such fantasies as having sex on the racquetball court; in a pool; while skindiving or skydiving; on a grassy slope near a lagoon; in a truck on the highway; in a redwood forest; at 4:00 A.M. or after a ten-mile hike; as a threesome (men especially seem to favor the fantasy of a man with two women) or a group; in an affair that entails no guilt, consequences or problems; and by being "taken," as in the Marlon Brando seduction scene in *Last Tango in Paris*.

Many people get turned on just reading about other people's fantasies, in books like Nancy Friday's *My Secret Garden*.

PAIRS Exercise: Sexual Turn-Ons—What Arouses You?

The focus in this exercise is on all kinds of sensual and sexual arousal, genital and nongenital alike. It is about discovering what makes you aware, however subliminally, of your erotic feelings and alive to the sexual charge between you and your partner. Take some private time and answer the following questions about you and your partner as honestly as you can in your journal.

WHAT AROUSES ME SENSUALLY AND SEXUALLY?

What are my earliest memories of sensual and sexual experiences?

What were my early erotic fantasies?

What kinds of erotic fantasy most turns me on now? (Remember: in this connection nothing is too odd or flaky—it's fantasy, not behavior.)

What kinds of setting (place, time, music and other conditions) put me in the mood for tenderness or sex or both?

What parts of my body are most erotically responsive, and to which kinds of stimulation (fondling, stroking, licking, kissing and so forth)?

In what sequence do I prefer to have those parts stimulated, so that sexual arousal builds best?

What other kinds of stimulation might help to make me sexually interested or aroused (tenderness, touching, sexual talk, pictures, films, pornography and so forth)?

What things that I do (or would like to do) to or for my partner most turn *me* on?

During lovemaking, what kinds of special stimulation (words or acts, mine or my partner's) most heighten my excitement? For example:

Stopping and starting
Taking more time
Being stimulated in several areas at once
Kissing (prolonged deep kissing, neck kissing)
My partner kissing or tonguing my breasts, nipples, face, lips, neck, ears, body, penis, scrotum, clitoris, entrance to the vagina, area between lips of the vulva, inner thighs, lower abdomen, buttocks, palms, fingers, feet, toes)
Genital licking
Sexy language
Talking about sex
Talking during sex
Music during sex
Lights on during sex
Talking about sexual fantasies
Playing out sexual fantasies
Sex in different parts of house or elsewhere
Sex in different positions
Sex to music
Sex by candle or firelight
Lying together nonsexually
Intercourse with both of us climaxing
Intercourse with only one of us climaxing
Erotic fantasy
Stimulation through reading pornographic material

Exchanging fantasies
Clitoral stimulation
Seeing my partner nude
Being seen nude
Caressing (body caress, face caress, foot massage, back massage, back stroking, other)
Hands on breasts
Mouth on breasts
Fondling my partner's genitals
Having my genitals fondled
Stimulating my own genitals with my partner watching
Watching my partner masturbate
Oral sex (tonguing, kissing or licking genitals): me stimulating my partner as foreplay to or through climax, my partner stimulating me as foreplay to or through climax; masturbating my partner
Using a vibrator on myself or on my partner
My partner using a vibrator on me
Sex without intercourse
Intercourse without orgasm
Joint viewing of: hardcore pornographic films or videos, "soft" porn
Other?

What sexual positions most satisfy or excite me?

After sex, what do I need to prolong the contentment and pleasure?

What do I like best about our sex life now?

> What do I most appreciate about my partner as a lover?
> What would I like my partner to do to make our lovemaking more of a pleasure?
> Is there anything else I want or need to make sex more satisfying or enjoyable?

Be assured that whatever it is, your preference, wish or fantasy is far from unique; your partner may even share it. While it is important that you share your wishes and preferences with your partner, you have an option about sharing your fantasies or keeping them to yourself, for your own arousal. For some people sharing fantasies is a turn-on, for others it is a turn-off.

If your partner doesn't respond enthusiastically when you first mention certain erotic wishes or preferences, don't let it be the end of the world. Some changes may not come, and some will come more gradually—as you acquire new skills for exchanging information and giving and receiving pleasure and gain confidence in yourselves.

PAIRS Exercise: Sexual Turn-Offs

In the last exercise, you listed the things your partner does or could do that give you pleasure. Here, you are to list what turns you off, whether in a sexual or in a broader sense. This exercise can put you in touch with things you often feel negative about but haven't really been acknowledging. It may also make you realize how relatively trivial some of the things are that bother you. As you compile your list, notice whether it is easier for you to identify what bothers you than what brings you pleasure. If so, begin trying to focus more on the pleasure and less on the obstacles to it.

Another function of this exercise is to clarify what truly matters. For a lot of people, four-letter words for sex (especially those that seem hostile or aggressive) are a turn-off; for others they're a turn-on! If one of you is turned off by something your partner considers a turn-on, there is no way you can get together if you never confide or honor each other's feelings.

Here are some turn-offs that have cropped up on the lists of PAIRS participants:

Not talking to me all day and then wanting sex
Always having to take the initiative
Doing the same thing all the time (always the same position,
    a lack of creativity, a ritualistic approach, no variety)
Partner's not shaving (face, legs, underarms)
Telling dirty jokes
Farting
Not cutting the hairs in your nose or ears
Picking your nose
Laughing too loud
Wearing too much makeup
Body odor
Unclean genitals (when you don't wash before sex)
Talking too much
Boasting
Using foul language
Too clingy a manner
Prudishness
Hesitant touch
Rough touch
When you are silent or unresponsive or emotionally
    detached (just lying there expecting me to "do it to you")
When you are depressed (or I am)
When you use sex as a weapon or a bribe
Drunkenness (mine or yours)
Fatigue
Heavy pressure at work
Interruptions or the threat of interruptions (the kids, the
    phone, the doorbell, someone else barging into the room)
Pressure to arrive at mutual orgasms
Fat
Foam jelly contraceptives
Limits on time
Lack of ambience
Teasing that goes nowhere
Being taken for granted
Being compared to others or comparing this time to last time
    or to some other time

Take as much time as you need to list your turn-offs frankly in your journal. You may want to add to the list over a period of several days.

Compare your list of turn-offs with your list of turn-ons. Do you see any patterns? Be attentive to whether your list of turn-offs is far longer than your list of turn-ons. Remember that if it is easier for you to say what bothers you than it is to say what brings you pleasure, your biggest obstacle to pleasure may be your own negative attitude toward it.

PAIRS Exercise: Sensual Pleasure Date

When you've both finished writing your lists of turn-ons and turn-offs, make a luncheon date with each other, arranging to meet somewhere away from home. On the way, stop at a store and buy a massage oil with an aroma you think you will like. At lunch, share your lists, preferably reading them aloud to each other. (This isn't always practical, but do it if you can. Something about the naughtiness of it makes it a memorable experience.) Remember, the fantasies needn't be acted on: They can remain fantasies. But for many couples it's a turn-on to share them.

Talk about your lists. Remember, this is not the time for arguments or defenses. You are seeking information, not agreement. By listening, your partner does not necessarily agree to stop doing what puts you off; he or she simply agrees to become aware of it and to appreciate and consider the information.

Make a Sensual Pleasure Date for the evening of the same day. Allow forty-five minutes, and decide in advance who is going to be giver and who the receiver of pleasure. Agree on whether or not the date should culminate in intercourse, or whether it should be decided by the mutual whim of the moment. If sexual performance has been a problem for either of you, however, you probably should specify that there is to be no expectation of sex—that for now you will focus on the sensual pleasures you may not normally focus on. The giver will set the scene: privacy, music, candlelight, a shower or bath together beforehand—whatever will please the receiver.

As receiver, you will lie unclothed on your stomach, partially covered with a large towel, while your partner gives you a gentle, leisurely body massage. You do nothing but take in pleasure and let your partner know what does or doesn't give you pleasure. Afterward, you can go quietly to sleep, or bond or reverse roles—whatever is your pleasure. Later, you can tell your partner what you especially liked.

Either the same night, or soon after—and some couples make their pleasure dates for Saturday and Sunday mornings—reverse roles, and let the one who was giver of pleasure become the receiver. Make an effort to have each session be leisurely and last the same amount of time as the other.

In your journal, write any insights that came to you as a result of this exercise. Couples sometimes find that an exercise like this helps give them a clearer focus on such issues as giving and taking, initiating and following, work and pleasure.

- Did you find it hard to take time for pleasure?
- Did you find yourself watching the clock, or preoccupied with fairness (for example, who got the longer turn)?
- Did you find a focus on sensuality a distraction, a pleasure, a relief? If you are traditionally the caretaker, did you find it difficult to be the receiver of pleasure? Did you find yourself wanting to tell your partner that he or she was doing it wrong, and how to do it "right"?
- Did your partner learn from the information?
- Or was it pleasure, pure and simple?

In the weeks ahead, make a conscious effort to set aside time for sessions or moments of sensual pleasure, and record in your journal the effect that these have on your relationship.

EXPLORING SEXUAL PREFERENCES

This exercise helps you explore what will give you even greater sexual pleasure. First, look through your lists from the questions on pages 255–7 and place a checkmark next to (or copy into your journal) those things you would like to experience or to experience more often. Then write "no" next to (or copy onto a second list in your journal) those things you do not enjoy and do not really want to experience. Add any behavior that is missing here.

When your partner has had a chance to respond to this exercise, set a time to compare answers, discuss similarities and differences in your perceptions and desires.

Then make two sexual dates during which you will each take a turn making love to your partner. When it is your turn to be the initiator, make love to your partner the way you would *like* your partner to make love to you. If your preference is making love to soft music and candlelight and being slowly caressed from head to foot before you begin focusing on genital stimulation, set the stage, and then caress your partner the way you would like to be caressed, at the pace and with the touch you would like to receive yourself.

Take turns on this, and allow for days in between when your partner's lovemaking will reflect what you have shown him or her and vice versa. Don't be afraid to try new things, and when you discover that something delights you and you aren't sure your partner is aware of it, speak up.

The point of this exercise is to find out what each of you likes. You may not know yourself what you like until you begin to explore. What makes one of you feel good may not necessarily be what makes the other feel good, but to the extent that you learn each other's arousal triggers, you will both benefit. Your partner's arousal validates your effectiveness as a lover and inevitably increases your own excitement and satisfaction. Lonnie Barbach says it nicely: "If we're going to make beautiful music together, you have to learn my song."

FUNDAMENTALS FOR GOOD SEXUAL ADJUSTMENT

Good sexual adjustment requires understanding and accepting yourself, your body, your *sensual* and your *sexual* feelings—recognizing that no matter what they are, they're probably legitimate. We know much about the universe, about how to master the environment and guarantee the satisfaction of our physiological needs. We can now begin to acknowledge and fulfill our emotional, relational, spiritual and sexual needs. In many ways, our sexual adjustment is the fulcrum upon which all of that turns—for sexual fulfillment between two loving partners can provide the individual maturity, serenity, security and generosity that permit us to thrive and ultimately contribute to society.

Here are a few fundamental suggestions that apply to all of us:

Be aware of and take pride in your sexuality; it is one of the most powerful and constructive forces in your life.

Be genuine and spontaneous in giving it expression. Know what turns you on and share it with your partner. Whatever it is, rest assured that you share it with much of mankind, though not necessarily with your partner.

It's okay to ask for sex, but since your partner can't *always* be on the same wave-length, don't let rejection destroy you. On the other hand, when you're asked and you don't feel like it, for whatever legitimate reason, don't make it a "rejection" but rather a provisional postponement, with a considerate and honest explanation.

Encourage your partner to ask for sex whenever he or she is in the mood. Tell each other which approach to asking for sex works best with you.

Never use sex as a bargaining tool.

Make it your business to find out what turns your partner on. Don't make any assumptions in this area.

Show appreciation for your mate as a person before and after, as well as during, sex. And during sex, engage your partner's mind and feelings as well as his or her body.

Be familiar with and enjoy your mate's *entire* body.

Talk freely about your sensations and feelings.

Become aware of and learn to experience the real pleasures of foreplay and afterplay, without undue focus on performance, athleticism or orgasm.

With the appropriate manner and timing, tell your partner what you need in order to be sexually satisfied. Make it clear that you're hoping for the same honesty from your partner.

Sex isn't necessarily a serious matter. Be as relaxed and childlike and playful as you wish. If you're going about it right, you will feel different ways at different times, and they're all fine.

Don't confine your tenderness and amorousness to the times

when you want or expect sex. Take and give pleasure in spontaneous and undemanding caresses, and keep "romance" alive in other ways that have special meaning for your partner. Consult your partner's "Caring Behaviors or I Love it When" list (created in Chapter 17) from time to time to remind yourself of what has special meaning for him or her; then take time to bring her the fresh flowers she loves to be given, or to make him the special dish that makes him feel you care.

Finally, don't be afraid to let yourself go. Be willing and eager to accept all of the risk of being totally yourself. Only then can you and your partner become truly intimate.

Take a moment to write in your journal notebook about what you are beginning to realize.

SECTION V

Putting It All Together

■   ■   ■

And in bowing to the forbidden and the impossible, we become a moral, responsible, adult self, discovering—within the limitations imposed by necessity—our freedoms and choices. And in giving up our impossible expectations, we become a lovingly connected self, renouncing ideal visions of perfect friendship, marriage, children, family life for the sweet imperfections of all-too-human relationships.

—*Judith Viorst*, Necessary Losses

20

The PAIRS Tool Kit

■   ■   ■

*A*s we reach the close of our journey together, it's useful to review how many concepts we've touched on; how to nurture an intimate relationship; becoming a detective about your own history and understanding yourself and your own uniqueness; understanding your partner; how to negotiate conflicts and resolve conflicts and differences; how to build pleasure into your relationship.

The Tool Kit on page 268 is a list of the concepts we've covered. I hope that everything on this list is now familiar to you. Remember that Bonding involves both emotional openness and physical closeness. The ability to meet this intimate need leads to pleasure, desire and feelings of love. The inability to meet this need leads to pain or the anticipation of pain (which is perceived as danger), and the resulting impasse as we run in fear, fight in anger or freeze. Our fight-or-flight response may be based on present reality or on our history and decisions we made regarding love, trust and closeness to another person.

The stress communication styles (the Computer, the Distractor, the Blamer and the Placater) are our way of dealing with emotional pain or the anticipation of not getting our needs met, but our style

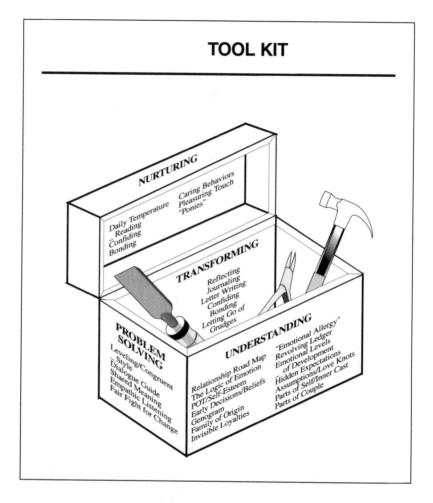

TOOL KIT

NURTURING
Daily Temperature
Reading
Confiding
Bonding
Caring Behaviors
Pleasuring Touch
"Ponies"

TRANSFORMING
Reflecting
Journaling
Letter Writing
Confiding
Bonding
Letting Go of
Grudges

PROBLEM SOLVING
Leveling/Congruent
Style
Dialogue Guide
Shared Meaning
Empathic Listening
Fair Fight for Change

UNDERSTANDING
Relationship Road Map
The Logic of Emotion
POT/Self-Esteem
Early Decisions/Beliefs
Genogram
Family of Origin
Invisible Loyalties
"Emotional Allergy"
Revolving Ledger
Emotional Levels
of Development
Hidden Expectations
Assumptions/Love Knots
Parts of Self/Inner Cast
Parts of Couple

often also becomes the problem and prevents intimacy rather than enhancing it.

To be sure that we don't use these styles, there are a number of things we can do. We can Level in order to assert ourselves in our own behalf, using the Dialogue Guide as one way to share what is inside. We can use the Empathic Listening mode or a Fair Fight for Change to negotiate differences. All of these help us assert ourselves without blaming. We can use the Haircut or Vesuvius rituals for rage release. We need to be able to Listen. We need to show caring through our behavior, and we need to share decision making, not out of fear, but because we want the relationship to thrive and our partner to be happy. When we solve problems, we need to include both thoughts and feelings: Any time I omit yours or mine, I am not going to come up with a solution that works.

We need the ability to have fun, to ride the pony and not just clean the barn. This is the positive behavior that leads to pleasure for both.

We need to explore how our early conditioning interferes with pleasure in our lives today. What kind of early decisions did you make? What inhibitions do you have? What do you need to change so that it doesn't contaminate your present relationship? If we do not look to the past to illuminate the present, the past may very well contaminate the present.

One thing we know about relationships is that the differences between partners are less important than the ability to talk about these differences easily, confide in each other and trust each other with our hearts and with our minds, as well as with our bodies. The presence of differences or areas that need work does not mean that we have a bad relationship, but rather that our skill in discussing differences and arriving at something we can both live with happily is vital.

I hope that the PAIRS exercises in this book have helped you learn about yourself, as well as provided you with skills for sharing this learning with your partner. When two people are emotionally open to sharing, all kinds of marvelous things can happen, but it does take two. My hope is that both of you feel more comfortable being able to talk about any of these things.

Skills learned but not used are easily lost. We need to continue the Daily Temperature Reading. We need to ask, "How are you?" daily and really *want to know*. We need to continue to build trust by confiding and to continue caring behavior without feeling that our partner is controlling us, but because *we want the relationship to win*.

Staying in touch with our partner and not letting problems pile up is not impossible. Sometimes, though, it is hard. I would recommend spending an hour together at least once a week to keep the ledger open and clear, to keep each other informed, to renegotiate expectations as the need arises. Changes need to be talked about, not made arbitrarily or unilaterally.

STAYING IN LOVE AS LOVE CHANGES

As our journey together draws to an end, I leave you with certain observations about creating and sustaining *positive change* in intimate relationships.*

Change is the one thing you can count on in relationships. Relationships change as circumstances change and as the needs, desires and experience of the partners shift. At the same time, *resistance to change is normal* and should come as no surprise, even when change clearly makes sense. We resist change because we are used to the old way and *we are afraid of what we do not know.* When you find yourself resisting a change that you suspect makes sense, you might tell yourself or your partner, "I'm afraid, but I'll try it anyway." Acknowledge the fear. The only way to find out if things can be different is to try changing them. You can always go back to the old way if the new way doesn't work out.

Lasting change requires four steps:

1. Knowing what you'd like to change
2. Changing it
3. Sustaining the change
4. Sustaining it under stress

Then you have it!

Your partner is more likely to respond to a request for a change if you *express it as a request for a positive change in behavior instead of as criticism.* For example, "I wish you would give me a compliment every day," instead of "You never appreciate me," or "Could we take turns choosing the restaurant?" Instead of "We always eat where you want to eat." Learn to tactfully teach your partner what you need. Add regularly to the list of caring behavior you would like from your partner, and pay attention to your partner's list. Developing the ability to confide and work through issues is the only way to overcome the bad habit of distancing and holding grudges.

We are far less open to change when our self-esteem is low, whether from inner or outer assaults. Therefore, it makes sense to request changes in behavior when your partner's self-esteem is high—when he or she is feeling valued, appreciated, respected, competent and loved.

*Adapted from *Helping Couples Change* by Richard Stuart, Ph.D.

In deciding how and when to make such requests, become aware of your partner's feelings of worth and consider how your request will affect him or her.

People don't change from one behavior to another because the first behavior is wrong. If they did, we would all find it easier to stop smoking, drinking, overeating, overspending, procrastinating and so on. We can accept changes (whether suggested by our partners or not) only when our *own* experiences, needs and cycles of growth make us ready for them. That process may be enhanced by a good relationship or a perceptive and caring partner, but it cannot be fabricated out of whole cloth. At some level we, too, must desire the change— and we must realize *the price we may be paying of pleasure in our relationship* for not changing.

Both parties must participate if the relationship is to change. Changes that are compelled or coerced are unlikely to be accepted or to last. Nobody wins if one partner feels that he or she is lost. Eventually the loser will distance or want to get even. Either you both win or you both lose, because *the relationship* either wins or loses.

Assume the best, not the worst. Both of you have a vested interest in improving the relationship. Therefore, assume goodwill. Don't act as if the minute you relax your guard your partner will go back to his or her old ways. Take responsibility for your own attitudes and commitment. Assume that your partner will do the same. Focus your attention on where you are now, not on your regrets from the past. Think of positive current goals, rather than brooding about old grievances.

If you want to change a complex system, plan to take a series of small steps. For instance, to change the basic nature of your relationship from one of distance to one of closeness, begin with small caring gestures, greeting your partner at the door, a welcoming hug, daily sharing of confidences, bonding and the commitment to confide and encourage the same in your partner. Do the things you can do to improve the relationship, such as remembering birthdays, not giving unwanted advice and honoring your partner's requests. Do it for yourself: for the pleasure a mutually fulfilling relationship will bring you!

Expect a pattern of two steps forward and one step backward. Temporary regression is a normal part of growth, especially during times of stress. Don't feel defeated by it. After an accumulation of learning, you may regress for a while to the level you were comfortable with earlier—and then go forward again until the new behavior feels comfortable. While one of you is practicing the new way, the other may drop back to the old way but will usually catch up again and, if the new way is maintained, will often improve on it.

Regression sometimes stems from the fact that a part of us wants to test the changes we're making, to see if they can be counted on, as if to say, "I want to see if we are really going to keep this up." If you have gotten to a point that feels wonderful, a regression may feel devastating, but if you step back and look at things objectively, you will probably see that things haven't dropped back to where they were when you began. With each successive regression, the recovery time is shorter, and you will be dealing with each other on a different level. *You will know you have overcome the old patterns when you can sustain the new behavior under stress.*

PAIRS Exercise: The PAIRS Relationship

Now prepare yourself for one final exercise.* Take quiet time to clear your mind and relax. Take several long, deep breaths.

Imagine an ideal relationship. Picture yourself as part of this couple. How does your day begin and end? What do you do that makes this relationship work so well? What does your partner do? What do you have as a couple that makes your relationship so special?

Now picture your partner and you spending the day with another couple. Imagine the four of you together, relaxing, talking, laughing, having a delightful time. Feel the pleasure in the time you spend together. Your friends decide to ask you for some advice. They ask, "What do we need to do to have a relationship as good as yours?"

What do you say?

Reflect on your answer. Then write your response in your journal. As you think about your answer, think about what you have learned that can help you bring your picture to a reality in your life.

*Adapted from *Training in Marriage Enrichment* by Don Dinkmeyer and Jon Carlsen (Circle Pines, MN: American Guidance Service, Inc.), 1984, p. 112.

MOVING FORWARD

By now, maybe you are familiar enough with PAIRS techniques to modify the exercises to suit your individual needs. There's no limit on how much you can improve your relationship so long as you truly want the relationship to work and are willing to use the PAIRS knowledge to work at improving it.

At the same time, expect an imperfect relationship. The human condition itself is far from perfect. We are all subject to disappointment, loss, illness, uncertainty and some form of discontent—usually at the most unexpected and inopportune times. Indeed, the more intimate you become, the more completely you love your partner, the more vulnerable you are to your partner's pain and anxiety. It's a small price to pay, however, for the joy and contentment of a genuine and dynamic intimate relationship.

PAIRS is like a box of carpenter's tools designed to help you build a foundation that will sustain lasting love. You are the architect. It takes practice to learn to use the tools with ease. It is said that you have to do something a new way at least forty times before you can change an old habit. So start practicing. It may take a while. But it's worth it, for the joy and contentment of a lasting intimate relationship.

A FINAL THOUGHT

As you reflect on your journal entries and the exercises you have experienced, be aware of the growing wisdom you bring to your relationship.

Give yourself and your partner a special message of appreciation for this journey you have taken together. Appreciate your own willingness to take risks in behalf of a fuller, more creative and joyful life. Go forward with a new sense of yourself and the possibilities of your relationships. And go with confidence.

For Those of You Who Want More!

■　　　■　　　■

The PAIRS exercises that have been described have been proven to be effective in developing new, more joyful relationship skills. They are an important part of the PAIRS program. By practicing the skills, you can make significant progress in building a foundation for a lasting love relationship, one that is a prime source of personal growth, healing, empowerment, and transformation.

There are many other powerful PAIRS exercises that have not been included in this book, as they don't lend themselves to book presentation. The complete PAIRS (Practical Application of Intimate Relationship Skills) program is a 120-hour course that is offered nationally and internationally by trained leaders. It provides a carefully sequenced, guided series of lectures and dynamic experiential learning that offers the opportunity to develop new perceptions and skills, to learn from other group members as well as from the leader and to share with your partner in even far greater depth.

If you are interested in taking the PAIRS course, call or write the Foundation for an information packet, a schedule of workshops and seminars and a list of leaders in your area.

The PAIRS Foundation was established in 1984. It is a nonprofit, nonsectarian, educational corporation that was developed to design and to offer programs for the prevention of marital breakdown. Applauded by psychotherapists and participants alike, the PAIRS program is considered the most comprehensive, uniquely effective course in the field today. The Foundation offers the following direct services:

- Workshops and classes for couples
- Workshops and classes for singles
- Lectures on relationship issues for the general public
- Therapy for couples and individuals
- Literature and audiocassettes
- PAIRS leader training for mental health professionals

For further information, call or write:

The PAIRS Foundation
3705 S. George Mason Drive, Suite C-8
Falls Church, VA 22041
Phone: 1-703-998-5550; 1-800-842-7470
FAX: 1-703-998-8517

BIBLIOGRAPHY

Adams, Teresa McAlister. *Living from the Inside Out*. New Orleans, LA: Self published, 1987.

Assagioli, Roberto, and Servan-Schreiber, Claude. *A Higher View of the Man-Woman Problem. SYNTHESIS I—The Realization of the Self*. Redwood City, CA: 1974.

Bach, George, and Torbet, Laura. *The Inner Enemy*. New York: William Morrow, 1983.

Bach, George, and Torbet, Laura. *A Time for Caring: How to Enrich Your Life Through an Interest and Pleasure in Others*. New York: Delacorte Press, 1982.

Bach, George, and Wyden, Peter. *The Intimate Enemy*. New York: Avon Books, 1968.

Barbach, Lonnie. *For Each Other: Sharing Sexual Intimacy*. New York: Doubleday, 1982.

Barbach, Lonnie Garfield. *For Yourself: The Fulfillment of Female Sexuality*. New York: Doubleday, 1975.

Benton, Walter. *This Is My Beloved*. New York: Alfred A. Knopf, 1943.

Berg, Louis, and Street, Robert. *Sex: Methods and Manners*. New York: McFadden Books, 1962.

Berne, Eric. *Games People Play: The Psychology of Human Relationships*. New York: Random House, 1964.

Boszormenyi, Ivan, and Spark, Geraldine. *Invisible Loyalties*. New York: Brunner/Mazel, Inc., 1984.

Bradshaw, John. *Healing the Shame that Binds*. Deerfield Beach, FL: Health Communications, 1988.

Bradshaw, John. *Homecoming: Reclaiming and Championing Your Inner Child*. New York: Bantam, 1990.

Branden, Nathaniel. *If You Could Hear What I Cannot Say*. New York: Bantam, 1983.

Branden, Nathaniel. *Honoring the Self: The Psychology of Confidence and Respect*. New York: Bantam, 1983.

Branden, Nathaniel. *The Psychology of Self-Esteem*. New York: Bantam, 1969.

Buber, Martin. *I & Thou*. New York: Charles Scribner's Sons, 1958.

Casriel, Daniel. *A Scream Away from Happiness*. New York: Grosset & Dunlap, 1972.

Cosby, Bill. *Love and Marriage.* New York: Bantam, 1989.

de Beauvoir, Simone. *The Second Sex.* New York: Alfred A. Knopf, 1952.

Dinkmeyer, Don, and Jon Carlsen. *Training in Marriage Enrichment.* Circle Pines, MN: American Guidance Service, Inc., 1984.

Firestone, Robert. *The Fantasy Bond.* New York: The Glendon Assoc.–Human Sciences Press, 1985.

Forward, Susan. *Men Who Hate Women and the Women Who Love Them.* New York: Bantam, 1986.

Friday, Nancy. *My Secret Garden.* New York: Simon and Schuster, 1973.

Fromm, Erich. *The Art of Loving.* New York: Bantam, 1956.

Gaylin, Willard. *Rediscovering Love.* New York: Viking Penguin, 1986.

Gibran, Kahlil. *The Prophet.* New York: Alfred A. Knopf, 1982.

Gibran, Kahlil. *A Tear and a Smile.* New York: Alfred A. Knopf, 1967.

Gordon, Lori H. *Love Knots: A Laundry List of Marital Mishaps, Marital Knots, Etc.* New York: Dell 1990.

Gottman, John, et al. *A Couples' Guide to Communication.* Champaign, IL: Research Press, 1976.

Gould, Roger. *Transformations: Growth and Change in Adult Life.* New York: Simon and Schuster, 1978.

Goulding, Robert and Mary. *Changing Lives Through Redecision Therapy.* New York: Brunner/Mazel, 1979.

Gray, John. *What You Feel, You Can Heal!* Santa Monica, CA: Heart Publishing, 1980.

Haley, Alex. *Roots: The Saga of an American Family.* New York: Doubleday, 1976.

Harris, Thomas. *I'm OK, You're OK.* New York: Harper & Row, 1967.

Hendrix, Harville. *Getting the Love You Want.* New York: Harper & Row, 1988.

Herberg, Will. *The Writings of Martin Buber.* Cleveland, OH: The World Publishing Co., 1956.

Heschel, Abraham Joshua. *God in Search of Man: A Philosophy of Judaism.* New York: Farrar, Straus & Cudahy, 1955.

Hooper, Anne. *Massage and Loving.* New York: Henry Holt and Company, 1988.

J. *The Sensuous Woman.* New York: Dell, 1969.

Janov, Arthur. *The Anatomy of Mental Illness.* New York: G. P. Putnam & Sons, 1971.

Janov, Arthur. *The Primal Scream.* New York: Dell, 1970.

Janov, Arthur. *Prisoners of Pain: Unlocking the Power of the Mind to End Suffering.* Garden City, NY: Doubleday, 1980.

Kahn, Michael, and Lewis, Karen. *Siblings in Therapy.* New York: W. W. Norton, 1988.

Keyes, Jr., Ken. *The Power of Unconditional Love.* Coos Bay, OR: Love Live Books, 1990.

Kushner, Harold. *When All You've Ever Wanted Isn't Enough: The Search for a Life that Matters.* New York: Summit Books, 1986.

Lair, Jacqueline, and Lechler, Walter. *I Exist, I Need, I'm Entitled.* New York: Doubleday, 1980.

Lerner, Harriet Goldhor. *The Dance of Intimacy: A Woman's Guide to Courageous Acts of Change in Key Relationship.* New York: HarperCollins, 1989.

Lidell, Lucinda, et al. *The Book of Massage.* New York: Simon and Schuster, 1984.

Liebman, Joshua Loth. *Peace of Mind.* New York: Simon and Schuster, 1946.

Liedloff, Jean. *The Continuum Concept.* New York: Warner Books, 1977.

Lynch, James J. *The Language of the Heart: The Body's Response to Human Dialogue.* New York: Basic Books, 1938.

M. *The Sensuous Man.* New York: Dell, 1971.

MacLean, Paul D. *Man & His Animal Brains. Modern Medicine,* February 3, 1964.

MacLean, Paul D. *A Triune Concept of the Brain and Behavior.* Toronto, Canada: University of Toronto Press, 1973.

Masters, Robert, and Houston, Jean. *Mind Games: The Guide to Inner Space.* New York: Viking, 1972.

McCarthy, Barry and Emily. *Couple Sexual Awareness: Building Sexual Happiness.* New York: Carroll & Graf Publishers, 1990.

McGoldrick, Monica, and Gerson, Randy. *Genograms in Family Assessment.* New York: W. W. Norton, 1985.

Miller, Alice. *Prisoners of Childhood.* New York: Basic Books, 1981.

Miller, Sherod, et al. *Straight Talk.* New York: Rawson Associates, 1982.

Missildine, W. Hugh. *Your Inner Child of the Past.* New York: Pocket Books, 1988.

Napier, Augustus Y. *The Fragile Bond.* New York: Harper & Row, 1988.

Napier, Augustus Y., and Whitaker, Carl A. *The Family Crucible.* New York: Harper & Row, 1978.

Nerin, William F. *Family Reconstruction: Long Day's Journey into Light.* New York: W. W. Norton, 1986.

Paul, Drs. Jordan and Margaret. *From Conflict to Caring: An In-Depth Program for Creating Loving Relationships.* Minneapolis, MN: CompCare Publishers, 1989.

Peck, Scott. *The Road Less Traveled.* New York: Touchstone (Simon and Schuster), 1978.

Pelletier, Kenneth R. *Mind as Healer, Mind as Slayer: A Holistic Approach to Preventing Stress Disorders.* New York: Dell, 1977.

Pittman, Frank. *Private Lies: Infidelity and the Betrayal of Intimacy.* New York: W. W. Norton, 1989.

Progoff, Ira. *At a Journal Workshop.* New York: Dialogue House Library, 1975.

Progoff, Ira. *Depth Psychology and Modern Man.* New York: McGraw-Hill, 1959.

Progoff, Ira. *The Dynamics of Hope.* New York: Dialogue House Library, 1985.

Progoff, Ira. *The Practice of Process Meditation.* New York: Dialogue House Library, 1980.

Rich, Penny. *Pamper Your Partner: An Illustrated Guide to Soothing and Relaxing Your Mate with the Sensual Healing Arts.* New York: Fireside Books (Simon and Schuster), 1990.

Richardson, Richard. *Family Ties that Bind.* British Columbia, Canada: Self-Counsel Press, 1984.

Sager, Clifford J. *Marriage Contracts and Couples Therapy: Hidden Forces in Intimate Relationships.* New York: Brunner/Mazel, 1976.

Sager, Clifford, and Hunt, Bernice. *Intimate Partners: Hidden Patterns in Love Relationships.* New York: McGraw-Hill, Book Company, 1979.

Saint-Exupery, Antoine de. *The Little Prince.* New York: Harcourt, Brace & Company, 1943.

Satir, Virginia. *Conjoint Family Therapy.* Palo Alto, CA: Science and Behavior Books, 1967.

Satir, Virginia. *The New Peoplemaking.* Palo Alto, CA: Science and Behavior Books, 1988.

Satir, Virginia. *Self Esteem.* Berkeley, CA: Celestial Arts, 1975.

Satir, Virginia. *Your Many Faces.* Berkeley, CA: Celestial Arts, 1978.

Satir, Virginia, and Baldwin, Michele. *Step by Step: A Guide to Creating Change for Families.* Palo Alto, CA: Science and Behavior Books, 1983.

Scarf, Maggie. *Intimate Partners, Patterns in Love and Marriage.* New York: Random House, 1987.

Scarf, Maggie. *Unfinished Business: Pressure Points in the Lives of Women.* New York: Doubleday, 1980.

Sheehy, Gail. *Pathfinders: Overcoming the Crises of Adult Life and Finding Your Own Path to Well-Being.* New York: Bantam, 1982.

Siegel, Bernie S. *Peace, Love & Healing.* New York: Harper & Row, 1989.

Stone, Hal, and Winkelman, Sidra. *Embracing Each Other—Relationship as Teacher, Healer and Guide.* San Rafael, CA: New World Library, 1989.

Stuart, Richard. *Helping Couples Change: A Social Learning Approach to Marital Therapy.* New York: The Guilford Press, 1980.

Tannen, Deborah. *You Just Don't Understand.* New York: William Morrow, 1990.

Vargiu, James and Susan. *Subpersonalities. SYNTHESIS I.* Redwood City, CA: 1974.

Viorst, Judith. *Necessary Losses.* New York: Simon and Schuster, 1986.

Warner, Dr. Samuel J. *Self-Realization and Self-Defeat.* New York: Grove Press, 1966.

Weigert, Edith. *The Courage to Love.* New Haven, CT: Yale University Press, 1970.

Whitfield, Charles. *A Gift to Myself.* Deerfield Beach, FL: Health Communications, 1990.

Whitfield, Charles. *Healing the Child Within.* Deerfield, Beach, FL: Health Communications, 1987.

Wile, Daniel B. *After the Honeymoon: How Conflict Can Improve Your Relationship.* New York: John Wiley & Sons, 1988.

Zilbergeld, Bernie. *Male Sexuality.* New York: Bantam, 1978.

INDEX